THE INTERNET BUBBLE

INSIDE THE OVERVALUED WORLD OF HIGH-TECH STOCKS

—AND WHAT YOU
NEED TO KNOW TO AVOID
THE COMING SHAKEOUT

THE INTERNET BUBBLE

ANTHONY B. PERKINS

and

MICHAEL C. PERKINS

HarperBusiness
A Division of HarperCollins*Publishers*

HarperCollins books may be purchased for educational, business, or sales promotional use. For information please write: Special Markets Department, HarperCollins Publishers, Inc., 10 East 53rd Street, New York, NY 10022.

FIRST EDITION

Designed by Elliott Beard

Library of Congress Cataloging-in-Publication Data
Perkins, Anthony B.
   The Internet bubble: inside the overvalued world of high-tech stocks—and what you need to know to avoid the coming shakeout / Anthony B. Perkins and Michael C. Perkins.
     p.   cm.
   Includes index.
   ISBN 0-06-664000-8
   1. Internet industry—Finance.   2. Online information services industry—Finance.   I. Perkins, Michael C.
HD9696.8.A2P45   1999
025.06'332—dc21   99-37288

99 00 01 02 03 ❖/RRD 10 9 8 7 6 5 4 3 2 1

To Julie and Kristin, the sunshine of my life.
—AP
To Alex and Claire, with love and affection.
—MP

CONTENTS

Prologue—Playing the Internet IPO Game   ix

Introduction—The Internet Stock Bubble   1

Internet Mania   11

Venture Capital Cowboys   35

Kleiner Perkins Caufield & Byers:
   Leading the Venture Capital Herd   67

The I-Bankers Embrace the Internet   105

The Great Biotechnology Bubble   135

Internet Companies in a Gilded Age   149

The New Economy   175

Cult IPOs, SCAMS, and Other Hazards
   of Internet Investing   195

Investing in an Overheated Market Environment   209

Epilogue   229

Appendix A: Calculating the Bubble   237

Appendix B: Bubble Calculation Methodology   **241**

Appendix C: Company Lists   **247**

Bibliography   **253**

Acknowledgments   **263**

Index   **267**

PROLOGUE: PLAYING THE INTERNET IPO GAME

*J*eff Bezos is a smart guy. He graduated summa cum laude from Princeton in 1986 with a double major in electrical engineering and computer science. But Bezos isn't just a nerd; he's ambitious and he likes to sell stuff. That's why he founded Amazon.com.

In 1994, while doing a stint on Wall Street as a hedge fund manager at D.E. Shaw, Bezos sat down and made a list of twenty things he thought he could sell online. He felt books had potential because with more than 3 million English book titles in print, even the largest chain stores like Barnes & Noble and Borders could carry only 150,000 at a time. "It was clear that computers and the Internet could be uniquely applied to organize, present, and sell the entire stock in a way that a physical store or mail-order catalogue couldn't possibly imagine," Bezos explains. He also realized that unlike a car or a sweater, people didn't have to test drive or try on a book; they could order it sight unseen.

Bezos chucked his job and pin-striped suits, packed up, and moved West. His destiny was to return to his computer-geek roots, immerse himself in the Internet, and become a multibillionaire along the way. So with classic entrepreneurial drive and passion, Bezos raised money from family and friends, built up the infrastructure over a year's time, and then launched Amazon in July of 1995.

After bootstrapping his company for several months, Bezos realized that to take Amazon to the next level he'd need more money and some help recruiting a top management team. It was time to get a professional venture capitalist on board. Bezos was in a good position to fetch a high valuation for Amazon's first professional venture capital round because he had real revenues and a significant customer list to show to venture investors. "We joked at the time that we would have to change our voice-mail system to say, 'If you are a customer, press one. If you are a venture capitalist, press two,'" he recalls. His must-have choice was John Doerr, the premier venture capitalist with one of the top firms, Kleiner Perkins Caufield & Byers (KP). But as it turned out, Doerr wasn't one of the investors ringing Amazon's phone.

Bezos is not one to leave things to chance. Instead of waiting around to hear from John Doerr, Bezos called him. Bezos said that given Kleiner Perkins's reputation in the Internet space, they should at least talk. Doerr agreed and was on a plane and in Seattle the next day.

Bezos wanted to split the deal between Kleiner Perkins and two other venture capital firms, Hummer Winblad and General Atlantic Partners, but Doerr preferred not. "He argued that if Kleiner Perkins owned the whole round, their partners could justify giving the company their full attention," says Bezos. This request seemed reasonable given that Amazon was selling only 15 percent of the company for an $8 million first-round investment, the biggest check KP has ever cut for a single-round investment in the firm's 25-year history. Before the check was even deposited, John Doerr got to work helping CEO Bezos fill out his management team with experienced professionals from both the software and retail business worlds.

In spite of this boost, several months later Amazon was still operating at a significant loss while the bricks-and-mortar booksellers like Barnes & Noble had started to take notice of the online opportunity. Bezos was deeply paranoid that they might storm his market and put him out of business. To hold them off, he needed a financial war chest fast. In the old days, Bezos would have gone back to the venture capitalists for more money, but this would mean selling stock at a low valuation and surrendering more of his ownership in the company, something he definitely didn't want to do.

Fortunately for Bezos, he was building his company at the beginning of the Internet boom era, when the public market was hungry to buy any new stock, as long as it had a *.com* in its name.

By taking advantage of pent-up investor demand and spinning some of the company's stock into the public market, Bezos could not only fill his war chest with cash at a much higher stock price than the venture capitalists would have paid, but he could also make a huge public relations splash about Amazon's market leadership. In John Doerr's words, it was time for Amazon to "put the puck on the ice" and raise as much money as possible to invest in scale and snatch the first-mover advantage.

Unfortunately, Bezos's timing couldn't have been worse. Amazon's IPO plans bumped right into the Internet market's winter 1997 mini-correction.

But Bezos did have an ace or two in the hole. He'd teamed up with a couple of aggressive investment bankers—the legendary Frank Quattrone and his longtime sidekick, Bill Brady. Both bankers were eager to do the Amazon deal. Recalls Quattrone, "We saw Amazon as a wave rider—as a business that would benefit from the Internet regardless of who the technology winners were."

Quattrone had something to prove, too. In April 1996 he and several executives had bolted from Morgan Stanley, where they had built its technology practice into the most dominant in the industry and opened up a rival office for Deutsche Morgan Grenfell (DMG) in Menlo Park. And a marquee deal like Amazon would be a great way to best his old employer as well as his longtime archrival Goldman Sachs. "We told Amazon we would go through a brick wall to get their deal done," says Quattrone.

And Quattrone and Brady were seasoned enough to see an advantage in the slow market for Internet stocks—it would mean having less competition when telling the Amazon story to the big institutional stock buyers like Fidelity. And as they hit the road with Bezos selling "The Earth's Biggest Bookstore" to institutional investors all over the country, the company's deal book filled with interested investors.

But how much to charge for the stock? Amazon's original S–1 filing proposed $13 per share, but the huge demand for Amazon's stock created a last-minute debate between bankers and management over whether the company should go out at $17 versus $18 per share. Given that Amazon proposed to sell 3 million shares at its IPO, the decision between choosing $18 instead of $17 meant a difference of stuffing an additional $3 million into the company's coffers.

When Bezos, Quattrone, and Brady met in New York in March 1997, they were joined on the phone by John Doerr and Scott Cook, an Amazon board member and cofounder of Intuit, maker of the financial software package Quicken. The haggling started right away. Bezos had no doubt about the best price; he wanted to go out at $18 per share. Quattrone and Brady were more cautious; they recommended $17 per share, thinking they could sell the stock more easily to the institutional buyers. "The safe thing was to price it at $16," says Quattrone. "Seventeen dollars would have been bold, and $18 would have been incredibly aggressive."

Meanwhile, Doerr and Cook played devil's advocates, challenging Bezos on his motives. "It wasn't easy to articulate the benefits of a $17-per-share price, but it was easy to articulate the benefits of $18," Bezos asserts. So $18 per share it was.

By the time the Amazon team went on the road to sell the stock in May 1997, the Internet stock market was ticking upward. Without ever having made a dime of profit, the company raised $54 million in its public stock offering. Amazon was valued at a whopping $475 million. As usual, Bezos's shrewdness paid off, as he and his family retained 41 percent of the company stock. John Doerr and Kleiner Perkins kept a little over 14 percent.

But Amazon's stock value didn't soar to a billion dollars like that of the many Internet IPOs that would follow. "The stock initially popped to $29 per share," says Quattrone. "But it came under pressure because Barnes & Noble sued them and a lot of people were shorting the stock; the price actually came down to the issue price." For the company's next infusion of cash, Amazon skipped the equity route and instead hired DMG to raise another $75 million in debt financing from a group of banks.

By the summer of 1998, with more than 600 employees and heavy investments being pumped into advertising, promotion, and more technology, Amazon had lost $27.6 million on sales of $147.8

million. Still paranoid about the competition, Bezos decided to float a high-yield debt/junk bond financing to raise an additional $325 million. This move had an extra advantage for the Bezos family, who still owned a commanding percentage of the company, by avoiding the dilution that an equity offering would have posed.

This time around, though, Bezos turned down DMG's plan to do the deal in favor of Quattrone's former employer, Morgan Stanley. Bezos clearly had visions of grandeur. While Amazon's stock had hovered around a full if not highly overvalued price of $90 per share, the junk bond was a gamble that in three years the stock would be closer to $300 per share, a rise of more than 233 percent. This would allow the company to refinance the debt in a second offering sometime in the future at a much more attractive stock price. "Placing our debt was all about flexibility," explains Bezos. "You can't predict what some of the opportunities might be and how much cash they might require."

By January 1999 Amazon stock had done a three-for-one split. The price was at $160 per share, equal to $480 pre-split. Amazon proceeded to raise more money through a $1.25 billion convertible-bond offering lead-managed by Morgan Stanley, said to be the largest offering of its kind in United States history. Bezos had raised the stakes again.

A year before Bezos dreamed up Amazon, a different story unfolded in Silicon Valley. In the summer of 1993, Jerry Yang and David Filo should have been working on their doctoral theses in computer science, but surfing the Net was a lot more fun. Their Ph.D. adviser was out of the country on sabbatical, so what the hell.

Hanging out night and day in a cramped, stuffy office trailer on the Stanford campus, Yang and Filo put together a catalogue of Internet sites. At first it was for their personal reference, but it gradually evolved into *David and Jerry's Guide to the World Wide Web*. Soon, hundreds, then thousands of Web surfers were accessing their guide. In a spirit of whimsy and refreshing self-effacement, Yang and Filo called their growing service Yahoo.

Like the Homebrew personal computer phenomenon of almost

20 years earlier, Yahoo was an organic, grassroots movement that only gradually evolved into a business enterprise. But when they realized they might have a commercial opportunity on their hands, Yang and Filo slapped together a business plan and began shopping it around to venture capitalists. The partners at Kleiner Perkins wanted them to merge with another budding online service they had already funded, Excite. Yahoo also got offers from America Online and Netscape to sell out for stock and come join those companies as employees. But Yang and Filo, wanting to remain independent, declined.

Eventually, they hooked up with venture capitalist Michael Moritz of Sequoia Capital, a first-tier firm that had built a pioneering image by seed-funding companies such as Apple and Cisco. A charming Oxford graduate with a British accent and a ready smile, Moritz had joined Sequoia in 1986 after serving as a business reporter for *Time* magazine, and he'd been looking for a big hit ever since.

Sequoia decided to invest $1 million in Yahoo ("gave is not a verb we use at Sequoia," says Moritz) and helped them recruit a stellar management team. With seasoned chief executive Tim Koogle and chief operations officer Jeff Mallett on board, Yang and Filo could now call themselves Chief Yahoos.

In the fall of 1995, Yahoo was running out of cash, so they raised $4 million from Reuters and Softbank.

Within a few months, Yahoo's online traffic had doubled, they had signed up more than 80 advertisers, and they ran live news feeds from Reuters. Most amazingly of all, Yahoo was making a profit; an unprecedented feat for a company started during the early Internet boom.

These developments were not lost on Softbank. Its president, Masayoshi Son, came to Silicon Valley to see Yahoo in their off-campus digs, a dumpy out-of-the-way place with a leaky roof. The entrepreneurs ordered in pizza and Son laid out his proposal to buy out Yahoo completely. Instead, Yang, Filo, and Moritz agreed to sell some of their stock to Softbank for a total of $30 million, while another $70 million came directly from Son into the business.

As Moritz puts it, "We watched our competitors getting bigger allies and realized that to grow faster we needed some big trains. We wanted to avoid getting gauzumped by the competition."

A team from Goldman Sachs also came calling at the urging of a young Goldman associate, Victor Hwang, a friend of Yang's from his undergraduate days at Stanford. Although initially dismayed by the informality of the operation, the Goldman team was impressed enough by the Web traffic numbers to do more research and eventually agreed to underwrite Yahoo's initial public stock offering.

Yahoo had its own reasons for doing a public offering. Unlike search engine companies such as Excite, Infoseek, and Lycos, Yahoo didn't need the cash to build, operate, and maintain a technology back-end to run its business. Instead, Yahoo focused on funneling its resources into building a brand name as the leading Web indexer and ultimate navigational portal for the Internet. Yahoo's early strategy was to position itself more as a media company that would build its image leveraging big-time and creative advertising campaigns, in the same way the early tycoons of television and radio broadcasting did. More than just raising big bucks, an IPO would also give Yahoo the serious public exposure it needed if it were to become a household name and the leading contender in the emerging Web services space.

"We didn't want to risk having the other guys go public while we didn't," says Jerry Yang. "Not only would they have the extra cash, but they could also use the stock as currency to acquire other companies. To have Excite and Lycos out there consolidating the market while we couldn't would've been a huge mistake." He adds, "I also think the market at the time was clearly receptive to a story like ours."

So in February 1996 Yahoo's executives, bankers, and venture capitalists got together in the company's newer and only slightly nicer offices in Sunnyvale to discuss the offering. At the meeting the Goldman Sachs team reported that the demand for the stock was already high. They hadn't even built their offering book yet, and the requests to buy flowed in. Yahoo was a pure Internet play in a frothy market, and the bankers wanted to cash in; they figured they could charge up to $25 per share, allowing Yahoo to double up on its valuation.

"This was Goldman's first big Internet deal," says Yang. "They would have felt bad leaving money on the table because they knew if they kept their institutional customers happy, those clients would buy more deals down the line because they would have a sense of how to make money off the Internet."

But one of Yahoo's founders, the cerebral and normally quiet David Filo, was wary of getting too greedy; he wanted instead to reward investors by giving them a reasonable deal. The more experienced managers also realized if the stock started out lower and continued to go up, this would be great publicity for Yahoo and help boost its brand recognition, especially if their competitors' stocks dropped below their initial prices. Yahoo's team took the long view. "We didn't want to be viewed as a company that went up and then went down," says Yang. In essence, Yahoo wanted to create an investor brand as well as a company brand by establishing the best stock performance record among its competitors.

Since Softbank had just paid approximately $13 per share for the private stock holding, the team thought this was a good target price for the public offering.

In what they called "the fastest IPO known to man," Yahoo filed to go public in the first week of March and was a public company a month later. During that period, Goldman Sachs got over 100 Yahoo-related phone calls a day, and the bankers claim there was in excess of 100 million shares of demand for Yahoo's 3 million share offering.

In the first round of trading, the stock went up to $24.50 per share. Shares changed hands several times and peaked at $43 before coming down to $33 at the end of the day. The total market value came to almost $850 million.

In the months that followed, the market for Internet stocks went into a downswing, but Yahoo stock never traded below its offering price, unlike its competitors. Its branding strategy had succeeded.

• • •

Although Yahoo and Amazon are a study in contrasts, both are among the Internet elite and the darlings of Wall Street. Yahoo had followed the old rules: It was profitable before going public and had raised plenty of money in private financing before its IPO. Its founders David Filo and Jerry Yang each retained a 15 percent ownership in Yahoo, while Sequoia Capital ended up with 17 percent and Softbank, 37 percent.

In contrast, Amazon is still not profitable. Amazon founder and CEO Jeff Bezos avoided further dilution of his 41 percent stake in the company by choosing to do a junk bond debt financing and later a convertible bond rather than another public offering or any additional private financing. By June 1999 all three entrepreneurs—Yang, Filo, and Bezos—were paper billionaires, and the Internet Bubble was bigger than ever.

We chose to open our book by telling the inside stories about the Amazon and Yahoo IPOs because we feel they represent the high drama of life inside the Internet Bubble. In this world, entrepreneurs, professional managers, venture capitalists, and investment bankers all work together to plot strategy, make decisions, and raise big bucks at a rate of speed unprecedented in the history of business. Read on as we describe what it's like to live and win big during a mania that is still unfolding as we finalize the last pages of this book.

Doonesbury

INTRODUCTION: THE INTERNET STOCK BUBBLE

> It's a sucker's game.
> –Bill Sahlman, Harvard Business School

Welcome to the Internet Bubble, a world led by a brash new generation of entrepreneurs who command thousands of Internet startups, many loaded with venture capital or flush with cash from recent initial public offerings (IPOs). The upside to this world is that the Internet boom is real. The companies successfully riding the electronic highway have transformed the technology industry, while also creating quality jobs and real wealth along the way. The downside is that the mania surrounding Internet companies has translated into too much venture capital, too many Internet startups, and too many Internet IPOs, driving both private and public company market valuations to insane levels. By our calculations, the 133 Internet companies that have gone public since Netscape in 1995 could be overvalued by as much as $230 billion (see Appendix A, "Calculating the Bubble," for further details). In the last half of 1998 and the first half of 1999, investors caught up in Internet mania drove Internet stocks up 400 percent, while the S&P 500 Index and Dow Jones Industrial Average increased 18.9 percent.

Given these market conditions, it's our view that individuals who own stock in public Internet companies could experience a 50 percent-plus meltdown in the value of their stock holdings if they don't sell before the Internet Bubble bursts.

But before we get further into this story, allow us first to admit that neither of us has a background in the investment industry. And as the technology investor Roger McNamee counseled us from the beginning, if we tried too hard to play stock analysts in this book, we would leave ourselves open for some real experts to "cut you off at the legs."

So for this book, we played the role of reporters. Our analysis and opinion can be described best as summarized from interviews with over 100 industry insiders. We tapped the wisdom of some of the smartest and most successful players in technology and finance, from Microsoft's Bill Gates, to entertainment investment banker Herb Allen Jr., to veteran venture capitalist Don Valentine. Virtually all those we interviewed agreed with this book's basic premise that the Internet company market as well as the venture capital industry are ripe for a huge shakeout. As this book was close to completion, Wall Street's most influential Internet analyst, Mary Meeker of Morgan Stanley Dean Witter, predicted publicly that a significant adjustment in Internet stocks would occur sometime by the end of 1999. "I think a big correction would be very healthy. I personally would welcome it," she told *The New Yorker* in an article titled "The Woman in the Bubble."

The Internet Boom

Another important point we want to establish up front is that in spite of our skepticism regarding Internet company valuations, we firmly believe in the Internet as a catalyst for the growth of the technology industries and for profound change in our culture.

On one level, the Internet is an extension of Metcalfe's Law, coined by Ethernet inventor and 3Com founder Robert Metcalfe, which states that the value of any network increases by the square of the number of people using it. In other words, a network with 500 people plugged into it is 100 times more useful than one with only 50 people attached. Metcalfe's Law focused on the network of computers within a corporation tied together with local area networks. The Internet takes Metcalfe's Law to an entirely new dimension—we can now imagine a network that ties together not only corporate users but potentially every individual in the world.

And the numbers have started to bear out this growing social revolution: 35 percent of all U.S. households are online, and about the same percentage of U.S. adults use the Internet. According to International Data Corp. (IDC), some 160 million people around the globe are logged onto the Internet; by 2003, IDC expects that figure to mushroom to 500 million.

On the commercial front, at least 30 percent of U.S. companies now have a home page on the World Wide Web. Advertising on the Internet more than doubled in 1998 to $1.92 billion, for the first time surpassing the amount spent on outdoor advertising such as billboards. This number is expected to grow to $8 billion by the year 2002. Online commerce is also growing at exponential rates. IDC predicts that businesses and consumers, which spent a combined $50 billion online in 1998, will fork over $1.3 trillion for goods and services in 2003.

In 1995 John Doerr, of venture capital firm Kleiner Perkins Caufield & Byers, predicted that the Internet boom would be bigger than the PC boom. In Morgan Stanley's spring 1999 Technology IPO Yearbook, Doerr's prediction was confirmed, at least on a wealth-creation basis. Since its inception in 1994, the Internet industry has changed from an up-and-comer to the third-largest technology industry by market appreciation. By 1999 the market wealth creation by the Internet ($236 billion), on an equivalent basis, exceeded that created by the PC ($221 billion).

A Tidal Wave of Capital

This spectacular growth in both technology and the Internet has not gone unnoticed by investors of all kinds. In 1998 alone the venture capital industry raised 139 new funds and plunked over $17 billion in new capital into startups, representing an incredible 47.5 percent increase over the previous year—the biggest jump in the history of venture capital.

In the public market one distinguishing characteristic of the Internet boom is that the vast majority of the investors holding

Internet stocks today are individual investors, compared to the typical investor mix in a technology holding such as Microsoft, where institutional investors generally own at least 50 percent. Baby boomers, awakening to the fact that pumping money into the stock market, whether through mutual funds, 401(k) plans, or individual stocks, promises better returns than investments in real estate, bonds, or passbook savings, and have charged into the market with a vengeance. In 1990, stock holdings represented 21 percent of households' total financial assets; by early 1999 the share had more than doubled to almost 50 percent. From 1996 through mid-1998, the net inflows to domestic mutual funds exceeded $500 billion, bringing total mutual fund assets to $5.2 trillion.

There's also been a constant flow of international funds from Asia and Europe into U.S. stock markets, including the high-tech-dominated NASDAQ. Another contributor to the wave is the Federal Reserve's increase of the money supply circulating in the United States; it's grown at an annual rate of 11 percent. A large amount of the excess money has found its way into the stock market, fueling more speculation. This explosive growth in the money supply has contributed to a virtual tsunami of capital washing over America's markets and high-technology industry.

And the technology sector has continued to grow. In 1998, U.S. technology industries generated $955 billion in revenues, representing roughly 53 percent of all business capital expenditures. These totals also mean that the technology industries contributed 8 percent of the gross domestic product—about one-third of the growth of the GDP in recent years—and 37 percent of all new jobs. As in the 1920s, when the auto industry drove economic growth, today technology is the main driver and the third-largest industry in our economy, trailing real estate and health care.

The performance of the technology industries in the stock market has been equally impressive. At the end of 1998, approximately 975 publicly traded technology stocks had institutional research coverage, and the aggregate market value of those stocks was $3 trillion. According to Morgan Stanley Dean Witter, the 1,243 technology IPOs of the past 19 years represent $2.1 trillion of the total.

Much of this investor excitement has been, of course, encouraged by a steadily growing U.S. economy, with low interest rates, almost no inflation, and record high employment. Some credit goes to deregulation of business, increased efficiency and innovation, and effective corporate restructuring for competition in global markets.

Some see factors such as low inflation as evidence of a New Economy, maybe even a so-called Long Boom in which the rate of economic growth actually accelerates because of technology. As we show in a later chapter, if it is a New Economy, it's one full of paradoxes in which there is no unusual increase in the rate of growth. This perspective is important to understand because the New Economy is sometimes used to justify the huge valuations of Internet companies.

Technology's Gilded Age

In spite of this rosy economic picture full of venture capital and public money, the technology industry has been here before. Insiders who played the technology investment game back in the 1980s, when the personal computer industry was born, recognize the parallels between the PC Bubble and today's Internet version. Venture capitalist Jim Breyer of Accel Partners says about Internet mania: "It's emotion, it's frenzy, it's the fad, and 90 percent of the companies should never have gone public and will go out of business or hit very hard times."

Historical technology investment statistics support the cautionary analysis of venture capital veterans such as Breyer. Since 1980, 5 percent of all technology companies has generated 86 percent of total shareholder value appreciation. With the flood of newly public high-tech companies hitting the market, it's difficult to know just who those few winners will be. "You've got to kiss a lot of frogs before you find a handsome prince," says Mary Meeker of Morgan Stanley.

For example, five large technology stocks—Microsoft, Intel, Dell, Cisco, and Oracle—make up almost 65 percent of the total technology shareholder value for the NASDAQ Computer Index, which represents over 700 computer industry-related stocks. The top-performing technology companies of each new generation continue to dominate the market value of the entire sector. "The other companies are like a single shot of vermouth in a hundred gallons of Stolichnaya," says Paul Deninger, chairman and CEO of technology investment bank Broadview International.

Bill Sahlman of Harvard Business School points out, "People like to say that if you had bought Microsoft stock when it became public in 1986 at a $460 million market value, you would have made 122 percent per year over the last 13 years. That's great—but you've got to go through a lot of stuff to find a Microsoft. The likelihood at that point that Microsoft, run by a 26-year-old college dropout, would succeed was very modest."

Actually, the insiders control the market for public offerings. They're like the house in Las Vegas or Atlantic City—the insider will win in the end. "The game has always been rigged," says Sahlman. "And if after 30 minutes of this poker game you don't know who the sucker is, you're in trouble."

And the insiders get fabulously rich from these IPOs, while others seek wealth either through entrepreneurship or by investing in the Internet. This is why Roger McNamee, a longtime investor in technology, has dubbed our era "Technology's Gilded Age."

"As I make my rounds of Silicon Valley," says McNamee, "I am struck by the degree to which money has become the main concern. Where entrepreneurs and employees once dedicated themselves to building great companies, there is now a relentless pursuit of wealth and the toys—cars, homes, even airplanes—that come with it. They seem most motivated by the gold in this golden age."

"We're in one of the biggest speculative excesses of all time," confirms venture capitalist Bob Kagle of Benchmark Capital. "Money is thrown at companies long before they've proven anything or learned the disciplines that come from facing the market and its realities."

"Building a company is a hard job," says Bandel Carano, a venture capitalist with Oak Investment Partners. "We haven't figured out how to shorten the time it takes to build a real company from 10 years down to 1. Why do companies go public after one year now instead of 10? Because we've stopped putting the effort into actually trying to build a company. We've put our effort into building stocks, because you can do that pretty quickly. You can put together a team, spin a story, get rich quick."

There are always two groups of speculators at work in a bubble: the insiders and the outsiders. The insiders naturally have the edge; they can buy into investments before they bubble up. The outsiders, on the other hand, usually come late to the game and buy into the market at much higher prices and at a higher level of risk than they realize. They are left holding the bag when the bubble bursts, even as the insiders get rich.

So When Will the Bubble Burst?

While we feel a shakeout in the Internet stock market is imminent, this book won't predict exactly when this might occur. But it wouldn't take much to accelerate this shakeout process. As veteran technology banker Sandy Robertson points out, with stocks at an all-time high, an increase in interest rates or the reversal of the flow of mutual fund cash into the market could weaken stock market performance in a hurry.

This book will examine the forces creating the Internet Bubble and give outsiders the benefit of some insider knowledge, so that the playing field might be a little more level. In the process, we'll provide readers with a glimpse of how the behavior of Internet investors today is similar to that of investors during other manias. We will take a behind-the-scenes look at the financial wizards funding the current Internet craze, including the venture capitalists, led by Kleiner Perkins Caufield & Byers, who want not only to invest in hot new Internet companies, but also to create whole new industries. We'll also highlight the activity and practices of the investment bankers of high tech—how they compete for deals, spin shares, and help their favorite institutional investors flip stock.

Finally, for the benefit of individual investors, we profile some of the most popular Internet companies and what they tell us about the market today, and suggest how the outsider can learn to invest wisely, just like an insider. We conclude with an open letter to Internet stockholders that, to the best of our abilities, summarizes the Internet Bubble phenomenon in all its glory and in all its shame.

Doonesbury

INTERNET MANIA

> **We have never had something so disproportionally publicized by everybody in the world as the greatest coming of anything ever as the Internet.**
> —Donald Valentine, Sequoia Capital

In the last five years, individual investors have poured millions into more than 2,000 Internet startup companies with nothing more on their minds than striking it rich. And as with any gold rush, some speculators have cashed in big. Below is a chart of the top ten performing Internet stocks that went public before May 1999 that tells the story. Shown here are the annualized return for these stocks. What's astounding is that the percentage increase in the stock prices given below is not even calculated from the IPO price, but from the closing price at the end of the first trading week when the normal investor would be able to buy these stocks.

Company	Percentage Return
Healtheon	3339 %
eBay	3269 %
AboveNet	1853 %
AmeriTrade	1105 %
MessageMedia	886 %
Go2Net	872 %
CMG	792 %
InfoSpace	681 %
E*Trade	652 %
Bottomline Technologies	611 %

But manias are nothing new. The classic historic case of a mania, of course, is the tulip mania of seventeenth-century Holland. The country's extremely prosperous mercantile culture created a place, as the historian Simon Schama puts it, "where a glut of capital washed around looking for a place to settle," and in which "thousands were eager to squander what disposable income they had in the irrational hope of instantaneous wealth." And this wasn't just the elite, but "modest folk" such as artisans, millers, weavers, carpenters, smiths, maidservants, and barge keepers. People of all grades converted their property into cash and invested in tulip bulbs.

There was about a two-year buildup of the tulip market before it took off in the year 1636—and then came crashing down for good in April 1637. At the peak of the mania, tulip prices doubled or tripled by the week or even the day, and the object became to snap up the tulip shares and then off-load them at a choice markup.

People eventually saw that this frenzy couldn't last forever. And when the full panic hit, prices dropped by the hour, and the tulip shares became worthless. Those who had borrowed to buy the bulbs went bankrupt. "Substantial merchants were reduced almost to beggary, and many a representative of a noble line saw the fortunes of his house ruined beyond redemption," wrote Charles Mackay in his classic study *Extraordinary Popular Delusions and the Madness of Crowds*.

More than 200 years later, America had its own version of tulip mania in the form of railroad stock speculation. Ultimately, many of the stocks sat underwater or failed completely as railroad bankruptcies piled up losses totaling $3 billion by the end of the nineteenth century. Around the same time, America also experienced the Comstock Lode silver rush. Historian Oscar Lewis describes Comstock mania:

Its silver mines became a sort of national anodyne, a sure avenue of escape into a land where every dream came true and every illusion had the substance of reality. All over America millions believed that there, granted the opportunity and a bit of luck, one's vision of wealth and power and prestige would surely materialize. The nation never had a more satisfactory wishing well.

After a concerted rush to buy silver stocks, the boom eventually collapsed, and the average investor lost out. In the end, only the insiders prospered. Lewis concludes:

Thousands were impoverished by the enormous stock losses . . . So widespread was this experience, and so painful, that the public was eventually forced to conclude that Comstock speculation was a losing game to all except the few who controlled the producing mines and who, having day-by-day knowledge of their prospects, knew in advance of the public when to buy or sell. Realization that the cards were stacked against them came slowly to thousands of bemused and hopeful gamblers.

The twentieth century has had speculative manias as well in the Florida real estate boom and the stock market frenzy of the 1920s. In both cases, many stories circulated of fortunes made overnight, and there was constant talk of prime real estate, hot companies, and surefire stock tips.

By 1927, though, the Florida land boom was a bust; nevertheless, stock prices rose on Wall Street and people continued to buy. "Thousands speculated without the slightest knowledge of the companies upon whose fortune they were relying," writes historian Frederick Lewis Allen. All sorts of people were in the market; it was a national mania that everyone expected to go on and on. A substantial portion of the American economy was supported by this wild rise in stock prices. Even one of the era's most esteemed economists, Irving Fisher of Yale University, got completely caught up in the speculative euphoria of the time; in the autumn of 1929, just before the Crash, he said, "Stock prices have reached what looks like a permanently high plateau."

The New Mania

Veteran technology investor Roger McNamee likes to distinguish between the industrial and technological manias that led to something lasting and mere fads such as the tulips that came to nothing. "There were a whole bunch of industries funded on the backs of gigantic manias, many of which led to great industrial revolutions," he says. "We like to speculate on things that are new and different—it's in our genes. When great new technologies come along, whether they are canals, railroads, autos, computers, or the Internet, everybody wants a piece of the action. Speculation tends to go hand in hand with entrepreneurship."

But McNamee also carefully explains that during these financial manias, which generally span a three- to five-year period at the beginning of any new industry boom, capital is infused rather indiscriminately into the industry. On the upside, this infusion of funds stimulates a huge burst of creativity, accelerates the development of new markets, and keeps the U.S. on top. Eventually, though, a Darwinian process sets in where the companies with sustainable business models survive, but the vast majority of startups implode and go out of business.

Investors in past industrial manias such as autos, steel, and canals were all big spenders who poured tons of capital into numerous companies. In the first decade of the twentieth century, 508 automobile companies were started, including Ford Motor Company; now only a few remain. The personal computer boom was similar. For the Internet boom, even more money is available as angel and corporate investors and even day traders have joined the mix, providing billions in risk capital. "The level of money and the level of company formations has skyrocketed—it's really quite amazing," observes Bill Gates.

But as is the case during all financial manias, McNamee suspects that the average dollar invested in the Internet space will have an extraordinarily low return. "It will be a number of years before the enabling technologies become standardized sufficiently enough for the Internet industry to take off," he believes. To bolster his case, he points to the increase in the wealth of Microsoft's chairman and CEO, Bill Gates, whose stock holdings were worth only $5 billion in 1990 but are worth over $90 billion in 1999. "Microsoft has been around for twenty years, but only in the last five has its value spiked," McNamee states.

Internet IPOs for Sale

As capital floods the market, companies not only get started faster, but go public sooner. Many have only a vague idea about what their strategy is, other than that it has something to do with "grabbing some Internet real estate." Says venture capitalist Ann Winblad of Hummer Winblad Partners, which has placed big bets on the Internet, "There are companies where, even if you squint, you can't figure out what their business models are." Winblad also points out that some are not companies at all, but merely a business built upon a single product.

So how do so many fledgling Internet companies get public? As in other manias leading to bubbles, there is a whole financial food chain that benefits from the process—in this case the entrepreneurs, the venture capitalists, the investment bankers, and certain large institutional investors and mutual funds. Venture capitalist Don Valentine of Sequoia Capital candidly calls it a "greed system" and states bluntly, "No one in the chain is doing this for altruistic reasons."

In the Internet boom era, venture capitalists are pushed by both their investors and the entrepreneurs they invest in to shoot quickly for an IPO. "When the market is hot, there's pressure to take your portfolio companies public because every other venture capitalist is," says Bob Kagle of Benchmark Capital, which funded eBay, one of the few Internet plays other than Yahoo that went public as a profitable company. Valentine offers a more sober motive: "To us, going public is just another means of financing the roll-out of a company. Yahoo is a good example."

But quick IPOs require willing investors, and the market over the last four years has demonstrated an insatiable demand for Internet stocks. "More than 95 percent of the other venture capitalists I work with like to say, 'The ducks are quacking; it's time to feed them,'" says Jim Breyer, managing partner of Accel Partners, whose Internet home runs include UUNET and Real Networks. But as investor demand rises, the quality of the companies generally sinks. "The quality bar to go public has been lowered and lowered and lowered," says Brad Koenig, managing director and head of the technology-investment-banking practice at Goldman Sachs.

But the investment banks willingly accommodate their investors' desires for technology IPOs so they can collect their 7 percent underwriting fees and sign on new clients to manage their follow-on offerings. And this banking environment has led to one of the most frothy IPO eras in history. "You have investment bankers leaning out of their shoes to find things to take public," declares Sequoia's Valentine. But the bankers make no apologies about taking fledgling companies public to meet this demand. "It's our job to put food on the stoop," declares Cristina Morgan, managing director at the investment bank Hambrecht & Quist. "If the cat eats it, we've done our job."

Investment bankers also make their money by keeping their big institutional clients happy. These investors control huge blocks of cash and use this financial power to bang on the bankers for big stakes in hot IPOs. And given the huge competition for IPO shares from the over three-dozen primary institutional investors around the U.S. that favor technology stocks, it's almost impossible for most individual investors to secure any IPO shares on their own.

Feeding this investment mania is the growing number of specialized funds such as Amerindo Technology, Munder NetNet, WWW Internet, Monument Fund, and one simply called Internet Fund, that hunger to buy technology stocks early in the game—including private mezzanine rounds early in a public company's life.

Geoff Yang, a venture capitalist with Institutional Venture Partners, says, "The irony of Internet mania is that everybody wants the same thing, but nobody is willing to take the pain on his deal, so companies that shouldn't be public are public. But no one, from investment bankers down to venture capitalists and the entrepreneurs, will sacrifice his deal if the public is willing to ride it."

What whets the public appetite for these investments is the innate human tendency of wanting to get something without necessarily creating something—a bit like the lottery. That's how, in 1920, Charles Ponzi convinced investors that he could pay them 50 percent interest for the use of their money for just 45 days. It was too good to be true. Ponzi took in $7.9 million, and the early investors were paid with funds raised from later ones before the whole scheme collapsed and the latecomers lost all their capital.

During manias, public investors tend to forget how much time it takes for viable companies to become established and for an industry to mature. "The investment maniacs in the public market end up sacrificing their net worth for the sake of the industry as a whole, something they obviously wouldn't do if they knew better," observes McNamee. "There's a thinning of the herd, and the greedy lose their capital on behalf of the insiders."

The added danger is that life in the Bubble also encourages the maniac speculators to overspend and overleverage themselves, racking up high credit card bills and other debt that could easily send them into a financial death spiral when the Bubble bursts. As stock prices today have escalated, so have consumer spending and debt. Debt as a percentage of personal income rose from 58 percent in 1973, to 76 percent in 1989 to 85 percent in 1997. Total credit card debt soared from $243 billion in 1990 to $560 billion in 1997. American families carry an average of more than $7,000 in credit card debt. And one American family in 68 filed for personal bankruptcy in 1998, seven times the rate in 1980.

Yet insiders continue to exploit the highly speculative environment. In some cases the mania encourages exploitation. In a 1996 interview with *Red Herring*, Michael McCaffery, president and CEO of investment bank Robertson Stephens, spoke bluntly about the nature of this public venture capital game. "You wouldn't find any venture capitalists in Silicon Valley willing to finance these companies with their own money at these prices. The professionals would never do that," McCaffery declared.

Just take a look at the stock prospectuses of these newly public venture companies—the risk sections are longer than the business summaries. In 1997 about one-third of the Internet companies completing IPOs lost money; in 1999 the same portion didn't even record any sales. Most of these companies have made no profit and have no idea when they will become profitable. Sometimes this vagueness is even seen as a virtue—that it's better to have no revenue than some revenue that doesn't grow very fast.

Part of the rationale for taking unprofitable companies public is the need to get out there to establish brand identity and to grab marketshare. But it's far from certain who the survivors, much less the big winners, will be. Many Internet companies just won't be around.

So the pressure of the financial food chain comes full circle, with the insiders pointing the finger at each other, even as they all reap the rewards. And the mania continues building toward the classic Darwinian shakeout that will follow.

Bubble Values

If most of the Internet companies will fail, and we still don't know who the ultimate winners will be, how do we value them? Stock security valuation is a challenge that goes back to the 1934 publication of the book *Security Analysis* by Benjamin Graham and David Dodd. Graham and Dodd tried to provide a logical way of evaluating stocks in the wake of the speculative frenzy that led to the Great Crash of 1929. In the 1920s, as in earlier decades, stock was valued subjectively, as much on the basis of rumor and "hot tips" as on anything else.

Graham and Dodd argued that share prices should follow a company's economic fundamentals, which they attempted to evaluate systematically. Their approach relied heavily on a company's historical earnings and on the balance-sheet values of tangible assets such as inventory, equipment, and the proverbial "bricks-and-mortar." Today, there is far greater emphasis on a company's future earnings power and on its intangible assets such as intellectual property and brand names, a measure especially true of Internet and software companies.

The traditional method of stock valuation tries to predict the long-term cash flows of a company, discounts those amounts back to the present, and then divides by the number of shares. As this process is much easier said than done, most analysts use a "good enough" proxy for cash flow called the price-to-earnings (P/E) formula in which you come up with an earnings multiple.

A further attempt to refine the formula for Internet companies is to do the proxy valuations based on EBITDA (earnings before interest, taxes, depreciation, and amortization).

The classic P/E ratio essentially shows how many more years of current earnings it would take to cover the current value of the shares. The higher the ratio, the more investors expect earnings to grow in the future. Beginning in 1950 and for several decades after, the typical P/E ratio was around 14. By the first quarter of 1999, the S&P 500 index average had a P/E ratio of about 31, and the S&P 500 Technology Index was almost 59.

P/E ratios still involve a certain amount of guesswork, and Internet companies must figure out what their income stream will look like in five years and what the real prospects for growth are.

Although the public market historically has had difficulty valuing new technologies and their growth potentials, the increase in stock prices, without question, has been wildly exaggerated for Internet companies. Yahoo saw its share price jump 584 percent in 1998, giving it a market value of more than $23 billion, which rose to $35 billion in the first quarter of 1999. Yahoo's P/E ratio got as high as 1,900. Amazon surged 966 percent in 1998 to a market value of nearly $17 billion, and as high as $21.4 billion, with a negative P/E ratio because it was still far from showing earnings in 1999. America Online rose 586 percent, giving it a market value of $71 billion, with a P/E ratio of over 275.

"There is no economic basis for these Internet stock valuations," admits Andy Bechtolsheim, cofounder of Sun Microsystems and an active angel investor in Internet companies. Bandel Carano of Oak Investment Partners agrees, "My view is that in the long run, technology businesses are worth between 10 and 20 times earnings, that's all. And it's 10 to 20 times the next 12 months' earnings, not five years out."

At some point, these darlings of cyberspace have to grow up and be valued like real companies. Money manager David Dreman applied a traditional dividend discount model to 10 go-go Internet stocks, assuming their earnings will grow a healthy 50 percent for the next three years, 25 percent for the five years after that, and gradually trending down to a mature 7.5 percent by the year 2020. Using this calculation, Yahoo, for example, should be valued at $13 per share instead of $161, and eBay at $6 per share instead of $187.

It's difficult to predict earnings for technology companies, partly because technology dislocations happen all the time. It's tough enough for franchises such as Microsoft and Intel to deal with this changing landscape, never mind the young technology company whose business model might be completely overthrown by unanticipated dislocations. This volatility is especially true in a new industry such as the Internet.

"When I got in the venture capital business in 1983, everybody had to own technology stocks," says Carano. "But by 1987, technology was considered an uninvestable asset class by professional money managers for exactly this reason—its unpredictability. Lots of people got burned. Right now, it's technology again, and they're willing to pay year 2005 earnings discounted back only 10 percent to justify today's stock price. Hello? It's hard enough to project Coca-Cola's next quarter growth rate, which is much easier to analyze than an Internet company's."

Bill Gates preaches the gospel of unpredictability even for Microsoft, which has grown at a steady rate of 40 percent-plus over the last 20 years. "Coca Cola will make its money off the same soft drink formula in 10 years. In those same 10 years, Microsoft will have had to completely reinvent all its products and our whole company," says Gates. "That's why I have always thought Microsoft was overvalued in the market."

Ultimately, the Internet space will become a bifurcated market, divided into two unequal groups. There will be the go-go stocks such as At Home, eBay, Yahoo, and Amazon, with top-flight venture capitalists, name-brand bankers, thorough analysts, and lots of business press and with them astronomical valuations. Then there will be all the other Internet stocks, whose stock prices will eventually be underwater.

Morgan Stanley's spring 1999 Technology IPO Yearbook noted that from February 1997, half of the 42 Internet IPOs that followed Netscape's IPO in August 1995 were trading below their offering prices. This meant that, excluding Netscape, investors had therefore lost over $375 million in market capitalization. By January 1999 the situation had reversed. Of the 78 Internet IPOs on record until December 1998, 83 percent had seen their market values appreciate by an incredible $156 billion (excluding $80 billion created by AOL).

Even while this trend has changed, Morgan Stanley's report still warns investors that many Internet stocks will prove overvalued. It again points to the fact that, since 1980, 5 percent of all technology IPOs has created 86 percent of the market value, and concludes that "the Internet will prove to be no exception" to this rule. Don Valentine corroborates this from a venture capitalist's perspective. "If you look at 20 or 30 years of history, a Sun Microsystems or a Cisco Systems happens only once in a while," he says. "There aren't many companies like that for the long term. We venture capitalists, by exception, create great companies."

There have been different attempts to justify the valuation of the go-go stocks that don't take into account fundamentals such as revenue growth or profit margins. One attempt uses Web site traffic as an indicator of at least relative valuation of a company with competitors. "Yeah, people come up with all these metrics to try to justify the stock price today. It's all bullshit," says Bruce Lupatkin, former head of research at Hambrecht & Quist and a longtime technology analyst.

A more serious alternative to P/E ratios is a method called Economic Value Added (EVA), which tries to measure the level of growth required to justify the current stock price. But when Amazon hit a price of $214 per share (pre-split), the EVA formula showed that its revenue would have to grow almost 60 percent per year for 10 years, reaching annual sales of $63 billion by 2009 to justify its price.

By comparison, Microsoft's growth has averaged 43 percent per year since it went public in 1986. Amazon would have to outpace Microsoft to reach the level of growth needed to make Amazon's stock price reasonable at even $214 per share. Yet Amazon stock went up to more than $350 per share, with a market value of nearly $17 billion in late 1998, after CIBC Oppenheimer analyst Henry Blodgett, now an Internet analyst with Merrill Lynch, set his 12-month target price for the stock at $400 per share. Not long after, Amazon stock did a three-for-one split. By the end of the first week of January 1999, the split stock price was up to over $160 per share. Pre-split, that would equal $480 per share. Amazon's market value was more than that of JC Penney and Kmart combined.

That companies keep their stocks pumping up by splitting their prices on a regular basis still bewilders industry players and has become an inside joke. Roger McNamee was in rare form last spring while addressing an audience of institutional investors in San Francisco: "Betting on Internet stocks, it's actually pretty easy. Here are the rules: 50 bucks a share is cheap; $150 a share is fairly valued; but at $200 a share, the stock is cheap again because that means you are about to have a four-for-one split."

The disconnect between business fundamentals and stock prices is real. Morgan Stanley Dean Witter's index of 73 Internet companies collectively lost $1.5 billion in 1998 yet had a combined market value of $115 billion.

"I've spent a fair amount of time trying to make an argument for the valuation of these Internet companies," says Lise Buyer, Internet analyst and director of the technology group at investment bank CS First Boston. "I can't do it. So I fall back on the Graham and Dodd comment that the buyer of such stocks is not making an investment, but a bet on a new technology or a new market. They are in an odds setting rather than a valuation process."

Say Hello to Mo

It's important to note that the go-go stocks have been boosted largely by momentum investors—people who aren't afraid to buy high, with the bet they can sell for even higher. Momentum investors buy the stocks simply because they're going up in price, not because of a company's underlying sales, earnings, or other business fundamentals. This kind of investing is driven by a certain herd psychology—if an IPO becomes "hot," the momentum investors stampede all over each other in anticipation of a huge price jump. They must buy the stock because others are buying it; people try to outguess the fashion in the stock market. Ultimately, they are looking for the "greater fool" who will pay more for it than they did.

In recent years retail day traders have driven momentum investing. These traders tune into business news networks like CNBC and CNNfn for continuous 24-hour coverage to help them with their investing. They also do online research and tap into Web sites such as Silicon Investor and The Motley Fool, where they can chat with like-minded people. Naturally, they use services such as E*Trade, Charles Schwab Online, and Discover Online to trade online. At an average fee of $15 a trade, online brokerage commissions are about 70 percent lower than what they were even three years ago, making the online services even more attractive to users.

An estimated 5 to 7 million day traders were online in the first quarter of 1999; their number was projected to go up to 10 million by the end of 1999, and perhaps as high as 18 million by 2002. Their activity accounted for 25 to 33 percent of all retail trading and was increasing quickly. Overall, online day traders accounted for about 14 percent of the stock market's daily trading volume, and about two to three times that for many Internet stocks. In many cases, day traders had taken over the main trading of Internet stocks from the major institutional buyers. In November 1998, for example, the average trade size of Yahoo was 438 shares, 453 for Amazon, and 310 for eBay. In February 1999 more than three out of four trades in Amazon, Yahoo, and eBay were for 1,000 shares or fewer, far smaller than the typical blocks of thousands of shares institutions usually trade.

The day-trading frenzy ultimately carried over to the stocks of the very companies profiting from their business—Charles Schwab, E*Trade, Ameritrade, and others. The stock price of Schwab, for example, soared 40 percent in one five-day period in April of 1999 to over $150 a share, giving it a market value of more than $61 billion—more than the combined value of Wall Street firms Merrill Lynch, Lehman Brothers, Paine Webber, and Bear Stearns. Concurrently, shares of Ameritrade went over $173, and E*Trade hit $125, an increase of 50 percent.

Day traders might buy an Internet stock at $94 in the morning and sell it at $96 in the afternoon, in what's really a form of gambling. *The Economist* has dubbed this phenomenon "cyber casino" in which "shares of firms with almost no track record, are being bought by investors with no experience, at prices that appear to make no sense." The magazine adds that "the casino capitalists who spend seven or eight hours a day at their PCs trading Internet shares appear to be stark, staring mad."

CS First Boston Internet analyst Lise Buyer agrees. "It's Vegas now, unless you happen to be familiar with what some company is doing. From the outside we don't know what the Amazons are planning. Maybe it's a steal, but I sure don't know," she admits.

Some of the trading is done on margin—in other words, with borrowed money. Some traders have 50 percent margin accounts with their brokerages; half the price of the stock purchase is paid with the buyer's own money and the other half with money borrowed from the broker.

This type of gambling not only drives up the valuation of certain stocks but also greatly contributes to their volatility, since momentum investors like to unload their shares quickly at the beginning of what looks like a significant decline in price. "One of the most amazing things about the Internet Bubble era is that investors have been completely desensitized to one-day price drops—almost irrespective of the magnitude," says McNamee.

Even with these wild fluctuations in stock prices, day traders not only hope to get rich, they expect it. According to a survey by the Institute of Psychology and Markets, the average investor, online or off, expects an 18.6 percent annual rate of return on stocks. With dividend yields what they are, even with the Dow Jones over 10,000, that kind of return would put the Dow at 45,000 in 2010 and at 210,000 a decade after that.

Hope Floats

Another factor that drives up Internet stock prices is their generally narrow float, the limited number of company shares available to public investors. In January 1999, while 51 percent of Yahoo's shares were available for public trading, only 35 percent of the stock of Amazon, At Home, and C/Net was; eBay had a mere 9 percent available. The entire float of most of those stocks could be turned over in less than a month. Amazon's actually turned over twice a week in January 1999.

When demand is high and the supply is limited, the prices of these stocks skyrocket. Their super-high prices result from too many buyers chasing too few shares.

One main reason for the small float is that venture capitalists and other insiders keep more of the stock from their Internet start-ups for themselves. In the first half of 1998, these companies offered only 31 percent, on average, of their total capitalization to public investors, therefore allowing insiders to retain more decision-making power after their companies go public. It also positions them to sell their stock at a greater profit following the significant share appreciation typical in bubble markets.

Many insiders can sell after 180 days following the IPO. The selling of shares by Internet company insiders picked up considerably in the fourth quarter of 1998 and the first quarter of 1999. In March 1999, right as the 180-day lockup ended, executives and other insiders at eBay filed to sell $1.1 billion worth of stock. By then, eBay stock, the best-performing IPO in 1998, had appreciated more than 25-fold from its IPO value in September of 1998, and its market capitalization was $23 billion. The insiders sold the secondary offering of 6.5 million shares of eBay at $170 per share in April.

Breaking the Record

The IPO historic record-breakers are among the go-go stocks or onetime darlings to watch out for. These stocks start out with an offering price at anywhere from $9 to $28 per share and skyrocket on the first day of trading, often to over $1 billion in total market value. In recent times, this IPO group has included Earthweb, Theglobe.com, eBay, Marketwatch.com, iVillage, and Priceline.com. "We call these gigastocks," jokes Andy Kessler of Velocity Capital, which made a boatload of cash betting on its own gigastock, Inktomi, which provides search engine technology for Web sites.

Earthweb, for example, is an online provider of technical information and computer software for Web site designers. But Earthweb gets its revenue from advertisers and had not turned a profit by the time of its IPO on November 10, 1998. It lost $7.8 million in 1997 and had lost $5.3 million in the first nine months of 1998. It sold 2.1 million shares, a 27 percent stake, on its first day of trading as its stock price soared from $14 per share to a closing price of $48.69—a 247 percent gain.

Just two days later, Theglobe.com, which helps clients design Web pages, went public. It offered 3.1 million shares at $9 per share, and the first-day closing price was a whopping $63.50, a record 606 percent gain! Its market value was $622 million, even though the company had $11.5 million of losses in the first nine months of 1998. By the end of the year, its stock was down to just over $32 per share. And by July 1999 was around $18 per share.

The online auctioneer eBay is even better known. On September 24, 1998 it went public at $18 per share; seven weeks later its stock was up to $174 per share and its market capitalization was a staggering $7 billion. During that period, eBay's stock turned over at a rate of more than 5 million shares per day on five separate days, a stunning record of activity, given that eBay's float was only 3.5 million shares. By the end of 1998, eBay's stock had multiplied 10 times within 10 weeks, amounting to an increase of more than 1,400 percent and a stock price of over $240 per share. It took Microsoft four years to achieve that kind of stock price growth.

In 1998, Internet offerings jumped an unbelievable 70 percent, on average, in their first day of trading. In 1999 the IPO frenzy increased, as almost a quarter of the offerings done in the first quarter of 1999 and a whopping 57 percent of IPOs in the second quarter were for Internet-related companies.

Marketwatch.com, a financial news Web site owned by CBS, went public at $17 per share and closed at more than $80 per share on its first day of trading—up 474 percent. Nearly 10 million shares of Marketwatch traded, even though only 3.1 million were issued, meaning that the original 3 million shares changed hands at least three times during the first day. Before the IPO, institutional investors had put in orders for more than 100 million shares.

Not far behind Marketwatch was Priceline.com, an online service that allows users to locate their favorite prices for airline tickets and hotel reservations. Priceline issued 10 million shares that were originally priced at $16 per share, but which opened at $81. Its closing price was $69, an increase of 331 percent.

iVillage, an online service specifically for women, was another hot first-quarter IPO, going out at $24 per share and closing at over $80 after soaring as high as $100 on the first day of trading. The first trade of the day was valued at more than $95—despite accusations by a former company CFO about inappropriate accounting, and the fact that there was already plenty of competition in the market. It also didn't seem to matter that iVillage had lost almost $44 million in 1998 and $21 million a year earlier.

iVillage was also significant because it signaled a trend toward an initial offering price for Internet stocks over $20 per share. It seems companies got tired of leaving money on the table when they knew the market would support higher pricings. The sense was that companies should raise as much money as they could while the mania lasted.

"The first thing we told our companies was, 'Go sell your stock. Take advantage of it,'" says Sandy Robertson, cofounder of the investment bank Robertson Stephens. "It's like the way the old Green Bay Packers coach Vince Lombardi used to tell his running backs to run for daylight. When you see the daylight, go for it." Edmund Cash-man, head of the syndicate desk at investment bank Legg Mason Wood Walker, is even more blunt: "It's the Wall Street way. We're all greedy as hell."

But someone still had to buy these Internet shares in the after-market frenzy. "People are buying Internet stocks as if they're Beanie Babies," says Internet analyst Lise Buyer of CS First Boston. "A Beanie Baby is worth 23 cents, but temporarily I've got to pay $20 for it. And I'll pay even $150 for it, until I'm no longer inter-ested, and then I'll say, 'Damn! it's just a piece of felt and some beans. What was I thinking?'"

It All Started with Netscape

Perhaps the most famous Internet IPO is Netscape's, whose offer-ing on August 9, 1995, generated a frenzy of interest. Internet analyst Mary Meeker calls that date "the start of Year One in the online era." One venture capitalist traces the current Internet mania back to the Netscape IPO. "What you found," he says, "is that certain traders, mostly institutions, made a lot of money from the quick rise in Netscape's stock."

Netscape's IPO started with a share price of $14 that doubled to $28 per share the day before the offering, and went from 3.5 million shares available to 5 million. The stock closed its first day of trading at $58.25. In the aftermarket, the stock went as high as $87, but by 1997 it had dropped almost as low as its offering price. It finally crept back up into the 20s and 30s in 1998.

Paul Deninger, chairman and CEO of technology-investment bank Broadview International, says, "If you bought Netscape just after the IPO and held it, you were screwed. If you bought Netscape within six months of the IPO, you were screwed. You were so far underwater you can't even imagine." Fortunately for Netscape, the company was eventually bought by AOL in late 1998 for $4 billion, a hefty premium over what their stock price was trading at on the day the deal was inked. In spite of this handsome price, the sale of

Netscape marked a rather unceremonious ending to Netscape's fairy-tale story as an Internet pioneer. Just two years earlier, Netscape had commanded 80 percent of the Web browser market; now it clung to barely half of it. As one pundit put it, "Netscape devolved from a browser business into a schizophrenic quilt of a part-portal, part-enterprise software, part-browser company."

In retrospect, the early publicity from Netscape's IPO may have backfired. "I think they went public a year to eighteen months too early," says Jim Breyer of Accel Partners. "If they had waited, and had not charged for their Internet browser but continued to build a presence with it, instead of tipping off Microsoft the way they did through their massive public offering, Netscape would have been fundamentally more successful long term. It was a strategic mistake."

As Michael Cusumano and David Yoffie point out in their book *Competing on Internet Time: Lessons from Netscape and Its Battle with Microsoft*, Netscape's overpriced stock also put pressure on the company's management to constantly meet Wall Street's high expectations on a quarterly basis. One result was that Netscape felt it had to keep charging for its Internet browser for the sake of the additional revenue, while Microsoft gave its browser away and grabbed more and more marketshare.

The Strange Case of K-Tel International and Other Internet Wanna-Bes

To recognize just how absurd the mania has gotten, look no further than K-Tel International, a company best known for selling the music recordings of fading pop stars on late-night television.

Before marketing such music compilations as "70s Teen Heart-throbs," K-Tel sold contraptions like the Miracle Brush lint remover and the Veg-O-Matic vegetable slicer and dicer. It branched out into music when it began selling a compilation titled "Hooked on Classics," in which classical music was played to a disco beat. In 1984, after disco slumped and K-Tel's investments in oil, gas, and real estate went south, the company went bankrupt.

Eventually the company pulled out of bankruptcy, and until April 1998 its public stock was very thinly traded, with only a few hundred shares changing hands on most days. This all changed when K-Tel suddenly announced that it planned to open an Internet record store. Its stock jumped from about $4 per share to almost $40. According to the *New York Times*, company founder Philip Kives of Winnipeg, Canada, who owned 80 percent of K-Tel, quickly sold 2.6 million shares after the stock price spiked up.

By October 1998 the share price had slumped again to about $8. Yet in early November, K-Tel announced it would sell music on Playboy's Web site as well as in a nonexclusive way on Microsoft's MSN online shopping channel. K-Tel's stock immediately shot up 93 percent. On some days more than 20 million shares changed hands, which was impressive, given that only 8.3 million shares were available for trading, 4 million of which still belonged to company founder Philip Kives.

Apparently, it didn't matter to stock buyers that K-Tel had lost money in three out of the previous four years, posting a loss of $3.1 million in the last quarter before the Playboy announcement. Or that the market for selling music online was already crowded, led by powerhouse Amazon and its nearest competitor CDNow. In fact, Amazon had featured billing on Microsoft's shopping channel, while K-Tel was only one of six others listed in the music and video section. And only 121,000 people had visited K-Tel's Web site in September 1998 compared with 2.2 million for CDNow during the same month.

By November 1998 K-Tel International was in danger of getting delisted from the NASDAQ stock exchange, since the company's total assets of $900,000 had fallen well below the minimum requirement of $4 million to stay listed. The company obviously did not have the tens of millions of dollars required to compete on the Internet. Not surprisingly, the threat of delisting caused K-Tel's stock to plunge from almost $40 a share to $10.

But K-Tel isn't the only ridiculous example of an Internet wannabe. Books-a-Million, an Alabama-based company with a little-known chain of bookstores in the Southeast, suddenly announced on

November 25, 1998, that it planned to sell books on the Internet. The company's stock rose from $4.38 per share the day before the announcement to $47 only three market trading sessions later. On one day, more than 8.2 million shares changed hands, driven by day traders, with the average trade for the overall session being only 437 shares. Company executives sold their shares like crazy. A report in the *Wall Street Journal* helped spur a general sell-off, and the stock dropped to $14.94 per share.

The Internet rumor-mill only got worse. At the end of 1998, a motorcycle maker named Bikers Dream merely suggested it might set up a Web site to sell motorcycle parts, and suddenly its stock was the hottest in America. The stock jumped 167 percent in one day, with shares changing hands eight times as frenzied day traders swapped the stock back and forth. The next day, the stock came back to earth with a thud when traders finally realized that the company's Web site wasn't even up and running.

Around the same time, clothing wholesaler Active Apparel Group began promoting its Internet debut in news releases and on CNBC. Active's Web site was also not up and running, but this didn't keep investors from bidding up the company's stock price from $1.25 per share to as high as $25. According to the *New York Times*, several company officers and executives took advantage of the surge and sold close to $1 million of their shares. The share price plummeted thereafter, and was still below $5 per share in February 1999, even though the company's Web site was actually operational by then. Active Apparel nearly got delisted from NASDAQ and ended up listed on NASDAQ's less prestigious small-cap stock exchange.

These company stocks are just a few examples of some that have reached irrational heights over the last four years simply because they had the word "Internet" or *.com* briefly associated with them. This kind of craziness led Rick Berry, director of equity research at J.P. Turner & Company in Atlanta, to quip, "The frenetic buying of Internet stocks is going to make the tulip buyers of the seventeenth century look like value players."

Doonesbury

VENTURE CAPITAL COWBOYS

There are more venture guys doing more deals with more dollars at higher prices than ever before. In the Internet boom there is just more of everything.
  —Roger McNamee, Integral Capital Partners

*I*n the supply-and-demand chain of the Internet Bubble era, venture capitalists (VCs) are the suppliers. Since the Netscape IPO in August 1995, VCs have poured billions of dollars into hundreds of Internet startups. Each of the 133 companies that are part of our Internet Bubble calculation (see Appendix C or www.redherring. com/internetbubble for a complete list) received some form of venture capital.

The VC Internet frenzy is fed partly by the increasing number of investors who have jumped into the game. Beginning in the early 1990s, huge public pension funds started allocating large sums of money to venture capital investments. And who could really blame them? While the average venture capital rate of return over a 30-year period is estimated to be an impressive 23 percent, in the last five years the best funds have brought in rates of returns between 50 percent and 150 percent—ungodly numbers which seduce even the most mild-mannered institutional investor.

In 1998 alone, 139 new venture funds were created, with more than $17.3 billion of new capital committed to companies, an increase of 47.5 percent over the previous year.

Venture Capital Investments

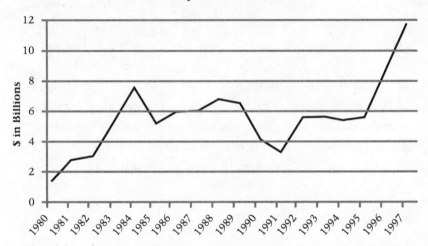

In addition to the professional VC firms, the number of corporate investors has grown rapidly. Technology blue chip companies such as Intel, Microsoft, and Hewlett-Packard have joined the VC business, investing billions with a vengeance. Since 1996 Intel has sunk $2.5 billion into 200 companies in the largest venture program in the U.S. Intel's senior vice president Les Vadasz boasted to us in May 1998, "We will invest $300 million this year in start-ups—all equity deals." And many of Intel's investments such as Inktomi, C/NET, Verisign, eToys, and Broadcom have turned into huge Internet boom stocks.

The other significant wave of venture capital investor that has emerged in the market over the last few years is the "angel" investor. The term "angel," originally applied to wealthy individuals who financed Broadway productions, now refers to cashed-out entrepreneurs who pump their personal wealth into young companies. This usually meant shelling out $50,000 or maybe $100,000, but recently these angels have raised their financial stakes and directly compete with venture capitalists, often to their chagrin. "The problem with angels is that they take vacations," says Michael Moritz, the partner at Sequoia Capital who sniffed out and seed-funded Yahoo.

Whether the new and old investors get along or not, the huge inflow of venture capital to fund the commercialization of the Internet should be no surprise. Whenever any new huge commercial idea has popped up in the U.S. market, from railroads to the personal computer, risk-loving American investors have historically jumped into the opportunity with both investment feet, and the Internet is no exception. So when the most powerful people in Silicon Valley meet for breakfast at Buck's Restaurant—presided over by owner and self-proclaimed "Big Cheese" Jamis MacNiven—to plot their next moves in the Internet boom, they are merely continuing America's time-honored gold-rush tradition.

The great irony of the Internet boom era will be that the very VC community that's pumped up the Bubble with new startups it's taken to market will also be the perpetrators of its explosion. By oversupplying the market with new companies, the VCs will satiate public investor appetite, and demand, particularly for overvalued Internet stocks, will evaporate. It happened in the personal computer boom, when the VCs funded too many personal computer and disk-drive companies, and it will happen again with the Internet.

This chapter examines the VC industry from its early roots to the multidimensional business it has evolved into today. We cover early success stories such as Intel, Apple, and Cisco and the generational changes in the VC business from the early venture days to the Internet boom era. Most important, we present a venture business that has too much money chasing too many Internet deals. More specifically, this economic environment has led to outrageous company valuations and an undisciplined investment market. It is our view that when the Internet Bubble bursts, there will be a shakeout not only in Internet companies but in the venture capital world as well.

Venture Capital Pioneers

Venture capital in America is nothing new. In some form—whether as angel investing from high net-worth individuals, classic risk capital, or even junk bonds—venture capital has been instrumental in financing everything from canals, railroads, steel, and automobiles to the information-technology industry. One of the most active VCs in the Internet space, Tim Draper of Draper Fisher Jurvetson, whose own Silicon Valley VC roots go back three generations, likes to recall Queen Isabella's investment in Columbus for inspiration. "She was the original seed capitalist," Draper enthusiastically told a Harvard Business School audience in the fall of 1998.

The first generation of info-tech VCs was not much different from America's early investors. In the 1960s and the 1970s, second- or even third-career businessman, playing largely with their own money, began investing in promising technologies and companies. "In the 1960s when I started, there were very few venture capitalists around, maybe 12 to 15 in the San Francisco Bay area," says Pitch Johnson of Asset Management, who made early, big bets on Amgen and Octel. This cadre of venture cowboys, which included characters such as Johnson, Bill Draper, Bill Edwards, and John Bryan, would lunch together every week at Sam's Grill on Bush Street in San Francisco and interview entrepreneurs. These meals would end by their asking the entrepreneur to step outside while they passed the hat to see how much money they would come up with.

But willing entrepreneurs in those days were hard to come by, so VCs spent a lot of time hustling around trying to find and create deals. Beginning in 1961, two of the modern pioneers of venture capital, Arthur Rock (credited with coining the phrase "venture capitalist") and the late Tommy Davis used to ring people up from their small office on Montgomery Street in San Francisco to let possible investors know they had found a deal, usually in electronics, and ask them to chip in enough money to make the deal work. "When the phone rang in our office, we would get excited because it might be a new deal!" recalled Rock. In the Internet boom era, Davis's successor firm, Mayfield Fund, receives over 1,000 new business plans per month.

Perhaps the most important contribution the early VC made was developing the legal and compensation structure for the business. Bill Draper and his lawyers at Cooley, Godward were the first to structure the modern venture capital partnership, where the general partners (the venture capitalists) typically charge the limited partners (the institutional investor) a 2 to 2.5 percent annual management fee on these funds as well as a 25 to 30 percent of the carry, or the percentage of the profits earned on the fund. This equation has translated nicely in the Internet era, when many VC funds reach $250 million in total and where the average general partner pulls down a couple of million in salary before he even places a successful bet.

Silicon Valley's Early Success Stories

Before Rock teamed up with Davis, his first Silicon Valley investment came at the request of Eugene Kleiner, then one of the scientists working under William Shockley, the Nobel Prize–winning inventor of the transistor (Kleiner would later cofound the legendary VC firm Kleiner Perkins Caufield & Byers). The idea Kleiner and his partners had for silicon transistors eventually became Fairchild Semiconductor, the mother of all semiconductor companies.

In a later fund Rock provided the seed capital for two other Shockley refugees, Bob Noyce and Gordon Moore, who also helped Kleiner start Fairchild. The company they pitched to Rock was, of course, Intel, and given their reputations (Noyce was general manager of Fairchild Semiconductor and the inventor of the integrated circuit, and Moore was also a distinguished engineer and Fairchild executive), they had little problem raising the money. In a 1994 *Red Herring* interview, Rock recalled the story behind raising seed capital in 1968 for Intel, the biggest hit of his VC career.

Gordon Moore and Bob Noyce had become disenchanted with Fairchild [Semiconductor]. Sherman Fairchild had died, and the new management of the parent company were kind of autocratic people located in Long Island who didn't understand how things worked out here. For instance, they didn't appreciate the concept of giving employees stock options, even though the year before Intel was formed, the semiconductor division of

Fairchild represented 110 percent of the company's profits. So, because of our long association, Gordon Moore and Bob Noyce contacted me to see if I could raise some money for a new venture they wanted to start that would focus on the semiconductor memory business. I told them I would, and we ended up putting together $2.5 million to start Intel. At $300,000, I think I was the largest single investor. The rest came from private individuals. We later raised another $3 million in a second round, and that was all the private venture capital that went into the company.

Amazingly, it took only $5.5 million in private capital to build Intel into America's most profitable corporation. Equally astounding, though, was the fact that the business plan it took to raise that money was only a page and a half long. "It was a document I wrote to sell the deal. But, of course, I don't think anybody turned me down," Rock said with a chuckle. "An unfortunate thing happened to the venture capital business. People started running their business plans by lawyers, who find all sorts of things left out that they think people might sue you over. Now we have huge business plans!" he moaned.

Today, seasoned VCs have tried to reverse the trend of bloated business plan summaries by using email. "If it can't fit in an email, it's too long to read," says Ann Winblad of Hummer Winblad Partners, who got word of some of her firm's biggest Internet success stories over the Internet itself.

The story behind the bespectacled and button-down collared Rock's later investment in Apple in 1976, which came through his affiliation with Intel, was quite different from his Intel experience.

Mike Markkula, who had just retired as a vice president at Intel, approached me about Apple. I was a little skeptical when I heard about Steve Jobs and Steve Wozniak. With their jeans, beards, and sandals, you might say they weren't exactly my style. But I went down to what I think was called the Homebrew Computer Show in San Jose. There were a lot of companies there, and I had never seen this before or since, but almost everybody at the show was crowded around the Apple booth trying to get a turn at their mock-up computer, which at the time was sold in a kit that you had to assemble. I literally could not get next to the booth. It was amazing! I thought it was great! I really thought there would eventually be a huge market opportunity. But, again, I was still a little uncomfortable with the two founders; it probably had to do with our age difference—both were barely 20 years old—but that's why I didn't invest more than I actually did, which was $57,000. Of course, I went on the board, and recruited Henry Singleton, who was the CEO of Teledyne, on the board. Markkula and the two Steves had recruited Mike Scott out of National Semiconductor to serve as president, so I began to feel a little better.

By the time Apple went public in December 1980, Rock's $57,000 investment was worth $14 million, and, if he had held all his stock, it would be worth $110 million (.019 percent of APPL's market in June 1999). Similarly, Rock's $300,000 investment in Intel has appreciated an incredible 20,000 percent since 1968 and is now worth over $624 million.

Rock, the initial chairman of Intel, remains on the company's board today, and served on the board of Apple until Apple competed against Intel in 1994 by joint-venturing with Motorola and IBM to build the PowerPC microprocessor. "Motorola had taken out an ad in the *Wall Street Journal* stating that they were taking Intel head on, and it was signed by Motorola, IBM, and Apple," Rock recalled in the *Red Herring* interview. "Within a week of the ad, articles started appearing in *Business Week* and other major publications stating that Apple and Intel were going to have head-to-head competition. Once I had decided I had to get off one board or the other, it was perfectly clear to me which board I would remain on. I own twice as much stock in Intel as I do in Apple, and I have been on Intel's board for 25 years, versus 13 years on Apple's board."

In spite of such early successes, the total amount of new money committed to venture capital in the 1960s was only about $100 million annually, and that number increased gradually in the first half of the 1970s. What opened the way for modern venture capital was the "prudent man rule" of the mid-1970s that allowed American institutional investors to allocate hundreds of millions of dollars for illiquid investments such as venture capital funds. "Institutional investors became the fountainhead of money," says Don Valentine legendary general partner at Sequoia Capital, also an early investor in Apple. "It allowed our funds to grow from $5 million to $50 million to $150 million."

The liberalization of investment rules in the 1970s and a decrease in tax rates on capital gains made increasing commitments to venture capital feasible and attractive. Overall, in the late 1970s and early 1980s the funds available for venture capital investment increased sharply—they shot up from $100 million in 1975 to $1.3 billion in 1981. Most of the new capital came from institutional sources, a tremendous windfall not only for Sequoia Capital but for other early venture capital firms such as Mayfield Fund from Menlo Park, the East Coast's leading VC firm Greylock Management, and the increasingly influential Kleiner Perkins Caufield & Byers.

The other big development of this time was the emergence of NASDAQ as the primary stock exchange for most of the venture-backed high-tech companies that did not qualify to raise money on the New York Stock Exchange. NASDAQ provided a ready outlet for numerous successful initial public offerings. Apple Computer, for example, was worth $1.8 billion on New Year's Eve 1980—more than Chase Manhattan Bank, Ford Motor Company, or Merrill Lynch, and twice as much as the combined market value of United Airlines, American Airlines, and Pan American. The success in the stock market of venture capital-backed companies such as Tandem Computers and Teradyne also gave the venture industry a real boost.

Changing of the Guard

By the mid-1980s, though, a change was in the wind. The Old Guard venture capitalists were joined by fresh-faced kids out of business school. While most of the Old Guard, and even some of the next-generation VCs who had joined them in the early '80s, such as John Doerr of Kleiner Perkins, had some industry experience, these young folks were making venture capital their first and primary career.

Members of this group included Stanford Business School graduates Geoff Yang, who joined Institutional Venture Partners; John Walecka, who was signed on by Brentwood Associates; and Harvard MBAs Jim Breyer, who landed at Accel Partners; Tim Draper, who started his own fund; Tench Coxe, who went to Sutter Hill Ventures; and Ofer Nemirovsky of Hancock Venture Partners. Another member of this generation, Bandel Carano of Oak Investment Partners, earned not an MBA but a master's in engineering at the age of 20, and has been described by Stanford's former Engineering School dean James Gibbons as "the smartest student ever to graduate from the school of engineering." Every one of these VCs is now counted among the most successful and wealthy of their generation.

"When I graduated from Stanford in '85, there were 13 people from my class who came into venture capital," says Yang, who made a name in the business early by funding two high-profile networking deals, SynOptics and Wellfleet Communications, which netted his firm a 2,000 percent return when the two companies merged to become Bay Networks. "Our entry into the business also signaled the end of the venture capital generalist era and the beginning of specialization," explains Yang, who chose communications technology as his specialty. Similarly, when Ofer Nemirovsky started at Hancock Venture Partners in late '86, he remembers "floundering around" for a year before sending a memo to his partners announcing that he intended to specialize in software deals.

Most significant, the entrée of this hoard of MBAs into the VC business meant that the new investment decision makers in Silicon Valley had little or no operating experience. It didn't take long for resentment to grow between the new VCs and the Valley entrepreneurs. The ill will between the two groups culminated in the legendary cover story in the June 1990 issue of *Upside*, drafted by the king of Silicon Valley lore Michael S. Malone, called "Has Silicon Valley Gone Pussy?"

These VCs—Rock, Valentine, Perkins, et al.—were very successful. Too successful, because their very success attracted not only half-assed competitors, but, worse, mountains of investment money. This money had to be invested, and that meant more people managing the funds. Unfortunately, the VCs were no more resistant to the siren call of respectability than their investment banking counterparts. And soon, the extra offices all over 3000 Sand Hill Road filled with venture pussies. By the mid-1980s, to visit a VC was to expect to be introduced to a parade of button-down, horn-rimmed post-adolescents in pleated flannel trousers. The older VC would intone proudly, "Randolph here just joined the firm. He's Choate/Brown/Harvard MBA" as junior shook your hand firmly and tried to conceal a supercilious smirk under a dewy upper lip.

Lessons Learned from the 1987 Crash

Before the 1987 market collapse, venture investing reached $4.18 billion, the peak for the decade. More money was committed than could be wisely invested, with inexperienced venture partners raising new funds and rates of return suffering accordingly. "I joined the business not long before the stock market crashed in October 1987," says Accel's Jim Breyer. "At that time, there were some new technology trends people thought would become important—artificial intelligence, pen computing, and robotics were all hot areas of investment. But they were all spectacularly unsuccessful."

However, despite these tough times, Breyer and the others regard the collapse of the IPO market in '87 as an important learning experience. Gone were many of the "me-too" deals that allowed VCs to make money by following the pack. Instead, younger venture capitalists had to dig more deeply to find investment opportunities.

These young VCs also responded to this challenge by finding mentors, just as John Doerr relied on Kleiner Perkins cofounder Tom Perkins to teach him the business. Bandel Carano, who had three home run investments early in his career—Parametric Technology, Synopsys, and Wellfleet Communications—received invaluable advice from Oak Investment's lead partner Ed Glassmeyer, who took Carano to meetings and, in Carano's words, "made me successful." Tim Draper, who also earned a huge early investment return by seed-funding Parametric Technology, had to look only as far as his father and grandfather, who pioneered the business of venture capital in Silicon Valley.

And there were still great investments made in the '87–'90 time period. Cisco Systems received a venture investment of $2 million in late 1987 from Sequoia Capital. In 1988 the company's sales were less than $10 million, but by 1997 they were $6.4 billion, and by late 1997 its market capitalization was $60 billion. And if none of Sequoia's original venture shares had been sold, they would have been worth over $6 billion by 1997.

Even though Cisco and other successful investments of this time provided some glimmer of hope, the initial public offering market dried up when the market crashed in the fall of 1987. According to financial research firm Securities Data Company, in 1987 the number of IPOs (51) and total dollars raised in these offerings ($774 million) were at historical low points and didn't begin recovering until 1991. In 1987 the average internal rate of return (IRR) on venture funds neared what one could earn in a passbook savings account at a bank: about 6 percent. The process that had created the initial boom had reversed itself. Institutional asset managers pulled back on their commitment to the venture capital industry, diverting capital to other sectors. "When institutional investors saw the dismal VC returns, they got the hell out of Dodge," explains Tim Draper, who at the time chose to raise his next fund from wealthy individuals at $250,000 a pop.

According to the National Venture Capital Association, capital commitments to venture capital firms plummeted, declining to a 10-year low of $1.27 billion in 1991. Under pressure, many of the venture firms imploded and broke up, and many venture capitalists exited the business. Most of the venture funds were 10-year limited partnerships, so one person was left standing to oversee what remained. Some of the portfolio companies were what the VCs call "the living dead"—they didn't go out of business but instead barely hung on, providing some jobs, eking out a payroll, but making very little, if any, profits.

But this shakeout was not necessarily a bad thing. "The most sane environment, if you had to pick a median for the last two decades, would actually be the 1992–1994 time period," says Jim Breyer of Accel. "We didn't have the backlash of the late '80s, but we didn't have the frothiness and the frenzy we've had in the last several years. In the 1992–1994 time period, we had very solid companies completing public offerings." He adds, "A company could not complete a successful public offering with top underwriters unless it had a history of profitability. Otherwise the underwriters didn't feel they could sell it to the right institutional buyers."

The Pussification of Silicon Valley Continues

With the advent of the Internet Bubble era of the mid- to late '90s and the influx of a couple more waves of young venture capitalists, the venture culture has gone through yet another transformation and is ripe for another shakeout.

"When I joined the venture capital business in 1987, that was also the year when Harvard Business School sent 30 percent of its graduates, its highest ever, to Wall Street. Three months later, the market crashed," says Accel's Breyer. "Today, we see extraordinary numbers of Harvard Business School and Stanford Business School graduates wanting to get into the venture capital business and into Internet entrepreneurship. It's an all-time high, and you can bet it's an indication that something's up." Bill Sahlman, longtime head of Harvard Business School's entrepreneurial studies, agrees. In a speech to East Coast entrepreneurs and VCs in the fall of 1998, Sahlman mused, "I figure that at least 10 percent of Harvard's MBAs want to become venture capitalists, suggesting historically we are at the top of the market."

The biggest downside to this new supply of Generation X venture capitalists is their inclination for a catfight. "It was much more collegial when I first got into the business," says IVP's Yang. "Now, you've got all these new firms coming in and a bunch of young, assertive people who want to make their mark. That part has made it a little less fun. They're ownership hungry. They're competing hot and heavy because they're absorbed by a gold rush mentality."

Breyer agrees, "The technology business has become trendy and faddish to an extent that it wasn't in the early '90s. Everything has happened more quickly than anyone expected, and that has driven venture capitalists to get very aggressive."

While these young VCs think they are geniuses, it's only because they have played the game during the Internet Bubble era, when returns have been fast and easy. And when you dissect their investment behavior, the newbie VCs often behave more like sheep, or "sheep following sheep" as someone put it—doing the same thing and making the same kind of investments as everyone else. And this "If you have a search engine company, then I better get one, too!" mentality is never more true than during technology booms and bubbles.

The personal computer Bubble is a great example. After all, where are the "me-too" computer products from Atari, Commodore, Kaypro, Tandy, Osborne, ITT, Fortune Systems, or Texas Instruments? All once looked like great investments but have long since been relegated to the PC dustbin.

Paul Deninger, chairman and CEO of technology investment bank Broadview International, is even more blunt about the caliber of the new Internet VC. "There are some real doofuses investing in the private equity market," he says. "All it takes is one doofus in a deal to drive the value up. All it takes is four doofuses to invest in the fifth, sixth, and tenth disk-drive company to totally screw up the market."

PC Booms and Busts

The ups and downs of the modern-day VC business since it was initiated in the early '60s are related to three technology booms: the personal computer, networking equipment and software, and now the Internet. Unlike the networking boom, the PC boom was characterized by a big bubble and its eventual explosion.

According to Don Valentine of Sequoia Capital, an early investor in Apple Computer, the problem with the early PC era was its undefined purpose and undefined markets: "When the PC was made, it was looking for an application. For years, people asked, 'It's nice, but what does it do?' The answer was, 'It doesn't do anything.'" He adds: "In 1978 we couldn't figure out who the customer was. Was it the education market? Was it the business market? You had a very embryonic product that didn't solve any problem. So it took a long time and there was a lot of wreckage; companies like Osborne and Commodore crashed because there was no market. In the beginning, there was no demand, no buyers."

(This attitude partly led Don Valentine and Sequoia to cash out early on its investment in Apple, thereby losing millions of dollars in future investment gains. This move underscores that even VC industry veterans such as Valentine often miss emerging new markets.)

"High expectations caused the air in the PC Bubble," says Bill Brady, a veteran technology-investment banker now with CS First Boston. "When 10 PC companies went public within a 2-year period of time, people finally had to face the fact that 7 of those companies weren't going to make it because they weren't viable."

An even better known example in technology finance circles of sheep following sheep is the Winchester disk-drive story documented by Bill Sahlman and Howard Stevenson of Harvard Business School in their famous case study "Capital Market Myopia."

From 1977 to 1983, venture capitalists invested an astounding $400 million in 43 disk-drive companies. Each company had competent management and aggressive financial projections, and each player needed only 10 percent of the potentially huge market to thrive. But the market could not sustain 43 new entrants, let alone the more than 100 domestic and foreign players active in the market at that time. The inevitable result was mayhem and a brutal mortality rate. It was no longer the old VC environment where too much capital was chasing too few deals. Inflated expectations had created a scene where too many VCs funded too many in each segment of the PC industry.

There were some benefits of the PC boom. The disk-drive business, although intensely competitive, resulted in a few, very strong, globally competitive American companies like Quantum and Seagate. By overfunding the birth of the industry, the United States became the world leader in disk drives, and consumers benefit from high-quality, high-capacity disk drives at low prices. In summary, a well-funded, competitive marketplace creates strong companies, high rates of innovation, and job formation, while enhancing the global competitiveness of the domestic economy.

Meanwhile, the VCs were the biggest moneymakers in the disk-drive business. Just as in the Internet Bubble era, VCs could generally hand over the shares in newly public disk-drive companies to their limited partner investors at reasonably high values and claim victory. However, Bill Sahlman also observes: "Typically, the public ended up holding the bag as competitive pressures resulted in major disappointments for post-initial public offering investors."

In their classic book *Venture Capital at the Crossroads*, authors William Bygrave and Jeffry Timmons document this lack of payoff for public investors:

> The public lost interest in speculative IPOs because—in sharp contrast to the returns of venture capital investors—theirs were dismal. . . . Public investors did better in IPOs of profitable companies that did not rush to go public, than in those of losing companies that did. . . . They got the message: Beware of venture-backed IPOs. After 1983, many of those IPOs turned out to be terrible investments. Some IPOs such as Victor Technologies and Priam went bankrupt, and investors lost everything. Conse-

quently, while holders of S&P 500 and Dow Jones stocks were enjoying record-breaking gains, public holders of venture-capital backed high-tech stocks were enduring losses, on average.

The best way to illustrate the reality of the PC Bubble and its impact on public investors is to take a 20-year look at high-tech investment bank Hambrecht & Quist's Technology Index below, and observe the market's ups and downs during the 1980s. The dramatic new rise in the Index in the late 1990s is, of course, the Internet Bubble as outlined in the book's introduction.

H & Q Technology Index

Networking: A Boom Without a Bust

In contrast to the sheeplike behavior in the midst of the PC Bubble and disk-drive mania, venture investing in networking startup companies such as Cisco Systems was much more calculated and sober. And it's no wonder that these investments came during a less frenzied time in both venture capital and the public stock market.

"In the beginning, the PC business did not solve a problem; it merely provided a glimpse of an emerging new market. But once the PC became somewhat useful, the next natural evolution was to link the computers. When Cisco came along, the environment desperately needed a solution," says Donald Valentine, an early investor in Cisco. "It was the company with the product that was a solution."

Bill Brady, part of the banking team at Morgan Stanley that took Cisco public in February 1990, agrees, "It was so clear if you read the prospectus. It was a whole new product. Network routers replaced bridges. It was logical. It had the best technology and a great market position." Yet as great as Cisco was, it was not a Bubble stock. "I think it had a $13 million revenue quarter before it went public. It was profitable for four quarters," says Brady. "We priced the deal at $18 per share and it went to $22. It didn't blow out, yet everybody knows the history of its stock price since then. Cisco was about as high quality of an IPO as the public could ask for."

But the larger point according to Valentine is that Cisco was one among many networking companies that succeeded. "For microchip and PC companies, there were lots of wrecks," says Valentine. "But, unique in the networking world, there are almost no busts." He adds, "What's different is that it's the first time a whole lot of companies were financed dealing with a precise problem—in this case, how to get the networks to work at all and to work at high speed. The customers came out of the woodwork to buy, overcoming all the market development problems and risks."

Back in the Bubble with the Internet

The recovery of venture capital returns beginning in 1991 and the emergence of the commercialization of the Internet's beginning in 1994 has pushed the pendulum back in the direction of overfunding.

One of the sure economic signs that we now live in a new technology bubble is the size of the venture funds raised today. Many of the top-tier venture capital funds have scaled up to funds of $250 million funds, including those for Sequoia Capital, Menlo Ventures, and Kleiner Perkins (their second in a row of this size). Another VC powerhouse, Institutional Venture Partners has jumped from $185 million in its previous fund to $350 million and Accel Partners to

$480 million. And Oak Investment Partners, which claims it's under-weighting Internet companies, still went from a total of $275 million for its previous fund to a whopping $600 million for its latest fund, handled by only six partners.

Without a doubt these massive capital inflows are a major cause of the Bubble. "The money has sloshed into venture capital," says Asset Management's Pitch Johnson, a VC since the early 1960s. "It hasn't flowed in—it's sloshed in and gone past the balance point."

The danger of huge venture fund sizes is that the managers get seriously overextended, and the quality time they can give to each deal goes down. Unlike companies with hardware and software products, the venture capital is not a scaleable business. When a firm's fund grows $200 million to $400 million, either each partner has to sit on more company boards or the firm has to recruit more partners.

"We only have a certain capacity," admits Sam Colella, general partner at Institutional Venture Partners. "It doesn't matter how much money you have. You can only do so many deals. You can only sit on so many boards." Another venture capitalist adds, "When you've raised a large fund, you cannot be an early-stage player who puts in a half million dollars in each deal, because you don't have the time. You've got too much money to put to work."

Pitch Johnson agrees. "The amount of help you get from your venture capital investor is not the same as it used to be," says Johnson. "And in many cases it's unsatisfactory. Guys run to too many board meetings; they haven't got time, and they're under terrible pressure to take their portfolio companies public."

The trouble is that the huge inflow of capital ultimately results in too much money chasing too few quality deals. "The capital rises, but the quality doesn't," says Johnson. And when capital rises, VC valuations skyrocket to Pluto. Average premoney private company valuations in 1997–1999, for example, were more than six times those for 1987–1989.

Paul Deninger of investment bank Broadview International elaborates, "Let's say three times as much money is in the venture business now that needs to be deployed in 1999 versus 1995. Are there three times as many quality deals? No. What does that mean? It means prices go up. And many companies get funded that shouldn't."

Michael Moritz of Sequoia Capital contends that hyped valuations will eventually come back and bite the overanxious VC. "We have a rule that we apply to venture investing. One is that price negotiation and valuation matters. The venture capital business lacks the continuous pricing mechanism of the public market, and one of the great ironies right now is that this mania has caused people to forget the importance of negotiation when it comes to valuation," explains Moritz.

Pushing and Shoving

There's no question that these investment trends have created a multitier venture industry. In the top tier are a small group of venture firms such as the venerable Kleiner Perkins and Sequoia Capital and the hotshot firm Benchmark Capital, that seeded eBay, the top-performing (up 1,300 percent!) IPO of 1998. These firms work with an experienced group of limited partners, win the best deals, and generally wield most of the power in the VC business. In the lower tiers are the less-experienced venture capitalists and entrepreneurs, funded by new entrant investors such as large public pension funds.

In this environment, top-tier venture partnerships are less interested in working in syndication with other venture firms and spend more time jockeying to become the sole investors in the startups they back. "There was a philosophy for a long time that it was better to syndicate, to share the work, share the risk, and have more deep pockets around when the subsequent investments were required. Venture firms are now going it alone and are very secretive about the deals they're doing," says Pitch Johnson.

In many cases the competition for deals is getting downright cutthroat as competing venture capitalists bad-mouth each other behind their peers' backs while they try to convince entrepreneurs to choose their brand and not the other guy's.

One angel investor who tried to secure a second round of financing from venture groups for one of his companies tells this story:

> I introduced the entrepreneurs to these four VCs thinking maybe one might be interested. Soon, all four are going crazy that this is their deal. So I say to the founder, "Well, let's start by raising valuation." So I call the VCs up. We raised the valuation from $6 million to $10 million. They all responded on the phone without talking to their partners that they would match the $10 million. I think during that day it got up to $15 million. This is in between VCs saying, "By the way, you need to know that this other VC is an asshole. You can call all his other board members. I'll give you the phone numbers of all the members of the boards he sits on and they'll tell you what a shitty contributor he is." All this personal stuff is going on while they're matching each other's offers.

Increased competition also means intense pressure to do deals quickly and with far less due diligence, or background research, than they should. "You have to make decisions faster and with less knowledge," says Art Marks a general partner with New Enterprise Associates. Venture capital partnerships also used to share due diligence when they worked together on deals. But in today's scramble to be the exclusive investor, this sharing of information has ended.

Corporations Join the VC Game

Even as venture capital partnerships beat up on each other in the competition for deals, some large corporations such as Intel, Microsoft, and Softbank have jumped with both feet into the venture funding game.

Intel, for example, has invested a remarkable $2.5 billion in about 200 companies since the mid-'90s. In 1998 alone Intel made more than 100 small investments; 80 went to new startups, about one-third of the deals were overseas, and 75 percent of them involved the Internet. Intel's strategy involves helping the overall market grow rather than making quick money, an approach they see as complementary to VC efforts rather than competitive. "We like to make sure the company has some other professional money, so we have other board members helping the entrepreneurs," explained longtime Intel senior vice president and board member Les Vadasz, who heads his company's strategic investment operation.

In other cases VCs and corporate investors also work together. One example is a combined $35 million investment by Microsoft, Compaq, Lucent, and Nortel in Accel Partners' Internet Technology Fund II. This fund is a component of Accel's larger $310 million venture fund. Another example is Microsoft's investment in New Enterprise Associates' venture fund NEA VIII. "We are using the premise of their investment in the fund as a way to introduce them to those companies which could benefit from a relationship with Microsoft," says NEA general partner Art Marks. "We are financial optimizers. We try to make the most of our investments." Companies like Microsoft especially help the VCs by buying some of their portfolio companies outright, providing high returns for the VCs. Two dramatic buyouts Microsoft made during the Internet Bubble era were for the fledgling startups WebTV and Hotmail. Microsoft purchased both companies, which had little or no revenue, for over $400 million each.

An interesting side story to the Hotmail deal was that in spite of the gigantic return Hotmail's VCs made on Microsoft's acquisition, Hotmail's lead investor, Tim Draper of Draper Fisher Jurvetson, thought it was too early to sell. "When Sabeer [Bhatia, Hotmail's CEO] returned from his first meeting with Microsoft, he had dollar signs in his eyes, and I thought, Uh-oh, we've got trouble," recounts Draper. And Draper's wariness paid off; the Hotmail's sales price eventually more than doubled because of his persistence that Hotmail remain independent. "I thought Hotmail could have been the next Yahoo," says Draper. Even Bill Gates admitted to us in February 1999 that Hotmail's perceived value had shot up tremendously since the acquisition in December 1997, and that Draper had the right instinct that it was too early to sell. "The guy at Microsoft who did the Hotmail deal had to slink around the office for a few months because everyone thought we had paid a pretty big price," recalled Gates. "In today's overheated Internet market, the same guy looks like a hero, because if we had to buy Hotmail today, it would probably cost a couple of billion dollars."

Angels Take Flight

A true indicator of a bubble environment is not only the over-abundance of money in increasingly large venture capital funds and the emergence of the more aggressive corporate investor, but the growing number of individual investors, loosely known as "angels," putting money into high-tech startups.

Many of these angels are cashed-out entrepreneurs with time on their hands and money to burn. In Silicon Valley these guys are epitomized by a group calling themselves the Band of Angels. Begun in January 1995 as an investment club with 12 members, they now have more than 120 angels in the group. The size of their investments has continued to spike up, from a pooled amount of $500,000 per startup to a blockbuster deal in summer of 1998, where 40 members of the Band invested a combined $4 million into a company called SendMail.

Yet the Band of Angels aren't the only ones looking for deals. Two of the cofounders of Sun Microsystems, Bill Joy and Andy Bechtolsheim, each put $1 million into the SendMail deal, bringing the angel funding to a total of $6 million. This compares with an average first-round venture capital investment of $6.5 million in high-tech startups.

Bright Light Technologies, a company providing a technology that combats online "spam," or junk e-mail, also got some heavy angel funding in 1998 from Band of Angels members as well as from Bechtolsheim, venture capitalist and Compaq board chairman Ben Rosen, and tech industry pundit Esther Dyson. These and other angels put in a combined $2.75 million, with venture capital group Accel Partners providing an additional $2.75 million, for a total of

$5.5 million of startup funding. Unlike SendMail, Bright Light at least had some professional venture capital funding.

While the recent level of angel investing expands the size of the overall venture pool available for promising new startups, it also impacts traditional venture economics. In the heat of competition between the angels and the professional VCs, private company valuations have skyrocketed, meaning VCs now ultimately pay more for less. Angel investors, for example, valued SendMail at an unprecedented $20 million at the time of their investment, and Bright Light raised its angel round at a $10 million valuation.

One main reason for these high valuations is that angels typically accept higher figures than do venture capitalists, in part because angels do less research on these companies and their markets and don't feel pressure to please limited partner investors. Hans Severiens, director of the Band of Angels, admits as much: "The angels are freer to invest on their gut," he says.

"I am actually skeptical of this angel experience," cautions Andy Bechtolsheim, who not only made several hundred million as one of the Fab Four that founded Sun Microsystems, but more recently sold his 11-month-old networking startup, Granite Systems, to Cisco for $220 million. "I think any start-up would be best advised to get money from a true VC. For major deals I don't think angels are a predictable source of funding."

Meanwhile, Bechtolsheim defends his own angel investments as primarily in the electronic development space he understands well, and "where I know the people and they know me." His role, though, is mostly passive—he does not regularly advise most of these companies or sit on their boards. He expects most of his companies to get acquired rather than to go public. He does admit that the red-hot SendMail and Bright Light deals he invested in are exceptions to his typical strategy.

Bechtolsheim isn't the only one skeptical of overinflated angel activity, in spite of his own high-priced investments. "Today's angels scare the hell out of me; they're so emotional," says Integral Capital's Roger McNamee.

Predictably, venture capitalists don't like the expensive competition from angels for early stage deals. "They don't deliver the value-added," says Winblad. "They might be there for a few rah-rah phone calls, but they don't wrap good business practices around the companies. They are not in the full-time profession of building businesses. I do it full-time. I have my money from institutional investors who won't give me any more unless I make money for them."

The abundant angel money that's jacking up company valuations is not always beneficial for the entrepreneur. If a startup's valuation gets ahead of itself, it becomes difficult for the company to grow into that valuation and to get additional private financing down the road. "It has created a chaotic effect," adds Winblad. "The capital structures are not done right."

Whether venture capitalists like it or not, the growth of angel funding of technology deals is part of the Bubble. In simple economic terms, angel money has greatly lowered the barrier to entry for Joe Entrepreneur to obtain venture capital. Many more companies—particularly Internet-related companies—are funded as a result.

Hey, Let's Go Start an Internet Company!

And just like during the PC Bubble era, many if not most of the Internet startups are "me-too" companies. In a variation on the sheep theme, Bill Sahlman of Harvard calls it "a lemming approach." He says, "It's like with the disk-drive companies—people have to have one."

This wanna-be venture mentality has translated into an astonishing investment total in the first half of 1999 of $11.4 billion. "Except this time around, VCs aren't funding 43 disk-drive companies. They're funding 43 of each flavor of Internet company," says venture capitalist Ann Winblad. "We auditioned 2,000 companies and we turned down a whole lot of them, but most of them got funded."

Venture capitalists typically divide the technology companies into dozens of specific sectors in order to analyze which companies are the best bets. The Internet boom has created several new categories of companies including search engines, e-commerce software, and several categories of online retail goods sites, the leader of which is Amazon. The VC first to fund what becomes the leading company in each sector (what author Geoffrey Moore refers to as the "gorilla" company) generally hits a big jackpot. In the overheated Internet market, three to four times the number of companies are funded to compete in each new sector than were funded during previous booms. "It used to be like a regional track meet where there were a few people in the high jump, a few people in the pole vault, and a few people in the sprint. Now it's like the start of the Boston Marathon," says Winblad.

One result of this mob at the starting line is that the startups' costs have increased four times as well. Investors now have to fork over huge sums to executive search firms to recruit the best talent, pay exaggerated salaries to keep the talent they find, and hire public relations firms much earlier than they used to.

Despite these costs, Winblad describes the prevailing venture industry attitude as that of a bunch of hungry settlers trying to grab land in a land rush. "Who cares if you can only pay attention to one-third of the companies you invest in. Get a bunch of them," she says with a touch of sarcasm in her voice.

Technology investment banking pioneer Sandy Robertson, who founded Robertson Stephens, one of the most active banks in the Internet space, has witnessed tremendous change in the flow of money in the startup investment market. "The 1970s were thinly capitalized," he says. "Other than Amdahl, probably no company got started with more than a million dollars in venture capital. The average was about $500,000 to $750,000 of initial capital." After this initial funding, these companies were expected to become profitable or the early investors and entrepreneurs became subject to a "wash out" financing, where their ownership positions would become severely diluted for not meeting their original business plans. "Nowadays startups are handed $5 million to $10 million of capital in their first rounds of financing," observes Robertson with a note of skepticism. "If the company doesn't get profitable on that money, oh that's all right, they're on track; in the next round, just double the valuation, and in the next one after that, double it again if necessary."

The underlying assumption is that the public market will help venture capitalists defray the cost of competition or perhaps even bail them out if they've picked the wrong horses. "With this huge injection of capital, companies are going public faster," says Robertson. "And they don't have to perform quite as well. If you've got the cash, you can erase the mistakes."

One prominent VC remarks acerbically, "My joke with some of the entrepreneurs we invest in is that when their companies start showing revenue and profits, their valuations will fall through the floor." When you look at the statistics, this is actually no joke. If a company shows a profit, that means an investor can actually calculate a price-to-earnings ratio, which, in the Internet Bubble era, generally translates into a much lower valuation. "If you place a bet on investing in a certain market valuation, and the company doesn't grow into that, you risk having nothing left at the end of the day," the VC says.

In investment banking–speak, public Internet company investors are currently engaged in investing in market capitalization rather than in sound fundamental companies. With the absence of revenue and profits, investors justify high market valuations based on untraditional, if not ridiculous metrics such as Web site traffic and page impressions.

Lise Buyer of CS First Boston, one of Wall Street's most influential Internet analysts, adds, "Eventually, investors and companies will figure out that you cannot pay employees and develop new products with Web traffic alone. You need revenue. Today investors don't care about revenue. But this absolutely has to change. Employees aren't going to buy new cars with Web traffic."

Benchmark Capital's Bill Gurley gave a much talked about example of this new valuation technique in his August 17, 1998 *Fortune* magazine column titled "Internet Investors Beware." He wrote:

Consider the absurd example of a Web-based company whose core service is to sell dollars for 85 cents each. This company obviously could achieve record visitors and page views at its Web site.

Revenue growth would easily set records, and it is quite conceivable that sales could reach into the billions within the first few quarters of operation. Apply even the most conservative Internet price-to-revenue multiple to this franchise and we are talking about a multibillion-dollar market cap. Perhaps you are questioning how this high-flying company will ever become profitable. Well, you are obviously forgetting that, with traffic like this, the potential for advertising and targeting will be tremendous!

In the same article Gurley argues that because Wall Street has swallowed the story that online customers, visitors, and page views are uniquely valuable, regardless of a company's profitability, entrepreneurs are rushing to the public market with Internet companies absent of any real business model. "The companies may achieve these traffic targets quite handily but still may have little chance at producing real value in terms of cash flow. With no focus on costs, it is easy to reach nonfinancial targets. This is the great thing about cash flow–based valuation: It's hard to sweep costs under the rug," he warns.

The Internet Shakeout

The bottom-line question is whether these Internet go-go companies can maintain their long-term market value. "The Internet industry dilemma to me is the same as the early PC one," remarks Sequoia Capital's Don Valentine. "You have to pace your investments in the Internet according to the value it creates for customers. The VC industry has gotten way ahead of itself in evaluating where the value exists, and the result is the funding and creation of unnecessary companies. What will we do with 2,000 companies? Do you think five years from now we will have 2,000 Internet companies? It's a repetition of the disk-drive mistake, the PC mistake. We always make that mistake when there is too much money."

Investment banker Bill Brady agrees, "You could compare the

number of PC and disk-drive companies that went public to the Internet companies that have blown out of the public gates in the last few years. Of all those disk-drive companies, how many are still companies today? It's like 10 percent. You could argue that only 10 percent of the public Internet companies will be viable in the long run."

The usual argument is that it's different this time. Even for the PC and disk-drive booms, venture capitalists at the time argued that the venture industry itself had improved and was therefore yielding higher-quality companies. There was more later stage follow-up financing, more added-value assistance provided to company management, better underwriters, and just better all-around technologies than before, they said.

The truth is that the venture funds raised in noneuphoric bear markets, for example 1987–1988, have done the best and have had the least wreckage, whereas those raised during the PC Bubble—especially 1982, 1983—have done the worst. "History tells you that the funds raised now will underperform," says Brad Koenig, managing director and head of the technology banking practice at Goldman Sachs. "So I think we will see some real correction here, and not only with Internet companies. There will be shakeout in hedge funds, in the money management business, and in investment banking. And there will be a shakeout in the venture capital business."

Setting the stage for the shakeout is the thousands of new venture capital sources funding the Internet, many of them with little experience outside a bull market. Basically, any new investor or venture capitalist who came into the business after 1992 has operated only in an easy-money environment. "I think for a venture partnership the most dangerous time is when everything is going well, or seeming to go well," concludes Michael Moritz, general partner at Sequoia Capital. "That's when the rot begins to set in."

Inevitably, VCs will have to go back to basics when the bull market ends. They'll have to be more cash conservative and willing to syndicate their deals to minimize risk; there will be no easy exits through quick IPOs or mergers. It will be a difficult adjustment, and many won't make it.

Without a hot IPO market, even the surviving venture investors will feel less sure of themselves. "Suddenly, you've got a lot of work to do working with your companies that don't make it out of the IPO gate," says NEA's Art Marks. "It will also get harder for your companies to raise money."

There are signs that this is already happening. "There are a lot of people baby-sitting a lot of companies wondering what the hell to do with them," declares Ann Winblad. And many of these can't even think about going public, even in a hot IPO market. She adds, "A lot of bunts in this game are concealed by acquisitions."

In essence, the venture capital world lives in its own distorted reality. One thirtysomething venture capitalist who started his career at the tail end of the burst in the PC Bubble worries that his peers have become so swept up in Internet mania that they have forgotten their economic lessons. "This is a repeat of a cycle," he states vigorously. "The only difference is that the financial markets are more extreme, and it's even easier to make money than it was in '83. If anything, it's gone to our heads even more."

Another concern is that many VCs appear to have taken advantage of the public investor drunk on Internet stocks. "The venture capitalists who have made the most money right now in this part of the cycle are the most promotional venture capitalists, the ones who hype the most and play into creating high multiples for their companies," the same VC complains. "It doesn't mean there aren't a lot of good entrepreneurs or venture capitalists, but when it becomes easier to make money by promoting stock than by building underlying businesses, people will shift their attention to promoting their companies."

The VC contrasts the Internet Bubble ethic with the old company-building ethic epitomized by Bill Hewlett and the late David Packard, the founders of Hewlett-Packard, the grandfather of all Silicon Valley companies. Instead of being obsessed with rapid growth and the golden lure of an early IPO, they concentrated on building an enduring, great company. Their aim was to build an enterprise profitable from the beginning, create a terrific place to work, and provide great customer service. The by-product of building a successful company was great wealth, but it's not what they thought about when they woke up in the morning.

Venture capital veteran Art Marks of New Enterprise Associates, whose Internet investment success stories include UUNet, Healtheon, and pcOrder.com, agrees with the younger VC's analysis. "The public market went from providing stockholder liquidity to raising needed capital for growth to financing growth plus creating buzz," Marks observes. "In the Internet era, the great hope is to be the firstest with the mostest."

Promotional skills and return on investment obsessions aside, the venture capital industry at large is overbloated and undisciplined. They may be chalking up some big scores today, but by oversupplying the market with young, unproven companies, they have set up the whole Internet market for a gigantic explosion.

Doonesbury

KLEINER PERKINS CAUFIELD & BYERS: LEADING THE VENTURE CAPITAL HERD

> **John Doerr is to his business what Bill Gates is to software.**
>
> —Stewart Alsop, general partner,
> New Enterprise Associates

The partners at venture capital powerhouse Kleiner Perkins Caufield & Byers (KP) are fond of swaggering into their annual Aspen, Colorado, partnership retreat and telling their investors how much market value their portfolio companies have created. And the numbers are impressive. Since the firm's inception in 1972, the $1 billion KP has invested in over 300 startups has turned into 127 public companies, including Compaq, Sun Microsystems, America Online (AOL), Netscape, Amazon, and At Home. The companies are now worth over $300 billion, generating over $75 billion in annual revenues and employing over 150,000 people.

While KP's annual return-on-investment numbers are not public, insiders say their combined funds since 1972 have generated an annual compounded rate of over 50 percent, with some of their recent, Internet-focused funds returning well over 70 percent—far outpacing the venture capital industry average of 23 percent, and putting the firm in the top 5 percent of all venture firms. KP's most famous partner, John Doerr, unabashedly refers to this type of venture capital success as "the largest legal creation of wealth in the history of the planet." And these totals don't even consider KP's active list of over 100 private companies, which also represents billions of dollars in potential market value and strategic influence in the technology industry.

All this moneymaking hasn't eluded the individual pocketbooks of the 12 KP general partners, either. KP has leveraged its record into raising a series of 12 increasingly larger funds to manage, most recently a $350 million fund, mainly from institutions, including university endowments such as those of Harvard, Stanford, and MIT, and nonprofits such as the Ford Foundation. KP's general partners command a 30 percent take of capital gains earned on their funds, and 3 percent annual management fees (based on the total dollar amount of each fund raised), demonstrably higher than the more typical 20 percent / 2 percent fee other venture firms command. In the October 26, 1998, issue of *Fortune,* the magazine estimated that the partners' individual take in just 1996 and 1997 alone, because of high flyers like Netscape and Intuit, was well over $200 million per partner. Senior partners John Doerr and Brook Byers are said to take the biggest slices of the pie, leaving the rest to be divided up by the other partners.

By putting these kinds of numbers on the scoreboard and exerting control and influence over its high-powered band of companies, KP has earned a godlike status inside the industry. "Kleiner Perkins is the only one with real power in our industry," says Sam Colella, general partner of KP competitor Institutional Venture Partners. "They are in a very different category." KP's Doerr refers privately to this perception of power as the "Kleiner Mystique," and he and his partners leverage this aura to win the hottest startups, recruit the best CEOs, and take their portfolio companies to the public market faster than any other venture firm in the business.

Doerr's partner Will Hearst III credits the innate competitive drive within each partner for KP's success. "We think about what the other firms are doing and why we might have missed an important deal. We analyze where we went wrong, and figure out if we can get back into a market and win," explains Hearst.

Part of this aggressive nature is revealed in how KP partners work with its network of companies to influence the direction of the Internet industry and gain collective advantages. The partners affectionately refer to their portfolio of companies as the KP keiretsu, a metaphor Doerr came up with in the 1980s that refers to the modern Japanese system of extensive cross-ownership within a family of companies that fosters mutual obligation. The most aggressive action within the KP keiretsu is generally targeted at destabilizing Microsoft, the software behemoth KP must conquer to gain control of the Internet industry for its top companies. And this high-stakes competition never rests. Just within this last year, two huge anti-Microsoft deals came down when two pairs of KP portfolio companies dramatically combined—AOL with Netscape and At Home with Excite. The goal in these two KP partner-orchestrated moves was clearly to consolidate forces in the Internet portal space and keep Microsoft's MSN online service a distant competitor.

In such efforts to seek advantage over Microsoft and dominate the Internet industry, KP, whether intentionally or not, has been a huge contributor to the inflation of the Internet Bubble. To stake out its turf, KP has funded some of the most richly valued Internet companies over the last 5 years, covering virtually every segment in this emerging market space. Incredibly, 15 of these companies have gone public, garnering a combined market value in excess of $150 billion.

When one looks between these numbers, one finds that this market value has been built upon the back of only $5.9 billion in total revenue and staggering combined losses of $26 million in the 12-month period ending March 31, 1999. The numbers look even worse if you subtract AOL's huge slice of the pie. What's left for the remaining 14 companies is $1.7 billion in revenues and a whopping $704 million in losses. By our calculation with AOL included, this portfolio could be overvalued by over $50 billion (or by 30 percent) if you assume a forward revenue growth rate of 65 percent. Also by our calculation, this total represents an incredible 40 percent of the total Internet Bubble, as described in the introduction of this book (see Appendix A "Calculating the Bubble" and the sidebar in this chapter for further details). Sadly, the retail stock buyers who own the largest blocks of stocks in these companies will inevitably get caught holding the bag when prices plummet back to reality.

This chapter tells the story of how KP found itself the biggest promoter of the Internet stock Bubble. We first focus on the founding investment principles of the partnership as seen through the eyes of legendary KP founder Tom Perkins and current lead partner John Doerr. Second, we examine the evolution and power of the KP network of companies and executive talent. Last, we describe how the partners first identified the Internet opportunity and then invested in companies such as Netscape, At Home, and Amazon, and finally, how KP has leveraged its advantages to cash in big (and early) in the overheated technology public markets.

The KP Way

The KP partnership was distinct in the venture capital business from its very inception in 1972. The founding partners, Eugene Kleiner and Tom Perkins, were well-known high-tech entrepreneurs, and both took joy in actively assisting the entrepreneurs they funded. Eugene Kleiner was a veteran of Bell Laboratories and Shockley Semiconductor Laboratory, Silicon Valley's first transistor company (founded by William Shockley, the controversial Nobel Prize–winning coinventor of the transistor). Kleiner, along with Gordon Moore and Robert Noyce (who later cofounded Intel), became one of the famous Shockley defectors who formed Fairchild Semiconductor, the mother of all semiconductor companies.

By age 40 Tom Perkins had established a legacy for working under his mentor and Silicon Valley godfather David Packard and driving Hewlett-Packard into the computer business, making it the company's number-one producer of revenues by the time he left. Along the way, he took $10,000 of his personal savings and built a startup company around a low-cost, easy-to-use laser he invented. His initial investment eventually turned into $2 million when he sold it to Spectra-Physics. "I guess I was already a de facto venture capitalist before I even raised my first fund," Perkins told *Red Herring* in a 1994 interview.

Their reputations as hands-on strategic thinkers separated Kleiner and Perkins from the number-crunching money managers on Wall

Street. "Kleiner and I characterized ourselves as technologists and entrepreneurs who could help start companies. We were the first industry guys to go into venture capital," Perkins recollected.

Kleiner and Perkins then picked partners who thought and acted like they did. Frank Caufield, Brook Byers, Kevin Compton, John Doerr, Will Hearst III, Vinod Khosla, Floyd Kvamme, Joe Lacob, Bernie Lacroute, Jim Lally, Douglas Mackenzie, Ted Schlein, and Russ Siegelman are all hands-on guys with strong technical backgrounds and competitive, impatient personalities who are often more ambitious than the entrepreneurs running the companies they invest in.

"Once we sign the check, we're on the team," Perkins emphasized. "We consider it our responsibility that the company never run out of money, we help them hire the right people, and we help them identify the risks and put those risks behind them. If anything, we have been accused of being too involved," he admitted.

This hands-on approach has allowed KP to build billion-dollar companies from scratch and create huge new industries. Even their first $8 million fund in 1972 (one of the largest venture capital funds raised in those days) was distinguished by two gigantic hits, Tandem Computer and the first biotechnology company, Genentech. Both companies were founded by KP partners Jimmy Treybig and Robert Swanson, respectively, in spare rooms at the firm's first offices on Sand Hill Road in Menlo Park. "Both Tandem and Genentech were high-risk deals," explained Perkins. "If we have any kind of investment formula, it's that we try to isolate whatever the biggest risk is in a given deal and structure our initial investment so the money is used to eliminate that risk.

"In the case of Genentech, clearly the biggest risk was whether or not God was going to let us create a new form of life," Perkins remembered with a laugh. "And with Tandem, we had to prove we could develop software that could work in a multiprocessing environment. The market opportunities were clear and exciting, but there were big scientific and technical risks in both deals."

John Doerr, who earned his KP stripes sponsoring the firm's investments in Compaq, Lotus, Sun Microsystems, Netscape, At

Home, and Amazon, among many other successes, concurs with his mentor that the secret to venture capital success is to get the risks out of the way early. And KP prefers some risks over others. "There are basically four risks we have to confront in each deal. There is technical risk: Can we split the atom? There is people risk: Will the key players on the team stay together? There is financial risk: Can we keep the company well-financed? And there is market risk: Can we get the dogs to eat the dog food?" Doerr explains. "The most dangerous of these risks is market risk. Removing market risk is expensive," believes Doerr. "We're risk-takers, but we'll take a technology risk over a market risk any day of the week." KP partners find market risk deadly because it often doesn't become obvious until after a company has blown through millions of dollars.

But while KP doesn't want its startups spending its precious dollars educating consumers, they have built their track record upon anticipating huge markets—such as compatible PCs and the Internet—and boldly launching companies right when these new industries are ready to explode. "We look for markets that are going to change, by at least an order of magnitude, the technologies that can make it possible, and great teams," says Doerr. Genentech gave birth to the modern biotechnology industry; Sun Microsystems led the move from mainframes to client-server computing; Compaq put PCs in corporate America; Lotus introduced consumers to spreadsheets; Intuit put personal finance on the PC; and in the Internet era they are betting on online services AOL (combined with Netscape's Netcenter), Excite/At Home, e-commerce portal Amazon, and a whole slew of other fledgling public and private companies in the e-commerce, media, and technology backbone space.

The willingness of KP to swing for the fences clearly separates the firm from the venture capital pack. Doerr explained this approach to us in a 1995 *Red Herring* interview:

The venture capital industry is very fragmented. There are 400 venture firms, right? So how can any one firm develop significant market share? Only by focusing on initiatives, which means several KP partners working together to help build companies and opportunities in specific areas, such as wireless communications, interactive media, and Internet/online services. If KP really hustles, we hope to see perhaps half of the really good projects in an area. But we can't do everything. Our goal is quality, not quantity. You also have to develop competence and expertise in an industry to earn the right to advise entrepreneurs.

Even KP's competitors in the venture business concur that focusing its investments on huge potential market initiatives is one of the firm's primary strengths. Geoff Yang of the top venture capital firm Institutional Venture Partners (IVP), which raised a $350 million fund in April 1998 to focus on "brave new world" investments à la KP, told us that this practice is what he admires most about KP. "I think when they create an industry initiative, they tend to refocus the whole partnership in one form or another toward those initiatives," says Yang.

IVP started focusing on the Internet in early 1994 when it provided the startup capital for Architext (which eventually became Excite), along with Vinod Khosla at KP. But Yang admits that IVP made this investment as a stand-alone deal, not as part of a firm-wide focus on the Internet. KP, on the other hand, had mobilized its entire firm toward making investments in the Internet space by this point, and Excite became one of over a dozen blockbuster Internet deals KP invested in before other venture capital firms even woke up to the online world.

In spite of KP's home run record, even its partners admit that some of their hits could have sailed farther out of the park. KP partner Vinod Khosla, who first came knocking on the partnership's door in 1982 as the founding CEO of Sun Microsystems, recounted recently how the computer workstation and server company he co-founded could have been worth five times as much as it is today. "I look at Cisco and can't imagine I was that stupid! Everybody at Sun, including John Doerr and [Sun's cofounder and current CEO] Scott

McNealy, missed Cisco as an opportunity," Khosla lamented while hitting his forehead with the palm of his hand. "Sun was out there from the very beginning saying that 'the network's the computer,' but we completely missed the networking system opportunity. And the first network router was just a piece of software—an application built on Sun's CPUs [central processing units, the brains of a computer]." And where would Sun be if it had seen that opportunity? "Sun would have had a $100 billion market capitalization—the size of Microsoft by now," contends Khosla.

Like other venture firms, KP has many deals that never get off the ground. In its most dramatic failure, KP tried to jump-start the pen computing revolution by backing GO Computer, whose handheld computer operating system was to convert the 25 million PC-illiterate and keyboard-adverse professionals into joining the digital age. What was supposed to be an $8 billion industry turned out to be dead on arrival as manufacturers turned out bulky, overpriced, and malfunctioning handheld computers that then-Apple CEO John Sculley referred to as Personal Digital Assistants, or PDAs. By September 1994, *Red Herring* featured a caricature of John Doerr posing in a faux rendition of Edvard Munch's painting "The Scream" under the headline "PDA Angst."

Ironically, in a largely underreported move that demonstrates KP's intense shrewdness as an investor, the firm did not lose money on its $3 million investment in GO. When it became apparent that the market was not going to emerge, and GO continued to burn money in research and development, the company was pushed into a merger with another KP company called EO, a maker of PDA hardware. AT&T, EO's biggest investor, agreed to ante up an additional $40 million in the combined company. But also as part of that deal, KP sold half of its EO stock to AT&T. After all the money had changed hands, the $7 million KP netted on this sale was as much as KP had invested in both GO and EO combined. Unfortunately, soon after the merger was inked, AT&T closed down EO for good and had to write off its entire investment in the company.

In his book *Startup*, which tells the GO story, cofounder Jerry Kaplan concludes: "In looking back over the entire GO-EO experience, it is tempting to blame the failure on management errors, aggressive actions by competitors, and indifference on the part of large corporate partners. While all these played important roles, the project might have withstood them if we had succeeded in building a useful product at a reasonable price that met a clear market need."

Doerr admits that the most important element for the success of the startup is hitting the market right, a skill he says requires equal parts "good judgment, sweat, and luck." The other key KP partner investment principles include personally using the technology, talking frequently with customers, and being passionate about products. "Most Silicon Valley startups get their technology to work but never squarely hit the marketing strike zone," Doerr told *Red Herring*. After pondering this final challenge, he added, "There's a tremendous marketing and management deficit in Silicon Valley."

Glorified Headhunters

The last reality—the severe management shortage of professional talent in the Internet era—is why John Doerr will whisper privately that he and his partners are often no more than "glorified headhunters." But this headhunting skill is one of their primary competitive advantages. The best example of this applied skill is the Netscape Communications startup story. "I think Jim Clark [Netscape's founder] will give us credit for helping assemble a first-rate team in under 90 days. Two vice presidents of engineering, vice presidents of sales and marketing, and world-class CEO Jim Barksdale," recalls Doerr. Barksdale was an amazing catch for Netscape, having previously been president of both McCaw Cellular and Federal Express. It's the ability to recruit this kind of executive talent that makes or breaks Silicon Valley companies. John Doerr is famous for going to extreme measures to convince the best talent to join a KP company, including flying his private Citation jet to pick up potential recruits and close the deal.

When we asked KP partner Will Hearst what was special about John Doerr, his answer was all about recruiting:

What makes John a great investor is his ability to recruit experienced management and come up with a complete team. Two rare commodities are engineering talent and management talent. John knows that people like Bill Joy [Sun Microsystems co-founder and the inventor of the Berkeley Unix operating system] are like .350 hitters in baseball. The eye-to-hand coordination of a batting champion like Tony Gwynn is just not the same as the average person's. I think John feels that the vision organ of Bill Joy or an Andy Bechtolsheim [another Sun co-founder, who sold his second startup, Granite Systems, to Cisco Systems in 1997 for $220 million after only 11 months in business] is just much higher than the average engineer. John makes a habit of staying close to these technology wizards and uses them as sources of deals, references, and due diligence.

In this way, the KP partners' role more closely resembles that of the Hollywood moguls of the 1930s and 1940s, whose power rose from their ability to sign up talent. Indeed, much of KP's influence comes from the hundreds of skillful managers the firm has placed in pivotal jobs over the past two decades. And a well-regarded manager in KP's talent pool, such as former GO Computer executive Bill Campbell, who was tapped to become CEO of Intuit, and Mike Homer, who ended up as executive vice president of Netscape, will always be presented with new executive positions and board seats on other KP portfolio companies.

Other instances of KP cross-CEO pollination include Intuit founder Scott Cook, who joined the board of Amazon, Netscape's former CEO Jim Barksdale, who sits on the board of At Home, and Excite/At Home's president George Bell, who sits on the board of Preview Travel.

In another impressive move, John Doerr aggressively recruited KPMG—Peat Marwick's vice chairman, Roger Siboni, to take the helm of enterprise software startup Epiphany. Part of what enticed Siboni was that Doerr told him KP would help him spread his risk by getting stock options from other KP companies in exchange for board participation. And true to Doerr's word, Siboni was sitting on the boards of Macromedia, Pivotal, and Active Software shortly after he was recruited. And if Epiphany doesn't work out, Siboni was also assured he could the join KP's "CEO-in-residence" program, a tradition started with Bill Campbell. "Even though I had achieved a high position within KPMG at a young age and was making a considerable salary, this was an opportunity I eventually could not pass up," recounts Siboni. As testimony to Doerr's persistence, it took him six months to talk Siboni into the job.

The most powerful members of the KP inner executive circle are also encouraged to join the Zaibatsu, a personal counterpart of the keiretsu, where a select group of former and existing KP entrepreneurs and industry insiders can invest in KP companies alongside the regular funds. The Zaibatsu's investments can be on a much grander scale than similar opportunities offered by top KP venture capital competitors such as Sequoia Capital or Institutional Venture Partners. While typical investments in their side-by-side funds average around $50,000, individual investments in the KP funds are more in the range of $75,000 to $300,000 per fund. In turn, members are expected to provide KP with the benefits of their own contacts and industry knowledge as well as with investment leads.

According to paperwork one Zaibatsu member gave us, Zaibatsu investors include KP portfolio company founders such as Netscape's Marc Andreessen, Intuit's Scott Cook, and Sun's Scott McNealy, as well as influential outsiders such as industry pundit Esther Dyson, former Sony USA president Mickey Schulhof, and Intel chairman Andy Grove. Ultimately, the Zaibatsu gives KP a network of influential friends and contacts who are loyal to the firm even beyond the normal functioning of the keiretsu. "You never want to bang on a KP company in public, because you might not get invited to invest in the next Zaibatsu fund," said one investor who pleaded to go nameless.

To keep the key players in the keiretsu well-nurtured and in regular contact with each other, KP also brings them together every year at its annual CEO summit in Aspen, Colorado. Executives of KP's hottest companies lodge at the genteel Aspen Meadows, home of the prestigious Aspen Institute. Here the likes of Amazon's Jeff Bezos, Marimba's Kim Polese, Excite's George Bell, and At Home's Tom Jermoluk can enjoy whitewater rafting or rock climbing under the brilliant spring sun before settling down to roundtable discussions about the future of electronic commerce or strategies for increasing Internet bandwidth. More important, there are numerous quieter and smaller discussions among the CEOs about how their companies might work together. "It's an amazing experience to be around that many quality players who yield so much industry influence," gushes Siboni. Doerr invited Amazon's Jeff Bezos to the firm's 1996 summit as a successful tactic to help close KP's exclusive $8 million investment in the company.

An interesting side note is that in spite of their tremendous success as investors, some of the KP partners harbor desires to run their own companies. "We all experience entrepreneur-envy from time to time," says KP partner Kevin Compton, who originally joined the firm as an "entrepreneur-in-residence" but eventually signed on as a partner. John Doerr at one point jumped into Sun Microsystems full-time to help them through a rough spot, and he also briefly considered taking the CEO job at Netscape. And when Will Hearst finally gave up the post as acting CEO of At Home, he admits it was very emotional for him to step down.

Part of this hidden entrepreneurial ambition is certainly driven by the financial upside. "You can make more money faster as an entrepreneur," Tom Perkins says. "I tell that to a lot of people who want to get into the venture capital business." Of course, this is moot, since KP partners become independently wealthy after only a few years on the job. But even for a partner like Will Hearst III, whose inherited wealth alone makes him a Forbes 400 member and the richest KP partner, racking up a big scorecard on his technology investments allows him to earn his keep. "In the old days, the venture guys talked about making millions of dollars; now they talk in terms of $5 million blocks," muses Marc Dicioccio of Lehman Brothers.

The KP Keiretsu

Industry pundit Stewart Alsop claims that John Doerr is to the venture business what Bill Gates is to the software industry. Doerr gains such a stature through influencing, and often commanding, the KP keiretsu of over 200 information-technology companies the firm has invested in and assisted over the last 25 years. Doerr admits that KP gets almost all its investment leads from entrepreneurs working within the keiretsu, and rarely has funded a deal that has arrived over the transom.

On KP's Web site (www.kpcb.com) the firm proudly boasts: "One of the most important elements within KP's concept of value-added investing is access to a network of shared information and knowledge referred to as the keiretsu. The partners at KP are proud to have facilitated more than 100 alliances among the keiretsu network of companies."

Roger McNamee, founder and manager of the highly successful technology fund Integral Partners, who also sits in the same offices as the KP partners, sums up the leverage of the keiretsu best: "I think the value of the keiretsu is really simple. There are network effects you need to leverage in order to succeed in Silicon Valley today. The keiretsu provides a low-drive, high-efficiency system for getting those effects."

While the wiry and hyperactive Doerr likes to play down KP's influence over these companies, particularly after they go public, each KP partner proactively encourages its companies to work together. They constantly introduce their family of entrepreneurs to each other and actively suggest licensing or marketing agreements, research collaborations, joint ventures, and, with the example of AOL's purchase of Netscape and At Home's purchase of Excite, even mergers and acquisitions. Sometimes this activity includes investing in each other. AOL has made multimillion-dollar investments in two other KP companies, including a coinvestment, along with Netscape, in the fledgling public travel e-commerce company Preview Media. But there is an art to peddling this kind of influence even for KP partners. "In our business, you can't just go up to a CEO and tell him or his subordinates to go do something," says KP partner Will Hearst. "You have to lead leaders; you can't lead their companies."

Khosla describes how KP's goals and the desires of the entrepreneurs in one of its portfolio companies almost came into conflict. In 1995, six months after KP had invested in Excite, Microsoft made an offer to buy the company for $70 million, which at the time seemed like a staggering amount to a group of young entrepreneurs. At this point, Excite had only a dozen employees, six of whom were under 23 years of age. While Khosla vehemently opposed the deal, he ultimately left the decision in the hands of the entrepreneurs. Because KP is so hands-on, Khosla explains, the ethic is for the partners to support the CEO. "The only time we work against the CEO is when we lose confidence in his abilities and think he should be fired. In all other instances, we follow the CEO's lead," Khosla explains.

Ultimately, Excite followed Khosla's advice and refused to sell to Microsoft, and the company went public in 1997 and eventually merged with another KP company, At Home, in January 1999 for a whopping $6.7 billion.

Walking the Slippery Slope

KP's critics charge that the firm sometimes pushes its portfolio companies too hard to work together or against some other portfolio company's competitor. "The keiretsu can be a mixed blessing, because a fine line exists between what's right for the company in isolation and what's right for the portfolio of companies," says Jerry Kaplan, founder of GO Computer, and more recently founder and CEO of another KP-backed company, OnSale. And as impressive as KP's keiretsu is, there is a certain danger that comes with grandiose ambitions to create whole new industries. Two recent cases exemplify KP's leveraging its interlocking company directorships to get deals done that many critics argue were over the top. Both stories include Excite.

The first story was when Excite paid Netscape $70 million to become the primary provider of Web search services featured on Netscape's Netcenter home page, an arrangement that guaranteed Excite millions of new page views a day. Insiders close to the situation contend that Excite's competitor Infoseek originally had a lock on this deal, but John Doerr, who sits on Netscape's board, and Vinod Khosla, who sits on Excite's board, went to work behind the scenes to cut Infoseek out.

As the story goes, John Doerr attended Netscape's executive vice president Mike Homer's wedding as the deal with Infoseek was about to come down. Doerr, knowing that Homer's best man and then-CEO of Intuit, Bill Campbell, had influence over him, asked Campbell for help. Doerr, who also sits on the board of Intuit, was overheard at the wedding saying, "If we want Excite to get this deal, throw Campbell on it."

Meanwhile, Khosla went to work for Excite, but told us that "the role KP played was only to put the companies together and suggest structures that were win/win for both parties." With Homer persuaded and Excite ready to play, there was only one obstacle left to overcome—Excite had only $9 million left in its coffers and therefore couldn't commit to the $70 million payment (to be paid in $10 million quarterly installments) to Netscape to close the deal. And Netscape needed a guarantee of payment in order to record the revenues to keep Wall Street happy. This is when Doerr stepped in again and said, "Well, Intuit will loan it to you." So Excite's management went back to Campbell and asked Intuit to loan them the entire amount.

(For the record, despite Netscape founder Jim Clark's and Mike Homer's confirmation of Doerr's participation in this deal in a *Fortune* article, Doerr denied any involvement. "I wouldn't do that," he told us at the annual National Venture Capital Association meeting in San Francisco in the fall of 1998. Khosla, while acknowledging his involvement, also contends that Doerr only became aware of the deal after it was a fait accompli.)

Intuit ultimately did a $500 million debt conversion in order to have the cash to lend Excite for its Netscape deal. According to an Intuit prospectus supplement dated May 21, 1998, Intuit provided a short-term, low-interest, unsecured loan of $50 million to Excite on April 30, 1998, "and may provide additional financing to Excite in the future." The prospectus also mentioned that Intuit held 2.9 million shares of Excite common stock, representing 13 percent of Excite's outstanding common stock at the time. It's also interesting to note that Excite would later complete a secondary public offering for $75 million, just enough to pay off its loan to Intuit.

Shortly after these transactions were completed, a founder of one of Excite's primary competitors marveled at the three-way deal. "The KP guys just did a nice little round trip where they got the public to finance Netscape, with Excite and Intuit being sort of a passing vehicle. And Netscape got to book the money as revenues, which I thought was really clever," he said.

"If I were Netscape, I would have been friggin' thrilled," said Cristina Morgan, head of corporate finance at Hambrecht & Quist, commending the deal. "In order to compete today, CEOs need to be as clever as possible. If that means using their backer's other relationships to get things done, then so be it. If it works, they are all geniuses. But if the money that so-and-so gave to so-and-so to invest in so-and-so goes down a rat hole, then you aren't a genius," Morgan cautioned. "Usually when that happens, you never hear about it."

Others we talked to in the industry were more skeptical. "I am very fond of getting critical mass leverage, but as a venture capitalist, I would avoid moving onto any slippery slopes that would endanger my companies," says venture capitalist Ann Winblad of Hummer Winblad. "If these kind of deals don't work out, they could potentially drag your company into shareholder lawsuits."

In the end, the Excite/Netscape/Intuit deal helped catapult Excite ahead of Infoseek into the number two position in the Web portal business behind Yahoo, and Netscape built credibility for its NetCenter portal for Web customers and boosted its revenues by $10 million a quarter for seven successive quarters. For Intuit's part, its finance and small business online service, Quicken.com, got a much-needed boost by being prominently displayed on Excite's Web site. "I don't know how much of this was public knowledge, but before this deal was done, Quicken.com wasn't getting any traffic at all, and was losing to Yahoo in the finance [Web site] category," explained Khosla

The other KP keiretsu deal that raised the eyebrows of industry insiders was At Home's purchase of Excite. At Home and Excite are startups created and funded in the finest KP tradition. At Home was actually conceived and named by John Doerr, and its original CEO was Will Hearst. After KP provided its initial financing, it gathered more funding for the company from a group of cable companies led by John Malone's Tele-Communications, Inc. (TCI), and later helped recruit many of the company's top management, including Tom Jermoluk, the CEO who eventually took over the company reins from Hearst.

At Home is theoretically trying to design the communications infrastructure that would allow cable companies to provide Internet access through cable. Excite was founded in 1994 by six Stanford students in their rented house in Cupertino. While the company raised its initial seed money from International Data Group, a technology trade publication company founded and run by billionaire Pat McGovern, Excite didn't really take off until KP's Vinod Khosla came in and held the young team's hand through endless strategy sessions and helped to bring in experienced managers. Since those early days, Excite has evolved from a simple search engine company to one of the Internet's most visited Web sites.

When the "merger" was announced in January 1999, it put a $6.7 billion value on Excite, a whopping 57 percent premium over its closing stock price on the same day. The irony of this purchase price is twofold. First, we would argue that given Excite's second position in the search engine company race, and the fact that it lost $37.6 million on a relatively meager $155.4 million in revenues in 1998, the company was grossly overvalued in the first place. By our Internet Bubble calculation (see Appendices), Excite was $4.5 billion overvalued by At Home. The fact that At Home paid such a high premium caused KP's investment in Excite to get a huge markup in value difficult to justify by even the most aggressive investment standards.

Second, even though At Home's stock was valued at over $10 billion at the time of the purchase, its numbers are just as bad as Excite's, having generated only a token $48 million in revenues in 1998, against $144.2 million in losses. The combined cumulative losses over the life of both companies is an incredible $350 million. "This is a funny-money deal of grandiose proportions," an experienced technology fund manager told us.

This is also a deal many people believe was made to keep At Home alive. "At Home needed content to move beyond being merely a distribution company with heavy dependence on the cable companies," says Frank Quattrone, a leading technology banker at CS First Boston. "There have also been rumors that some of the cable companies might not renew their distribution deals with At Home," cautions Quattrone. Facing these risks, Tom Jermoluk went to work. With $10 billion worth of paper stock value in hand, he began to look around for something of real worth to buy. "He paid a huge premium for Excite, but it didn't matter so much because the investors thought it was a brilliant move," says Quattrone.

But most industry insiders remain skeptical. "The merger with Excite was clearly a deal designed to save At Home," concurs Paul Deninger, chairman and CEO of technology investment bank Broadview International.

For the record, At Home CEO Tom Jermoluk declined our requests for an interview.

From Excite's perspective, CEO George Bell got nervous about his company's future when AOL bought Netscape. Bell told *U.S. News & World Report* the week the deal was announced, "I came home to my wife and said, 'I have to rethink everything I know about Excite.'" His big question was, How was Excite going to compete in the brutal Web portal competition in the shadow of the giants AOL/Netscape, Yahoo, Infoseek/Disney, NBC/Snap, and Microsoft?

Conventional wisdom in Silicon Valley has always been that, as in all media battles, only the top three portals will survive. From this standpoint, Bell's paranoia made sense, but the real question insiders are asking is: Why At Home? If customer reach and Web traffic are what makes portals king, Excite wasn't picking up any significant new users with At Home, which has signed up only 330,000 subscribers to its service to date. By comparison, according to Media Metrix, Excite had 14.2 million users visit its site in November 1998, and about 20 million people have used Excite's "My Excite" feature, which allows users to create their own individualized home page to include updates on their favorite stocks, sports teams, and news.

According to what the two companies' CEOs told the *New York Times* on the day the deal was announced, Excite is uniquely positioned to solve At Home's problems. "We can take what we know about [Excite's customers] and intuit their income levels and imputed demographic profile and whether they are likely to sign up for broadband services," said Bell, adding, "That's a powerful method of cross-promotion." Jermoluk also noted another benefit to the deal. "The hidden gem of the whole deal is how we'll implement their targeting and database technology to deliver advertising to the individual user," he said.

Excite's defenders also say that the real winner of the portal competition will be the company that can offer fast broadband services to home and office, thus allowing customers to easily download videos and music over the Internet, engage in video conferencing, and speed up the normally clunky Web site surfing experience. High-speed Internet lines also open the way to more efficient and reliable online shopping, banking, trading, and advertising.

Arguably, Excite should have remained agnostic on which pipe it was choosing. In addition to At Home's cable solution, new two-way satellites and a telephone wire technology called ADSL are both developing rapidly, and the portals that end up winning, we think, will offer their services across all platforms. By helping At Home focus on solving its customer acquisition problems, Excite may lose the bigger battle for customers and eyeballs.

The bottom line is that KP believes if its companies are to remain top players in the Internet battles against Microsoft, Yahoo, and the others, these are the types of inside deals they need to broker. Or so the reasoning goes. "With the industry moving at Internet speed, you need to create business partnerships to accelerate the success of your company," observes Phil Horsley of Horsley Bridge Partners, a long-time investor in KP funds. "The fact that KP can leverage the sister companies in its venture investment portfolio, where you have partners sitting on both boards, can be a real advantage."

The Internet Opportunity: Bigger than the PC

At KP there are benefits to working within the keiretsu other than keeping your established companies in play. Kibitzing among portfolio company founders and CEOs often provides the impetus for some of KP's most exciting new opportunities. Doerr was originally turned on to the Internet by his good buddy and Sun's tech wizard Bill Joy, who told Doerr he should jump into the Internet opportunity with both feet. This advice gave Doerr the confidence to invest in Netscape, the Web browser developer whose early success, in essence, gave birth to the Internet industry. Doerr says that KP's interest in the Internet was also confirmed by working with the KP portfolio company Intuit. When KP first invested, Intuit was a one-product company with $35 million in annual revenues. Five years later, it has over $400 million in revenues and a significant share in three software businesses: personal finance, tax preparation, and small business. "In three years the Intuit team turned a one-legged stool into a sturdy, deep-rooted stump," Doerr says. "Regis McKenna articulated the key strategy at one of our off-sites: 'The smartest entrepreneurs aren't providing either a product or service, but both.' [Intuit founder] Scott Cook and his team deeply understand that Intuit is not just a software company, but also a service provider building enduring relationships."

And Doerr's philosophy has proven right. Whether you talk about AOL, Yahoo, Amazon, or any of the great online companies created so far, the strategy to become both a product and a service has given them domination.

"In the early 1980s, the PC was driven by spreadsheets and word processing, and lowering costs in businesses. Now the killer applications leverage the top line—helping us inform, sell, educate, entertain, inspire, even govern. I believe the Net can have as much impact as the telephone, radio, or possibly television—it will certainly be bigger than the PC," Doerr explained prophetically to *Red Herring* in 1995. "Silicon Valley is no longer about silicon; it's about networking," he said. "In the 1980s, PC and hardware and software grew into a $100 billion industry—the Internet could be three times bigger."

This new awareness inspired Doerr to sign up one of his all-time best recruits, Will Hearst, who left his family's famous media business to join KP as a partner in early 1995. "Five years ago people would have wondered, Why add a media guy to a technology venture group? Will's a first-rate technology investor. But it's also clear that there are also major opportunities in new media," explained Doerr at the time. Hearst's first major assignment was, of course, to help launch At Home.

Netscape Takes Sail

Since waking up to the Internet opportunity, KP has funded more Internet deals than any other venture capital fund, pumping an estimated $300 million into over 53 Net-related startups.

Its first major play in the Internet space was a company founded by Jim Clark, the former Stanford computer science professor who had previously founded Silicon Graphics (SGI). In January 1994, Clark resigned from his post as chairman of SGI, the multibillion-dollar visual computing company, to start an interactive software company for the Internet, then called Mosaic Communications. "The Internet is more exciting than 3D graphics," Clark told *Red Herring* shortly after he founded the company and before taking money from KP.

At the time, Clark had bankrolled the company out of his own pocket, stating that "venture capital is good for the raw entrepreneur," which he obviously no longer considered himself to be. When pushed further about his wariness in dealing with venture capitalists, Clark recounted the story of his first startup. "When I started Silicon Graphics, I sold 40 percent of the company for $800,000 in our first round of financing. By the time SGI went through a couple of public offerings, I ended up owning only 1 percent of the company. In retrospect, that kind of hurts. So when I started Netscape, I decided it would be a better idea to fund the company myself, since by then I had some of my own money," he said.

Clark's new startup team included Marc Andreessen, the 22-year-old whiz kid, and his development team from the University of Illinois, which created one of the first popular Internet browsers, Mosaic.

"I've learned everything I know about the Internet over the last three months. I'm convinced that the Internet is the information superhighway, and that Marc Andreessen's vision is right on," Clark proclaimed to *Red Herring* at the time.

Netscape's initial plan was to make the best Internet browser and then market and sell it over the Web. If Netscape quickly gained market share and built a large installed base of customers, the company could build a strong brand and defend its position in the browser market. This task was not difficult because distribution of software over the Internet proved to be incredibly inexpensive. In the first huge sign of the commercial potential of the Internet, Netscape sold over 10 million browsers in just nine months. "There is no other distribution system in existence that would have allowed that," Clark bragged at the time. He then accurately predicted, "We see this potential for low-cost distribution of any kind of intellectual property—whether it be software, or pictures, or movies, or CDs, or anything that can be represented as bits—as one of the most revolutionary aspects of the Internet."

Eventually, Clark decided he could use the assistance of a seasoned venture capital team to build Netscape. Before presenting his deal to KP, Clark "halfheartedly" shopped Netscape, out of a sense of professional obligation, to the two venture capital firms that were original investors in SGI: New Enterprise Associates and Mayfield Fund. This time he wasn't going to give up 40 percent for only $800,000. Instead, Clark told the venture capitalists they would have to invest at an $18 million valuation if they wanted to get in on the deal into which he had already pumped $3 million of his own money. Mayfield never called him back, and NEA was interested only if they could get in at a $12 million valuation.

At this point, Clark revisited his dream with John Doerr. "John Doerr, God bless him, had the courage to pay what at the time looked like a very high price," recalls Doerr's friend and competitor Norm Fogelsong of Institutional Venture Partners. And in many ways, KP's willingness to pay a higher price to win the Netscape deal was vintage KP. In spite of its position of tremendous strength in the market, KP still has the reputation of not cutting the toughest, tightest deal with the entrepreneurs they work with. "We try to make sure the entrepreneurs make a lot of money, too," states KP's Tom Perkins. "We like to tell the entrepreneurs that the only time we're on the opposite side of the table is when we're cutting the pie in the first round."

"When Jim called about Netscape, he really didn't need our money," recounts Doerr. "He wanted help building the team and polishing the company's strategic plan. I guess we forced him to take the money. In fact, after we agreed to invest, I think it took four or five months before he even cashed the check."

Clark concurs that KP's greatest help, other than being early believers in the Internet, was their incredible recruiting skills. "These are the ways that top-flight firms such as Kleiner Perkins can really help out young enterprises. So I don't mind if they own a part of Netscape, because they've earned it," says Clark.

And the admiration is mutual. "The high human drama here is that Jim Clark and I have always wanted to work together," recalls Doerr. "I first met him as a professor at Stanford. But Jim started SGI after we had committed to Sun Microsystems, so we competed for several years. Jim Clark has an exquisite sense of taste for the confluence of different markets and technology. He also moves with an extraordinary sense of urgency."

By the time Doerr brought Jim Clark and Marc Andreessen in to formally present their deal to the KP partners at one of their sacred Monday morning general partner meetings in June 1994, Doerr and several of his partners had already worked with the two entrepreneurs to pound out their growth plan. Sitting in the expansive, glass-encased KP boardroom around a table that some partners jokingly refer to as the world's largest surfboard, Clark and Andreessen made their case about why their browser could become the new platform for the Internet era the way that Windows had become the platform for the PC era. Within 30 minutes the KP partners voted to invest.

Netscape would eventually use the $5 million KP invested and the proceeds of an August 1995 IPO to build one of the fastest-growing companies ever founded. But in spite of Netscape's early dominance of the Web due to the ubiquity of its browser, Doerr and his partners were always realistic about the company's long-term success. Doerr told *Red Herring* just before the company's IPO, "The company generates 80 percent of today's Web traffic. But Internet software is going to be extremely varied, vertical, and competitive." This observation was eventually proven right, however ironically for Doerr, when Netscape was ultimately forced to sell to AOL, after losing significant browser market share to Microsoft and losing the traffic battle to upstart portals like Yahoo and Excite.

Holy War with Microsoft

In a 1996 *New York Times* article, Bill Gates wrote, "The surging popularity of the Internet is the most important single development in the computer industry since the IBM PC was introduced in 1981. It is even more important than the advent of the graphical user interface, the use of on-screen pictures, and type fonts. Like the PC, the Internet is a tidal wave. It will wash over the computer industry and many others, drowning those who don't learn to swim in its waves." While Bill Gates admits that Microsoft was a little late to join the Internet game, he is widely credited for radically refocusing his company's strategy onto the Net in a matter of months, a corporate feat virtually impossible for most companies its size. So while Netscape and other KP companies had a good 12-month jump-start on Microsoft, they knew that ultimately they would have to turn and face the software behemoth.

One of KP's most visible offensive moves against Microsoft was in 1996, when the firm raised corporate money from IBM, TCI, Cisco, Oracle, and Sun Microsystems and formed its Java Fund. Java was a new object-oriented software language developed by Sun; its original premise was to allow software applications written in the code to run on any operating system, whether Windows, Unix, or the Mac OS, without any alteration. In the words of the outspoken Netscape cofounder Marc Andreessen: "The purpose of the Java Fund is to drive a paradigm shift that, if it plays out, would overturn Microsoft."

Soon after the Java Fund was created, CNN interviewed *Red Herring* about its prospects for success. While we recognized that KP's investment expertise and its vast industry relationships allowed little room for the firm's failure, we still questioned why KP would focus its fund on a specific technology. It had been our experience, for example, that those venture funds formed between the PC and Internet booms to target "multimedia" (i.e., CD-ROM content) were less successful than those more focused on the broader software industry.

Shortly after we returned to our office from CNN's San Francisco bureau, we received a call from a KP partner. "I don't think *Red Herring* understands exactly what we are up to with the Java Fund," he said. "The fund is actually targeted at Internet opportunities in general." Okay, we thought, but then why call it the Java Fund? "We are basically a bunch of frustrated marketing guys, and we thought that, given the plethora of new 'Internet' venture capital funds, we could get more attention if it was called the Java Fund," he explained. Not quite content with the spin, we pressed further. KP was still making a statement about the importance of Java, we insisted.

By the end of a long, fascinating conversation, the partner

finally admitted what was behind the new KP investment initiative: By stimulating the proliferation of Java technology, it could possibly become part of a new operating system for the Internet, thereby significantly loosening Microsoft's grip on the technology industry. "If Microsoft dominates the Internet era, we will end up merely funding companies we sell to Microsoft, and *Red Herring* will spend all its time writing about Microsoft—and that won't be much fun for either of us," he said.

A few days later, the entire *Red Herring* editorial team drove down to Menlo Park to have lunch with John Doerr. Right away we focused the discussion on KP's strategy to destabilize Microsoft by pushing Java. "Oh, no, no, no," said Doerr. "We gain nothing in our business by being ideological. Many of our companies do business with Microsoft—we consider them a partner." He also stated that he had offered Microsoft the opportunity to invest in its Java Fund in an effort to show the world, once and for all, that the battle between KP and Microsoft was mere myth. (Not surprisingly, Gates declined.) With suspicion still apparent in our eyes, Doerr kept on selling: "No single company can own the Internet—it's too big!" While we agreed with his premise, our view was that Doerr was just doing what he does best—being a good gamesman.

Doerr knew that proclaiming war on Microsoft wasn't smart. Many of KP's portfolio companies—such as Intuit, Compaq, and Pivotal—heavily depended on Microsoft. But he also knew that the Internet was causing a major new dislocation in the computer business, and Microsoft's position was, for once, vulnerable. Rather than compete with Microsoft in the press, Doerr was poised to take on the software giant in the market.

The creation of the Java Fund, therefore, drew the lines of competition between the KP keiretsu and Microsoft. Previously, Sun, Netscape, America Online, and other KP portfolio companies were happily and vocally chanting anti-Microsoft slogans, but this was the first time they had formally joined together in an open alliance.

Unfortunately, KP and Sun's original dream for Java to emerge as part of an alternative for the Windows operating system has yet to be realized. To date, Java has done nothing for Internet browsers except to slow them down, and it has yet to become the platform of choice for smaller, embedded Internet devices.

Java has, though, become an important programming language that makes developers more productive as well as a crucial middleware architecture that helps tie together disparate corporate computer systems across heterogeneous networks. The surge in the adoption of Java applications for servers and middleware, particularly for very large and small companies, has surprised even the most optimistic pundits. By 2002, according to the International Data Corporation, the size of the Java market should exceed $2 billion, with nearly 1.5 million programmers coding in the language.

In an interview with *Red Herring,* Sun's chief technology officer, Bill Joy, said Sun wasn't ready to concede the consumer market to Microsoft. "The PC of the next wave will be a combination organizer, pager, and cellular phone—a pocket-size personal communicator that's always on and always hooked to the Net," he said. And did he believe that this next wave would crash down on Microsoft? "That's why Gates is worried about Symbian [the new operating system for cell phones that the leading players such as Motorola, Ericsson, and Nokia are rallying around]. You combine this threat with the undisputed success of the PalmPilot—this must scare the heck out of Microsoft," he answered. Joy's theme for the future, he explained, is "simplicity for the consumer."

KP's initiative to lead the destabilization of Microsoft goes beyond the evangelization of Java, of course. In January 1999, the industry witnessed an example of the KP keiretsu strategy on steroids when Sun and AOL sliced and diced a third KP portfolio company, Netscape, to strengthen their positions as the two biggest players in the anti-Microsoft camp. By acquiring Netscape for $4 billion, AOL has made a major move to outflank Microsoft where it remains most vulnerable, in online media and electronic commerce software. On the media side, AOL hopes to build on its subscriber base of 17 million (a large portion of whom do not surf the Web) by absorbing the 16 million Web-savvy visitors to Netscape's popular Netcenter Web site. This is yet another industry event that shifts the competitive dynamics from pure browser plays toward content-rich portals—another potentially ominous trend for Microsoft. On the e-commerce software side, Sun has agreed to put its sales and marketing muscle behind packaging and selling Netscape's Internet server software for AOL.

While the deal certainly strengthens competition against Microsoft, it also acknowledges that Netscape ultimately had to throw in the towel in its battle with the software Goliath. Originally, Netscape's two founders, Jim Clark and Marc Andreessen, made lofty claims that Windows technology was going to become increasingly irrelevant as operating system functions became subsumed by their company's browser. This goal, while unrealistic, represented yet a second line of attack for KP, along with its Java initiative, in its war on Microsoft. Unfortunately, because of early arrogance and poor strategic and product execution, Netscape stumbled badly.

One could speculate that KP's attack on Microsoft extends beyond the business world. Shortly after the news broke that the Department of Justice had filed a complaint against Microsoft, the *Wall Street Journal* columnist Paul Gigot called to ask us if we thought John Doerr's close relationship with Vice President Al Gore had anything to do with the lawsuit. No one will ever know the answer to that, we responded, but it does tie in to the grand scheme of overall assault on Microsoft. And it is a matter of public record that three of the Justice Department's most vocal witnesses—Scott McNealy, Steve Case, and Jim Barksdale—are all CEOs of companies with KP partners on their boards.

Although the description of the keiretsu in action is admittedly part speculation, it does illustrate that KP and its 175-company-strong keiretsu is a force in the technology industry that has successfully challenged Microsoft's dominance. When we confronted Bill Gates directly over lunch at the World Economic Forum in Davos, Switzerland, in February 1999 about KP's strategy to prevent Microsoft from lording over the Internet in the same way it did over the PC, he would only say, "I hear things, and people tell me things, but I really can't say anything for certain." KP partner Russ Siegelman, who spent seven years working for Microsoft, supported his former boss's benign view on KP in a *New Yorker* piece in 1997: "Bill's view of venture capitalists is they're out to make money and they will do that any way they can."

But whether this is a concerted effort on KP's part or not, given the rising impact of the Internet across all industries and the consolidation of the anti-Microsoft forces, Bill Gates's position as the most powerful person in the technology industry is being challenged. "The Gates/Doerr competition goes back at least a decade, when Lotus [a KP personal computer software company investment led by Doerr] got its butt handed to it by Microsoft in the spreadsheet wars," observed a technology industry veteran friendly with both Gates and Doerr who preferred not to be named. "The battle continued when Microsoft took on Sun in the corporate computing market with Windows NT, and lives on today over the Internet," he said. With his growing political clout and his role as captain of the KP confederation of companies, no other figure looms larger in the Internet era than John Doerr.

Gaining the First-Mover Advantage

A big part of KP's strategy to win big in the Internet game is helping its companies gain first-mover advantage, which generally means raising big bucks through any means as fast as possible. Part of this tactic is leveraging what insiders refer to as the "Kleiner Mystique," a form of investor-relations pixie dust that KP has sprinkled on some of the most richly valued Internet companies in the public market. One longtime technology investor well acquainted with the Mystique says, "It's not by accident that Kleiner Perkins deals get much higher valuations than those of other firms. It's based on knowing how to optimize company pitches and the way they present data to Wall Street. KP is good at making their companies the center of attention." Sam Colella of Institutional Venture Partners observes, "If you are an institutional buyer playing in the public market and you look at an At Home, you say, 'Oh my god. KP is behind this deal. This could be a whole new industry. Geez, those guys have done it so many times. Yeah, I had better buy this.'"

In particular, the advantage of having John Doerr on a company's team helps create an image that it is bigger than life and thereby worthy of an equally fanciful market valuation. "The Internet is underhyped," is a classic Doerr remark when he's out peddling his Internet startups. Sun Microsystems CEO Scott McNealy refers to such promotional energy as "the Doerr sphere of evangelism—the art of selling some futuristic technology as the next big thing."

"He has used personal self-promotion to his advantage better than any venture capitalist on the planet—bar none—by an order of magnitude!" says Broadview's Paul Deninger. "Doerr has created a product category around the venture capital business, and he has successfully branded himself and Kleiner Perkins as the most powerful venture capitalists in the category," explains Deninger. "So is there any difference between what Bill Gates does and what Doerr does? One sells product, one sells valuation."

And the investment bankers we talked to who regularly fall over each other trying to win the next KP deal and take it public concur. "KP is given the benefit of the doubt," believes Mark Diocioccio of Lehman Brothers. "They have a cachet and a marquee name that comes from having made people money. They can do more aggressive things because people see them as having a lot of credibility," he says. Brad Koenig, managing director and head of the technology banking practice at Goldman Sachs, who has taken several KP companies public, adds: "KP has established a dominant position. John Doerr has the image, the brand, the perception that he and the firm can add significant value both through their business acumen and especially through their keiretsu network of companies. It's all larger than life!"

Two classic examples of KP companies that stood behind the Kleiner Mystique and moved quickly into the financial markets to gain market advantage are Netscape and Amazon. In the summer of 1995, when Netscape was a year and a half old, Doerr worked behind the scenes to convince the company's management that it was the right time to go public. Doerr thought Netscape should raise money while the market was hot on the Internet, and, more important, an IPO would give Netscape's browser business a huge boost. And it worked. "The IPO was one of the best marketing tactics we could have done," says Netscape founder Jim Clark. Indeed, the advertising value alone was worth market points and strength in the company's early days.

Amazon's founder and CEO Jeff Bezos recalls that before the company's initial public offering, he and Doerr agreed that "the Internet land grab" was in full swing, and that if the company didn't build a war chest to capture and retain customers faster than its competitors, it would lose out big-time. So just as in the Netscape case, Doerr convinced Bezos and the investment bankers that it was time for Amazon "to put the puck on the ice," that is, to heighten its image and raise some cash by taking the company public, in spite of its losses and the fact that most of the management team had been together only four months.

Doerr also regularly argues that in the Internet era, going public early helps create a liquid currency in the form of stock that companies can use for acquisitions. To make his case, Doerr likes to quote what has become known in Silicon Valley as Bill Joy's Law: Assume innovation will occur outside your corporation. Following this philosophy, all KP companies engage in acquisition activity and major corporate alliances. "You can't predict what some of the opportunities might be and how much cash they might require," says Amazon's Bezos.

As a postlude to Amazon's IPO, the company recently raised what their underwriter Morgan Stanley described in an ad in the April 1999 issue of *Red Herring* as "the largest convertible offering in history." To maintain its Internet land grab march, Amazon raised an incredible $1.25 billion convertible bond to offset its anticipated losses into the next millennium.

While KP has consciously cultivated a certain mystique to critically leverage its deals, it's clearly a paradoxical strategy that involves simultaneously keeping the firm and its companies in the spotlight, yet maintaining enough distance to create a certain mystery and awe. Doerr defended himself in an August 1997 *New Yorker* piece, saying, "People criticize me for being too grandiose, and it's probably true. But why not think big? Maybe you get a big belly flop. Or maybe you get the next Netscape."

But some skeptics in the industry are more cautious about the long-term success of companies that undergo such early hype. "I think you can go back and look at some of KP's biggest promotes— such as Dynabook, GO Computing, and 3DO—all those companies were presented as bigger than life very early," observed venture capitalist Bob Kagle of Benchmark. "I don't know how many truly bigger-than-life early companies have gone on to be great businesses yet. I think it's a short list." Kagle also pointed out that if one were to go through KP's portfolio carefully, one would find that many of KP's bigger successes were companies they invested in at later stages, after the companies had some momentum. "In some cases, like Sun Microsystems and Intuit, the companies were already demonstrating their success. So the benefits of this early game of hype get kind of fuzzy," says Kagle.

Also fuzzy is whether the early hype and ultimate overvaluation of the Internet Bubble stocks degrade the integrity of the technology financial markets. As one seasoned venture capitalist noted in a bit of a tirade when we brought up the subject:

> KP can argue lots of things: "Oh, look at our companies. We've raised a lot of money so we can hire a lot of people and we employ x number of people. Isn't that great. Look at all the wealth we create." They never seem to consider the damage that could occur if the whole thing crashes. They never wonder if they could be pushing the stock price up astronomically way ahead of its time. You have to remember that companies end up having to grant stock options to new employees at those crazy

prices. And even if the company does just fine, the stock still ultimately goes down to a normal valuation. Those employees end up being impossible to retain. It's just the wrong way to do business.

THE KP PORTFOLIO AND THE INTERNET BUBBLE

The following table presents the portfolio of the fifteen pub-licly-traded Internet-related companies KP has funded. As we mentioned in the introduction to this chapter, the KP portfolio represented 40 percent of the total Internet Bubble as of June 11, 1999. Also as of that date, none was trading under its IPO price, and thirteen were still unprofitable in the quarter ending March 31, 1999. Three of the companies—Amazon, AOL, and At Home—make up 87 percent of the total equity market capitaliza-tion of the entire pool of Kleiner-funded companies.

According to our Internet Bubble calculation (see Appendix A "Calculating the Bubble" for further details), the fifteen compa-nies as a group would need to produce annual revenue growth greater than 80 percent in order to justify their current market capitalizations. This percentage is consistent with the average required growth rate of the entire group of 133 companies we measured. Given this consistency in implied growth rates, one could note that KP's portfolio is not any more overvalued than the entire Internet Bubble portfolio. As a testimony to KP's mus-cle in the market, it is interesting to note that Amazon, AOL, and At Home are among the industry's eight $10 billion-plus market cap pure-play Internet winners, and the three companies repre-sent 34 percent of the total market value of the entire Internet Bubble portfolio.

Kleiner Perkins Portfolio of Internet Companies

($ millions) Name	Market Cap (6/11/99)	12-Month Revenue	Implied Future Revenue	5-Year Implied CAGR
Excite/At Home	$14,240.7	$252.1	$9,301.8	106%
Amazon.com	17,100.0	816.3	22,338.9	94%
America Online	107,700.0	4,190.0	70,347.9	76%
Concentric Network	1,170.0	96.4	764.2	51%
Healtheon	5,630.0	56.6	2,451.6	112%
Intraware	481.5	38.4	251.6	46%
ISS	1,180.0	45.8	513.8	62%
iVillage	894.6	19.3	779.1	110%
Marimba	910.7	20.2	396.6	81%
NextCard	1,890.0	1.1	823.0	274%
Onsale	314.5	235.4	164.3	-7%
Preview Travel	240.0	27.7	125.4	35%
Rhythms Net Connections	4,070.0	1.2	2,658.5	368%
SportLine USA	821.4	34.8	715.4	83%
Verisign	2,730.0	47.9	1,188.8	90%
TOTAL	$159,373.4	$5,883.3	$112,820.9	81%

Equity value implied by estimated forward growth rate of entire
Kleiner Perkins portfolio at:
50% = $ 65.3 billion
65% = $ 105.3 billion

Total Kleiner Perkins portfolio Internet Bubble contribution @ an
estimated forward growth rate of:
50% = $ 94.0 billion *
65% = $ 54.1 billion *

*Both figures would represent roughly 40 percent of the total 133 companies in the Internet Bubble calculation at similar growth rates.

Doonesbury

THE I-BANKERS
EMBRACE THE INTERNET

We sell stocks at whatever price the market will bear
on whatever day—that's our job.
—Michael McCaffery, CEO,
BancBoston Robertson Stephens

The grand facilitators of the Internet Bubble are the investment bankers. These pin-striped peddlers of IPO shares come
from large New York–based investment houses such as Morgan
Stanley Dean Witter and Goldman Sachs, and San Francisco–based
boutique banks like Hambrecht & Quist and BancBoston Robertson Stephens. As the underwriters of the IPO, these banks guarantee companies they take public that their sales team will sell an
agreed-upon amount of stock at an agreed price. If the investment
bank fails to unload all the shares to deep-pocketed institutional
investors such as Fidelity and Vanguard, they have to buy all outstanding shares themselves. For this guarantee, which rarely gets
called upon, the participating banks are paid a hefty 7 percent commission on the total capital raised in the public offerings they manage. After taking a company public, bankers usually continue to
work with their customers by managing follow-on equity and debt
financings. So, hustling for the IPO business sits at the heart of the
investment bankers' livelihood.

The technology investment banking business has been particularly lucrative in recent years. From 1992 through 1998, there were
a total of 826 initial public offerings for technology worth $48.8 bil-
lion. During that same time period, there were technology follow-
on stock offerings worth $59.5 billion. The commissions paid on
these offerings alone represent close to $8 billion. Within the tech-

nology sector, the Internet-related offerings have begun to dominate the IPO schedule. Over the last five years more than 130 Internet companies have gone public. (For the complete listing refer to Appendix A "Calculating the Bubble.")

This chapter examines the beginnings of the modern technology investment-banking industry, with a special focus on some of the early Silicon Valley pioneers in the industry as well as on the bigger New York–based banks that later joined the tech banking game. We look at how the Bubble helped foster an environment where two of the pioneers of technology banking sold the investment banks they created for top dollar to huge commercial banks, then turned around and started two new competing firms. We also examine the emergence of electronic investment banking and how it promises to rattle the industry. Finally, we look at some of the potential conflicts of interest in technology banking that are accentuated by Internet mania. Due to huge investor demand for Internet IPO shares and a highly competitive banking market, bankers often find themselves taking companies public prematurely and helping the banks' favorite customers spin shares and flip stock for huge gains. While investment bankers will never reap the same level of reward as the successful entrepreneur or venture capitalist, they are critical players in funneling the huge level of investment dollars into new companies associated with the Internet.

Technology Banking Pioneers

In 1965, long before the world knew the name Silicon Valley, Sandy Robertson, a partner with the New York–based investment bank Smith Barney, was dispatched to San Francisco to scare up some business and look for prospects. South of the city, Robertson discovered a growing new technology industry that included Fairchild Semiconductor, the first major semiconductor company, whose founders and early employees would later spin out and start most of the next dozen chip companies including Intel and National Semiconductor. Unfortunately, Robertson quickly found out that Smith

Barney wasn't interested in these companies. "By 1969 I was pretty frustrated," says Robertson. "We did a private placement for Spectra Physics, a laser company which was one of Tom Perkins's [who later cofounded the venture firm Kleiner Perkins] first venture investments, but the bank refused to take the company public." Robertson had problems trying to get people in New York to understand what kind of products these companies produced. "I'd go back to New York for our partners meeting and the guys there would say, 'Hey, Buck Rogers, how's our ray-gun company doing out there on the West Coast?'" Robertson recalls. After getting shot down on the Spectra deal, he had to walk across Montgomery Street in San Francisco and hand it to another East Coast transplant, Bill Hambrecht.

Just a year earlier, in 1968, Hambrecht had joined with an early venture capitalist out of Bank of America, George Quist, to form Hambrecht & Quist, a firm that combined venture capital with investment-banking services for small but rapidly growing companies in Silicon Valley. Over the years, H&Q grew into a major investment bank by underwriting deals that included Apple, Genentech, and many of the hottest IPOs during the Internet boom.

Meanwhile, Robertson left Smith Barney and eventually joined with Paul Stephens to raise $1 million to form Robertson Stephens investment bank, whose mission was to target hot new technology companies. Eugene Kleiner, later of Kleiner Perkins fame, invested in the firm as a limited partner. As for his old employer, Robertson reports: "Almost 10 years to the day after we started our firm, the president of Smith Barney came to my office and said, 'Gee, we're interested in technology; how can we work together?' I thought to myself, You're 10 years behind—you could have owned the place."

Despite the formation and reasonable success of specialized banks—now known as technology boutiques—such as Robertson Stephens and Hambrecht & Quist, financing Silicon Valley start-ups was not a huge business in the 1970s.

By the late 1970s, however, the big New York investment banks—the so-called bulge-bracket firms—decided to set up technology practices in San Francisco. While financing high-tech companies was still a small market—the average IPO deal size in those days was a paltry $10 million to $15 million in range, with very little merger-and-acquisition activity—even the larger investment banks began to recognize that something dynamic was happening out West. The now-defunct L. F. Rothschild was the first big bank to enter the market, and Morgan Stanley and its longtime archrival, Goldman Sachs, were all actively pitching their services to technology companies by 1980.

Opening the door to these bulge brackets were some of the best venture capital firms, such as Kleiner Perkins Caufield & Byers and The Mayfield Fund, who wanted the additional prestige and clout these New York banks could provide for their portfolio companies. "When I joined Morgan Stanley in 1977," says Frank Quattrone, now managing director and head of the technology group at CS First Boston, "the firm was basically an execution house for its existing blue-chip clients such as General Electric and General Motors. We expanded beyond that when the Kleiners and Mayfields began courting Morgan Stanley and Goldman."

Another factor was a rule change in the banking business that enabled bond issuers to switch banks more easily. This shift set off a mad scramble for clients among the investment banks, and some companies such as Exxon actually started to insource some of their investment-banking work. As a result, profit margins at the banks began to shrink, and they needed to find new markets for their services. High technology was a natural choice—it was growing fast, but it was underbanked.

A watershed deal was the public offering of Apple Computer in 1980, lead-managed by Morgan Stanley and joined by Hambrecht & Quist as another underwriter. "Steve Jobs, who felt he had a very large company in the making, wanted a large investment bank to be the banker," says Quattrone.

Ben Rosen, Morgan Stanley's electronics analyst at the time and an early user of Apple's computers, was instrumental in forging the connection between the bank and Apple. Rosen later gained notoriety as a cofounder of Compaq Computer and venture capitalist with Sevin Rosen.

Apple was actually the first IPO Morgan Stanley had done in almost 25 years, and more opportunities followed. In 1982 Kleiner Perkins asked Morgan Stanley to help arrange a private placement for its largest venture fund to date, $100 million, and a strong link between the two firms was forever forged.

Meanwhile, Goldman Sachs got its biggest break in the technology market when it took Microsoft public in 1986, thus legitimizing the bank's technology practice. Alex. Brown & Sons also had a good year in 1986, which included taking Sun Microsystems public.

Yet while the bulge brackets could offer a whole range of services, the boutique banks, living or dying by their technology deals, had the strongest technology research at the time, enabling them to participate in many technology IPOs even if they didn't lead them. This competition catalyzed Morgan Stanley and Goldman Sachs to build their own strong technology research teams and opened the way to additional business with technology companies that went beyond leading initial public offerings.

Despite its promise, the technology market remained cyclical and sometimes volatile. In 1983 the personal computer Bubble hit its peak, but when it burst in 1984, some very lean years followed for tech bankers, and it got even worse after the stock market crash of 1987.

The bulge-bracket banks had enough resources to survive, but some of the boutiques struggled. Busy chasing one high-tech initial public offering after another, they came up short when the IPO market dried up. And while some good companies such as Cisco and Microsoft did go public after the PC bubble burst, the crash of '87 nearly finished off some of the boutique banks.

"I joined Hambrecht & Quist in 1982," says managing director Cristina Morgan. "I believed technology was a driving force in our economy. I looked smart in the eight-month bull market of 1983. But, frankly, I looked stupid from 1984 to 1990. You might as well have not been in the technology business—being at Hambrecht & Quist in the eighties was a joke."

Technology banking veteran Stu Francis, managing director

and head of the technology practice at Lehman Brothers, provides a similar spin on his two decades in the business:

> When I started in the business after finishing at Stanford in 1977 and went to a dinner party and told people I was an investment banker, they said, "What's that?" In the mid- to late eighties when I went to a dinner party and said I was an investment banker, they said, "I just read about how much money you make." In the nineties when you tell people you're an investment banker they say, "Why aren't you retired?" I think that sort of sums it up. Investment bankers used to be behind the scenes working with their clients. Now certain firms and individuals have become much more visible. It's just a bigger-time industry.

The Life and Times of Frank Quattrone

Frank Quattrone, currently managing director and head of the technology group at CS First Boston, has been arguably the most dominant investment banker in technology over the last 15 years. Many compare Quattrone's impact on the development and growth of technology investment banking with that of John Doerr on the venture capital business. Like Doerr, Quattrone is a paragon of shrewdness, intelligence, business savvy, and aggressive salesmanship. Not coincidentally, both launched their careers about the time the personal computer industry took off, and they went on to share many deals, including Netscape and Amazon.

While Quattrone was finishing up his MBA at Stanford Business School, his future employer, Morgan Stanley, was taking personal computer upstart Apple Computer public. Buoyed by the success of Apple's IPO, Quattrone joined Morgan Stanley at a good time after graduation in 1981, and he spearheaded Morgan Stanley's California presence as a technology banking powerhouse. Along the way, he built a superior team of bankers, including Bill Brady and George Boutros, who complement his talents and can independently handle the biggest, trickiest deals.

At Morgan Stanley this team managed the public offerings and other financial services of the biggest names in technology, including Cisco Systems, Netscape, and SGI. Over time, Quattrone and his wily band of bankers and analysts built Morgan Stanley into the dominant brand in technology. Companies wanting to go public swarmed the firm, seeking the halo effect that comes with having the Morgan Stanley name stamped on an IPO prospectus. And if they were lucky enough to go with Morgan Stanley, their stock would be sold at premium prices, and they would have lots of after-market support and attention.

By April 1996, even though Quattrone earned an estimated $5 million a year, he and his team had grown restless at Morgan Stanley. In a move that shook the industry, Quattrone, Brady, and Boutros rounded up nine other associates and bolted from the Morgan Stanley mothership to form a new technology practice based in Menlo Park, California, called DMG Technology, under the umbrella of Deutsche Bank, a large international commercial bank and financial institution based in Germany. And this renegade team's goals were no secret. DMG's mission was to move quickly to create a technology corporate finance, merger advisory, and research services business that would eventually compete head-on with Morgan Stanley.

"There were a bunch of reasons for leaving Morgan Stanley," says Quattrone. "There were some compensation disputes in which we were promised certain things if our business performed, but these didn't materialize. Our group was more efficient and profitable than the other groups at Morgan Stanley, but we were still asked to keep our head count flat."

The tech practice added from 40 to 50 new clients a year to the firm, and the business had grown from $30 million to $150 million with the flat head count, yet when Quattrone asked for two more junior associates, which would cost Morgan Stanley $100,000 to $200,000 a year, he was turned down.

"This was one of the straws that broke the camel's back," says Quattrone. "The assistant to the associate drone in charge of new associates basically said, 'You guys have the highest ratio of associates and analysts to officers of any group inside the investment-banking division. You can't have them.'"

Aside from these disputes, Quattrone and his cohorts had caught the entrepreneurial bug, a contagion everyone in Silicon Valley catches. "Frankly, a bunch of us were 35 to 40 years old, and we had seen a lot of our clients start companies and pursue their dreams," says Quattrone. And it did not go unnoticed that these entrepreneurs earned tens to hundreds of millions more than even the highest-paid investment bankers. "It was our time to share in the American dream," explains Quattrone.

So Quattrone & Co. founded their "pure play in technology" with DMG in which they were purportedly offered 50 percent of the profits generated by their deals, an unprecedented arrangement in the investment-banking world.

What they didn't expect, though, was that none of the top technology analysts at Morgan Stanley—George Kelly, Mary Meeker, Chuck Phillips—would follow Quattrone to DMG. "They chickened out," says Quattrone. "We did DMG partly because these analysts felt so frustrated at Morgan Stanley. I fielded their complaints constantly. If I had known all of them would stay at Morgan Stanley, I wouldn't have left the bank."

Meanwhile, Morgan Stanley's old archrival, Goldman Sachs, hoped that the firm would be significantly weakened by the departure of Quattrone and his talented sidekicks, and could exploit this market opportunity while Quattrone established himself at DMG. But Morgan Stanley still did well: In the year following Quattrone's departure, Morgan Stanley's technology group raised $8.5 billion in 35 financings on a lead-managed basis and advised on 22 merger-and-acquisition transactions, while Goldman captured some 58 percent of the technology market during that time span.

At the same time, DMG, with only 4 percent of the market, came on strong in 1997, during which it took Amazon public and advised on 5 of the 10 biggest merger-and-acquisition deals. It handled an incredible deal load of over 100 transactions worth $23 billion and took in $200 million in fees, representing 30 percent of Deutsche Bank's overall banking revenues for 1997. "We had relationships and contacts in the technology community that were well developed," states Quattrone. "And by then, we had a research team that clearly rivaled Morgan Stanley and Goldman." He adds, "We tried to build a brand. And there was a buzz going around that, unlike other banks, which were necessary evils, you actually had a good time working with the DMG people."

Yet in the spring of 1998, the DMG party abruptly ended. Quattrone and his team bolted again, this time to CS First Boston, and this change received even more news coverage. Not long before they cleared out in June, even as rumors mounted of their imminent defection, Quattrone sent out a memo to reassure clients that said, "We are here to stay. Please trust us." But it was not to be.

Some industry watchers speculated that DMG had siphoned off too much of Deutsche Bank's profits, largely in the form of Quattrone's huge compensation package. But Lehman's Stu Francis thinks it was more than that. "Frank Quattrone is a very talented, capable banker who did what he needed to do to put DMG on the map and run the business the way he wanted to run it," Francis says. "But I can see why he left. Deutsche Bank's commitment to the technology sector had changed." Another competitor, Cristina Morgan of Hambrecht & Quist, points out that Quattrone, like John Doerr, has gained enough stature to pull off his personal branding play. "They should call wherever he works 'Frank's Bank' because that's what it is, at DMG, First Boston, or wherever he might go next."

Wherever he works, Quattrone maintains that if an investment bank wants to have a top-flight technology practice, it has to do more than just underwrite IPOs; it must have the experience and resources to advise companies on numerous financings as well as on mergers and acquisitions. "You have to have people who have lived through the cycles and have seen what can go wrong and who can provide the best advice to companies instead of just trying to hustle them into doing deals," declares Quattrone. "If the only thing you do is take a company public, and you lose the company right after that, you've made the investment but you never get your return on it. That was what happened to the boutiques; they didn't have the products."

And at the time of this writing, Quattrone proved once again that his team's magic still lives in the market. Since setting up its technology shop under Quattrone, CS First Boston has moved up from sixth place to third as the lead manager of IPOs sold in the U.S. and advised clients in over 40 mergers and acquisitions and strategic financings. These deals include participation in Amazon's $1.25 billion junk bond, the biggest convertible debt offering ever, and Computer Associates' $3.6 billion acquisition of Platinum Software (CS First Boston represented Platinum), one of the largest merger-and-acquisition transactions in the software industry. The bank also advised Ascend Communications when it was bought by Lucent for $24 billion.

Goldman Sachs vs. Morgan Stanley

When Morgan Stanley's top Internet analyst Mary Meeker was asked by *The New Yorker* in April 1999 if she had any regrets, she mentioned that Morgan Stanley had missed the opportunity to underwrite IPOs for Yahoo, eBay, and Amazon. She admitted that losing the Yahoo business was a "brain dead" mistake because she thought, at the time, that Yahoo wasn't ready to go public. Goldman Sachs was happy, of course, to sweep up the Yahoo business with no big bank competition. The Goldman banking team also outfinessed Morgan Stanley with its pitch to eBay's management to take the online auction company public. "We walked out of our meeting with eBay right then and knew that it didn't click," Meeker moaned to the *New York Times*. This loss hurt Morgan Stanley, because eBay ended up as the top-performing IPO of 1998.

And with Amazon, Meeker contended to *The New Yorker* that she wanted to do the deal, but was overruled by the senior management at Morgan Stanley because the bank had a long-standing relationship with Barnes & Noble, Amazon's main rival. Frank Quattrone and Bill Brady, while still at DMG, ended up snatching the Amazon business, a deal that helped establish DMG.

But Meeker didn't rise to Internet industry stardom by resting on her laurels. Still convinced that eBay would be the online auction category leader, she kept her relationship with eBay's management a top priority in her hugely hectic schedule. Meeker, for example, spent hours reviewing strategy with eBay's CEO Meg Whitman, even helping her review and critique her IPO roadshow presentation.

In the end, all Meeker's hustling paid off. When eBay initiated its $1 billion secondary offering in March 1998, Whitman insisted that her underwriters at Goldman share the offering with Morgan Stanley. Much to Goldman's chagrin, they agreed. "Morgan Stanley earned it," Whitman told the *New York Times*.

Meeker's persistence with Amazon also paid off. In spite of being stifled by her bosses (a decision that upset Meeker so much, she almost quit) she stayed in contact with Amazon's executive team and remained a big supporter. Amazon rewarded Meeker for her public endorsements by signing up Morgan Stanley to sell $500 million worth of their junk bonds.

In many ways, Meeker's experiences in dueling with Goldman and her former partner at Morgan Stanley, Frank Quattrone, epitomizes the longtime, often brutal rivalry among the big banks that fight in the technology space. All three firms focus like lasers on winning only the best Internet deals because in the long run, they know the banks with the best-performing IPO portfolio will reign supreme.

So far in the Internet investment banking game, Goldman appears on top. Along with Yahoo and eBay, Goldman's other big winners include search-engine technology provider Inktomi and the women's Web services company iVillage. Since the beginning of 1998 through mid-1999, Internet IPOs underwritten by Goldman such as these have surged an average of 293 percent. At Morgan Stanley, big gainers such as Broadcast.com and Priceline.com helped propel the firm's IPOs during the same period to an average increase of 175 percent. And both these firms have impressive IPO performance numbers even when you exclude the first day of trading, when enthusiasm for an IPO is at its height and Internet stocks have shown their biggest single-day gains. Goldman's IPOs after their first day of trading average 62 percent and Morgan Stanley's 46 percent.

When you compare the figures of these two investment-banking kingpins with those of the other large banks, you begin to see why entrepreneurs tend to put either Goldman or Morgan Stanley on their dream underwriter list. Donaldson, Lufkin & Jenrette's IPOs during the same period, for example, were up only 26 percent, and down 15 percent after the first day of trading. And Merrill Lynch, which has built up its Silicon Valley presence aggressively since it opened a technology practice in Palo Alto in 1996, saw its IPOs initially gain 79 percent, but only 17 percent after the first day of trading.

Selling Out at the Top of the Market

The boutique banks may be full of bravado, but, in the end, it's tough for them to compete with the full-service banking capabilities of the Morgan Stanleys and Goldmans. In 1998, for example, the four biggest houses—Salomon Smith Barney, Morgan Stanley, Goldman, and Merrill Lynch—raised over 50 percent of $8 billion in total proceeds raised in IPOs. "Indeed," quips one bulge-bracket banker, "the boutiques would not have existed in the first place if the venture capitalists hadn't needed them in the early days of Silicon Valley to take their portfolio companies public."

The bigger banks are in a stronger position to leverage their global brands and debt-raising muscle to win most of the big deals. In fact, with only a few exceptions, Morgan Stanley, Goldman, Merrill, and now the Quattrone-led CS First Boston generally cherry-pick their deals and leave most of the smaller and unproven Internet-concept IPOs for the tech banks. In 1998, when Merrill Lynch studied the possibility of acquiring Hambrecht & Quist, for example, it concluded that it would have taken on only about one-third of the deals H&Q had done to date. The other two-thirds—those that raised less than $50 million for an IPO and generally would not have led to additional business for the bank—Merrill considered too small to bother with.

"We're a technology brand," admits H&Q managing director Cristina Morgan. "By contrast, Morgan Stanley, Goldman Sachs, and the other bulge brackets want only the cool, the hot, and the big. They count on the speed dial from Kleiner Perkins, which sees these banks as some kind of guarantee that the stock offerings will only go up after the IPO, and therefore Kleiner Perkins funnels all the best startup companies in their direction."

The competitive reality led to the sale of three of the industry's top tech banks—Alex. Brown & Sons, Robertson Stephens, and Montgomery Securities—to large commercial banks. And the founding father of the technology-banking industry, Hambrecht & Quist, flirted with being acquired by Merrill Lynch, but ended up going public and remaining independent.

Other than competitive pressure, part of what inspired the sale of the tech banks was the deregulation of banking. In November 1996, a change in Section 20 of the federal banking laws allowed large commercial banks to own and operate investment-banking practices once again, knocking down a barrier set up by the Glass-Steagall Act, passed in the aftermath of the stock market crash of 1929 to curb the power of the money trusts that had controlled Wall Street.

More important, however, there was a growing sense by the firms' savvy principals that they were at the top of a very frothy market, and if they should ever cash out, the time was now. Alex. Brown was the first to go when it was bought by Bankers Trust in 1997 for $2.3 billion. "That got things going," says a boutique insider. "This looked like a pretty good time to cash in. The high was high enough, so we sold out." When Bankers Trust was in turn swallowed by a larger fish, Deutsche Bank, which digested BT at the cost of $9 billion in spring 1999, the investment banking arm was given the new name of Deutsche Banc Alex. Brown.

Robertson Stephens was next to go on the block after Alex. Brown when it sold out to Bank of America in June of 1997 for an eventual total price of $470 million. Later that year, NationsBanc bought Robertson's archrival, Montgomery Securities, for a whopping $1.3 billion. When NationsBanc then bought Bank of America, it decided to unload Robertson Stephens to avoid overlap with its earlier Montgomery Securities acquisition, so NationsBanc sold Robertson Stephens to BancBoston in September 1998 for $800 million, a huge premium over the price paid by Bank America. BancBoston, initially valuing Robertson at $400 million, paid double to beat out five other high-caliber suitors that wanted the invest-ment bank. "They said they'd pay full price if we gave them an exclusive look at it," a Robertson executive told us. "So they paid the absolute top."

To avoid immediate competition from an old pro, BancBoston paid Sandy Robertson a special compensation to stay out of the investment-banking business for at least a year after the acquisition. BancBoston also negotiated a penalty clause with Bank of America that would require them to pay BancBoston $400 million if they did not make good in keeping Sandy Robertson out of the business.

On the flip side, NationsBanc did not have a binding noncompete agreement with Thom Weisel, who founded Montgomery Securities in 1971. So when he left the bank in a huff in the fall of 1998, he set up a competitor to his old firm called Thomas Weisel Partners and attracted a number of his old partners and associates from Mont-gomery Securities—about 90 people in all. "Our agreement to join NationsBanc was based on Mongtomery's remaining independent and staying in charge of all capital-market activities," recalls Weisel. "But they wanted to fold us into the bank, which was a violation of the merger agreement and my employment contract." He adds, "If I had a chance to do it all over, I wouldn't do the merger. Montgomery would be doing just fine on its own. But I'm on to the next chapter." But given his wealth, why is he bothering? "This is what I am," says Weisel. "I don't know what else to do. I don't intend to retire." For those who know Weisel, this was not a surprising move. "Thom is the most competitive human being on the planet," says a longtime asso-ciate.

Montgomery Securities still fared well after Weisel's departure. By January 1999, mostly on the strength of its brokerage business, rev-enue at Montgomery was up 80 percent above the previous year, recovering nicely from the stock market meltdown in the latter part of 1998. However, Montgomery still struggled to build up its invest-ment-banking business, especially in the areas of technology and health care, in the wake of all the defections from those departments.

Net Bankers

While Thom Weisel pursues a more traditional route back into tech banking, the other two veteran financiers prominent in Silicon Valley lore, Bill Hambrecht and Sandy Robertson, are going electronic. Hambrecht, who cofounded H&Q back in 1968, has formed his own electronic investment bank, W. R. Hambrecht & Company. Located in a former warehouse in the city's design district, Hambrecht's new online investment bank sells new stocks over the Internet in a so-called Dutch auction, with investors setting the price. Robertson, who cofounded Robertson, Stephens & Company, is backing a competing online investment operation, E*Offering, a company 28 percent owned by E*Trade. E*Offering could open up the stock sales process even further, with new stocks available on a first-come, first-served basis.

Looking at the numbers, we think these two investment- banking pioneers are riding on top of yet another big wave in their already distinguished careers. By mid-1999, 52 IPOs had already parceled part of their IPO shares for sale over the Internet. "We are in the baby-step stage," says Bill Doyle, research director of online financial services at the consultancy Forrester Research, which projects that by 2003, as much as 12 percent of IPO shares will be sold online to individual investors. Forrester also projects that 20.4 million people will have Internet brokerage accounts. "First you had the discount brokers; now you have the emergence of the discount investment banker," observes a gleeful Michael Moritz of Sequoia Capital. Moritz is giggling because he and his partners, particularly Don Valentine, have been very vocal about what they believe have been overinflated investment-banking fees.

This time around, however, Hambrecht and Robertson aren't the only pioneers in town. Established firms like the Charles Schwab Corporation and DLJ Direct, the newly public online affiliate of Donaldson, Lufkin & Jenrette, already distribute shares online and help underwrite stock offerings. There is also an emergence of startup online investment banks much like W. R. Hambrecht and E*Offering. Wit Capital of New York, formed in 1996, had distributed stock in over 40 deals by mid-1999 and raised almost $80 million in its own IPO in May of 1999.

While online investment-banking promises to be incredibly lucrative, it will also be fiercely competitive. When the dust clears, this new industry will shape up much like the other service industries being dislocated by the Internet, with a combination of old and new dogs driving the business.

The Squeeze Is On

The emergence of electronic investment banking undoubtedly will put a serious squeeze on the fees associated with managing IPOs. This is good news for entrepreneurs as well as for all investors.

Typically, IPOs are arranged by a lead-manager investment bank (sometimes called a bookrunner) which gauges institutional investor demand by extensive marketing, acts as the lead underwriter, and arranges a syndicate of other banks to share the underwriting risk. Bankers also sit up late at night in smoke-filled boardrooms with company executives and lawyers to set the final IPO share price. For these services, the bankers typically charge companies 7 percent of the money raised from the IPO, in part to pay for marketing costs.

Most consider these fees rather exorbitant. "I think the banks are disproportionately compensated for what they do," declares Sequoia Capital's Don Valentine. "I'd like them a lot better if they charged no more than 5 percent."

Conceivably, Dutch auction systems, brought online by firms like W. R. Hambrecht & Company, could put the most pressure on traditional investment-banking fees. The auction approach has actually been in place for years and is used extensively for the resale of U.S. government securities. The issuer is the Treasury Department, and the underwriters are bankers designated by the Federal Reserve Bank of New York. Under this kind of system, potential investors set the terms of the IPO in an auction rather than by the traditional direct offer/preset price system of trading. Under Hambrecht's system, called OpenIPO, investors place bids over the Internet for the number of shares they want at prices they are willing to pay. When the subscription period ends, the managing underwriter tabulates the bids and reoffers the stock to the bidders at the highest price at which all shares are spoken for.

Since Hambrecht's new e-investment bank leverages the Internet as a new, low-cost research-and-stock-share distribution channel, the firm offers a lower overall banking fee of 4 percent instead of the traditional 7 percent for managing the IPO.

W. R. Hambrecht & Co. claims its system also counteracts many of the abuses traditional banks engage in for IPOs. The biggest conflict always centers on who gets the hot IPO shares first. Online auction proponents claim that their approach allows small-scale investors to compete with even big institutional investors who typically get allocated the most IPO shares because they yield the greatest financial clout with their bankers. A flyer Hambrecht uses to market itself reads: "One for me. None for you . . . Most investment bankers lead a very hard life. After they take care of each other, they have to take care of their friends. And after they do that, they have to take care of the people they'd like to have as friends. You can imagine that after all this hard work, there aren't many IPO shares to go around."

The reality, as private equity editor Stephanie Gates reports in her August 1999 *Red Herring* article "The IPO Tease," is that individual investors still need to jump through a number of hoops to get access to IPOs even through online services. She found that to make the shortlist of qualified IPO buyers, investors had to meet minimum asset or transaction requirements, or get lucky through a random selection process. Personal asset requirements in some cases were as high as $500,000. Some online services required numerous previous trades on their systems or that the investor fill out detailed reports on their personal financial status each time he or she wanted to buy an IPO. The bottom line on IPO shares, says Gates quoting Gartner Group analyst Chuck Shih, is that "the people who have a lot of money are still the ones who will make lots of money."

Meanwhile, CS First Boston's Frank Quattrone is skeptical of this system as a whole: "I just don't think high-quality companies will risk going with that kind of pricing formula, especially with such little research support undergirding it." He adds, "Think about it. If your business takes small companies public and trades their stocks and not much else, that's the low end of the business. That's what these electronic offering services are going after—you bring down the fees to where you can barely make a living."

Bill Doyle of Forrester Research does not believe fees alone will persuade companies to choose online investment banks as underwriters. "Given a choice between Goldman Sachs and E*Offering, what will a young company choose? Goldman—even if E*Offering offers to do it for half," says Doyle. "When Goldman leads a road show, people pay attention," he adds.

There's also a sense that these electronic offering services, because they might become bottom feeders, will get more companies out there that don't deserve to go public.

Our guess is that all the major investment-banking firms will eventually succumb to competitive pricing pressure from e-bankers and be forced to build extensive Internet sales-and-distribution systems of their own or acquire one of the new upstarts. They will also have to compete with online bankers who propose to further lower the cost of IPOs by using the Internet to conduct "road shows." (Traditionally, just before going public, a company's management and its underwriters travel around the country and meet with groups of analysts, fund managers, and other potential institutional investors to answer any questions about the company's financial information and short- and long-term outlook.)

Big banks such as Merrill Lynch have already rattled their traditional retail broker networks by going online, and Goldman bought a 22 percent stake in the online investment bank Wit Capital for an estimated $20 million. "The bigger firms are slow to react," says Walter Cruttenden, CEO of E*Offering. "This massive distribution will win," he predicts, because it has "the most people, the quickest service, and the lowest cost."

The emergence of online investment banking will no doubt significantly increase the supply of new companies going public. In the Internet Bubble environment, the annual number of companies going public has already swelled from 100 to 200. "The supply-and-demand dynamics will change because smaller-cap companies will have quicker access to public markets," says Sandy Robertson. (Robertson-backed E*Offering plans to focus on small IPOs—those worth $25 million to $50 million.) He believes that if online firms such as E*Offering can help jar the IPO door fully open, Internet stock prices as a whole will finally come back to earth. "Internet stocks are overvalued right now because there exists a pent-up demand for new public equities, particularly in the Internet and technology space," explains Robertson. "The Amazons and Yahoos are the most expensive stocks in history because they are the only game in town right now."

A System in Conflict

In spite of being the gateway to IPO funds, the investment-banking industry remains controversial in its practices. "The whole investment-banking system is in conflict," complains Sequoia's Don Valentine, and many in the banking business would agree with him. Herbert Allen Jr., the billionaire president and CEO of the New York–based investment bank Allen & Co., is one of them. Although Allen & Co. has brokered some major corporate mergers in recent years, including entertainment megadeals such as the Disney–Capital Cities/ABC merger, unlike traditional investment banks, it often doesn't charge a set fee for its work. And while Hambrecht is critical of the conflict of interests in the IPO game, Allen is equally critical of conflicts in the merger business.

"I don't know how you can set a fee before you know what value you have added to the transaction," says Allen. "Most of what Wall Street does in mergers and acquisitions is non–value added." Sometimes the bank just gives an opinion on what is pretty much a done deal. "That's not value-added, that's legal protection," says Allen. He further contends that it's unusual for a bank to come up with an original idea beneficial to both parties in a merger. "That kind of activity is in short supply," says Allen. Allen points to his bank's added value in helping Coca-Cola buy a stake in Columbia Pictures—the deal was completely in the bank's hands.

But Allen admits that the bank did not necessarily bring much to the table in the Disney–Capital Cities/ABC merger. The three main players—Michael Eisner, Warren Buffet, and Tom Murphy—had already worked things out before they called Allen & Co. "Whatever they wanted to pay us for the deal was fine with me. It was a privilege just to be involved," admits Allen.

Allen & Co. tries to promote discussion and dealmaking among these huge entities by hosting an annual retreat at Allen's Sun Valley, Idaho, ranch. About 40 major business institutions are represented, and executives like Bill Gates, Gerry Levin, Andy Grove, Rupert Murdoch, and Barry Diller come with their families. This retreat obviously differs from the typical scramble of technology bankers for IPOs, merger deals, and follow-on financings.

Yet even closer to Silicon Valley, investment banks such as Broadview International that specialize in technology-company mergers criticize their peer institutions. "We consider most investment banks securities firms because they sell securities as their primary business," says Paul Deninger, chairman and CEO of Broadview. "They do corporate finance work for companies, but companies are not their primary client—the institutional investor is their primary client. And they treat the IPO market as something meant to work primarily for the institutional investor." He adds, "These securities firms view companies as products, not companies. When they do an IPO or walk out on the trading floor, they call it 'product,' not 'the company.'"

"Our companies and our people are treated as meat," agrees Sequoia's Don Valentine. "The banks care only about getting the transaction done and collecting their commissions. They want the shares from our company to Fidelity on Wednesday or whenever; they don't give a crap about the company."

Further evidence of the meat trading is the lack of follow-up attention for some of these companies. Investment banks bother with certain thin-margin IPOs primarily because somewhere among these companies, a few could mature into tomorrow's Intel, Microsoft, or Cisco. And as a company grows, lucrative follow-on services could make up for the IPO's paltry margins. But if a bank doesn't judge the company to have this kind of potential, its research analysts usually ignore it. And without this coverage, the Fidelitys of the world will not buy it, so the stock languishes. "It's a ball-buster job to get anyone to pay attention to some of our quality companies," declares Valentine.

Stock Analysts in Denial

While gaining the ongoing coverage of top investment banking analysts is important to all public companies, in the midst of a volatile stock market, these analysts are often the last to give investors clues that there might be something wrong. Perennial optimists, analysts don't like to bear bad news. Consequently, they tend to be in denial if companies report weaker-than-expected earnings or if some global economic indicator portends a shrinking market for a company's products. Things will always get better next month, the analyst likes to say. There are exceptions, of course, but the lone skeptic might be regarded as a doomsayer, if not a traitor.

Besides a bias toward the positive, stock analysts at investment banks rarely come out negative because the companies they cover are often customers of their banks. More and more, analysts have become involved in the sales process. It's typical for analysts to visit prospective clients alongside corporate finance officers, who court stock offerings and merger-and-acquisition business while using positive coverage by these analysts as their best lure.

A 1998 study done by First Call, a Boston research group that tracks analysts' opinions, showed more specifically that analyst downgrades on stocks have become unusual in the last several years. In fact, recommendations to buy stocks have vastly outnumbered recommendations to hold or sell: Of 6,000 stocks tracked by First Call, more than a third were rated "strong buy," slightly less than a third "buy," and most of the rest were "holds." Only 1 percent were "sells." A study by Zacks Investment Research published in 1998 showed similar results. In an analysis of reports on 6,000 companies, only 1.4 percent got a sell recommendation, whereas there were 67.5 percent buys and 31.1 percent holds.

One practical consequence of these reports is that a high level of excessively optimistic analysis hurts investors' ability to gauge a stock's true prospects.

Chuck Hill, a former securities analyst and current research director for First Call, sees this slant as a product of fear among analysts that they might offend the firm's investment-banking departments or the companies they cover if they say anything negative. "There's some reluctance to put a sell on a stock," he says. "It's tougher now to be independent."

"It's a situation people have started looking at lately. Analysts are afraid to have sell recommendations or even hold recommendations because if they downgrade a stock, the bankers could lose their relationship with the company," admits Frank Quattrone. "Some companies consider the analyst's ratings in terms of giving out the more lucrative banking business. It sets up, clearly, a potential for a conflict that must be managed properly."

Critics charge not only that analysts do less original work and more readily present data that follows the company line, but also that few take the trouble to go out and talk to suppliers, customers, and competitors to get an accurate view of what's going on.

Bruce Lupatkin, former head of research at Hambrecht & Quist and a longtime technology analyst, agrees that the role of securities analysts at banks has changed and that they're more involved in the sales process. "It's not a green-eyeshade back-office crank-the-numbers thing," he says. "The analysts have become rock stars."

But with this role has come new pressures. "One is that the companies cut you off if you say anything negative. Your information sources dry up," Lupatkin says. "Also a bit surprising, the institutional community is unhappy with the change of recommendation. They shoot the messenger. They think, 'You just knocked my stock down two points. I didn't need you to do that.'" The bottom line ultimately determines what happens. "In the end, we give the clients what they pay for," says Lupatkin.

Herb Allen Jr., whose investment bank Allen & Co. does not employ securities analysts, also criticizes this trend. "I have a problem with the way security analysts on Wall Street are used today," he says. "They are usually fairly weak historians and very poor prognosticators. And if you use the analyst to get the investment-bank business, how trustworthy is his opinion going to be on the other side when he sells some poor jerk the stock? The system doesn't make sense to me."

Most institutional investors trust only about 20 percent of the analysts they consider intellectually honest. The rest are seen as "investment bankers in sheep's clothing."

This reality makes Herb Allen and other critics conclude that because the analysts from the banks have grown too cozy with the companies they cover, they serve more like cheerleaders or even front guys rather than as true analysts.

Stock Spinning

Another investment-banking practice called into question during the Internet IPO go-go days is what has become known as stock spinning. On November 12, 1997, *The Wall Street Journal* published a front-page article by reporter Michael Siconolfi titled "The Spin Desk: Underwriters Set Aside IPO Stock for Officials of Potential Customers." This article and others following it set off a storm of controversy in the investment-banking community, sparked an SEC investigation, and caused civil suits to be filed against some of the banks.

In his articles Siconolfi accused certain investment banks—

Robertson Stephens, Hambrecht & Quist, and Montgomery Securities in particular—of operating "spin desks" designed to allocate chunks of hot new stocks to the personal brokerage accounts of corporate executives, venture capitalists, and other decision makers sitting on the boards of companies whose business the banks wanted. The timely allocation of these stocks made it possible for these individuals to "spin" or "flip" the shares on the first day of the initial public offering for quick profits.

The *Journal* quoted one former recipient of such spin shares, David Cary, CFO of i2 Technologies, as saying, "It's as common as water, and you can have all you want."

While most shares must go to big institutional investors such as the mutual funds, a small number were said to be set aside in a "retail pot" for certain individuals. Robertson Stephens was reported to have routinely allocated about 10,000 shares of each IPO deal to the personal brokerage accounts of executives, venture capitalists, and other special customers.

Morgan Stanley was alleged to have allocated 1,000-share blocks of the Netscape IPO to some executives, including the CFO of the then privately held Arbor Software. Arbor later chose Morgan Stanley to manage its IPO.

Cristina Morgan, a managing director at Hambrecht & Quist, defended the practice in the *Journal,* likening it to free golf outings or fancy dinners for prospective clients. "What we're talking about is trying to solicit business," she argued. "We throw lavish parties with caviar. Is that not trying to influence them?" Likewise, allocating stock "is not illegal," she said. "It's not immoral. It's a business decision. If you sell doughnuts, you do everything you can to enhance the image of your doughnut shop to customers. You're just doing your job. That's what we're all doing."

When we later asked Morgan about the spinning controversy, she called it "a tempest in a teapot" and added, "The investigators found that the stock went to retail customers of Hambrecht & Quist who had every right to the stock. Those brokerage clients happened to be, in some cases, corporate finance clients of the firm entitled to allocations in rough relationship to their investing activities with the firm." Furthermore, the allocations "were so small as not to amount to a hill of beans." As for the *Journal* articles, she declared, "This was Mike Siconolfi's bid for a Pulitzer."

Asked about spinning, Brad Koenig, managing director and head of the technology-banking practice at Goldman Sachs, says, "I would say it's widely practiced in our community. Goldman Sachs did not engage in it, but I think some firms used it aggressively."

Stu Francis, a managing director at Lehman Brothers, says, "Well, Lehman never did it. I don't think anyone does it anymore. It began informally because venture capitalists and others wanted to buy the stocks. Then, as the industry got bigger and bigger and the IPO market got bigger and bigger, it became more of a standard practice. People slipped into spinning when it wasn't a problem, but it became a problem as the market got bigger."

The boutique investment banks such as Hambrecht & Quist and Robertson Stephens were believed to have engaged in the practice more than the New York–based investment banks because the boutiques' share of technology underwriting had been increasingly eaten into by the larger bulge-bracket banks.

A colleague of Francis at Lehman Brothers also ascribes the practice to "a somewhat looser culture and compliant environment in Silicon Valley's financial community than what you'll find in New York."

An executive from one boutique states, "It got out of hand. We saw some of the competition buying deals by giving an awful lot of IPO stock to the venture capitalists. It was getting a little flagrant, and it shouldn't have happened. The venture capitalists should be in the same category as the investment managers, who aren't allowed to buy these stocks."

The practice was probably not as extreme as *The Wall Street Journal* claimed, but the mere existence of such a practice is just one more indication of how some insiders, including venture capitalists, often have had access to the best stocks, far more than the retail buyer could ever hope to.

Flipping and Other Mutual Fund Schemes

It's not unusual in the Internet Bubble for an IPO stock price to triple or even quadruple in the early aftermarket and then decline thereafter. This pattern creates an ideal environment for another insider practice known as flipping: buying the stock once or more on the first day of trading and unloading it on the same day for a quick profit.

And it's no secret that investment-banking firms allow big institutional investors to flip, looking the other way while these investors dump hot new stocks at their whim, often within hours or even minutes of the stock's first trade. Meanwhile, the firm's stockbrokers get a commission of up to 4 percent of the value of an IPO trade, double the commission for most other stock transactions. And because the firms want to keep big institutional investors happy, since they are the source of huge trading fees, the brokers are not penalized for selling them the bulk of IPO shares, even though these investors also do most of the flipping. Mutual funds and pension funds have enough clout to avoid flipping strictures.

Since the primary client of the investment bank is the institutional investor, the IPO market is treated as something meant primarily for institutions. These investors view individual companies as a small and highly mobile part of their portfolios. They are not committed to these companies; if they don't like them, they'll sell them as soon as they can.

Flipping is critical to individual investors because a high proportion of IPOs perform poorly over the long haul, so "while institutions dump IPOs, retail is stuck holding the bag," says Lori Dennis, a former Merrill Lynch broker quoted in *The Wall Street Journal*.

A "flip report" prepared by investment bank Bear Stearns in 1998 showed that 15 of 33 institutional buyers of Bear Stearns–led IPOs quickly sold many or all their shares. "It's a major problem," says Bear Stearns chairman Alan "Ace" Greenberg. "They want it, then the minute they get it, they sell it."

Sandy Robertson, cofounder of the investment bank Robertson Stephens, explains it this way:

If you have a hot deal, when one of the big institutional investors asks you for some stock, you have to give it to them even though you think they're going to flip it, because they're giving you so many commissions all the time. Of the 100 institutional investors who buy the stock, maybe 15 want to own it over the long term. You can't say to a big mutual fund, "Oh, we know you're not going to hold it, so you're not getting any." They'll swear on a stack of Bibles that they're going to hold on to the stock. So you have to give it to them. That's why the trading volume is so high in the first couple of days after an offering, because there are four trades on one block of stock. You can't get around the flipping.

Some see a darker side to the public stock manipulations by certain large mutual funds. One venture capitalist even sees a kind of Ponzi scheme in the way the largest mutual funds buy and sell IPO stock in overheated aftermarkets. He believes these manipulations are a product of the whole interdependent food chain of investment bankers and analysts, mutual fund managers, venture capitalists, and entrepreneurs operating in the midst of a momentum-investing environment in search of the greater fool.

"If I want to buy a highly promoted IPO," he says. "I look for a CEO and a group of venture capitalists who are very promotional and spend all their time weaving a story for the press. As a mutual fund, I then buy up the float in the hot aftermarket."

The float is that amount of stock still available for public trading after an IPO. For Internet companies, notoriously little stock has been available, making those stocks ripe for manipulation. Demand is high, but supply is limited. In the case of Yahoo in mid-1998, on average, only 8.9 million of its 93 million shares were traded—because of the demand, the price took off. And at the time, only about a third of Amazon's 49 million shares outstanding were available for trading; the entire float could be turned over in a month.

"The guys who own a lot of these small-float Internet stocks might have $100 million or $200 million worth of position in a company," says the skeptical venture capitalist, "and they can put in $10 million of buy orders to have the stock go up even in a market that's going down 200 points." He adds, "In a market that's heading up, they can keep pushing that stock up further. It becomes very controllable with these little tech stocks. So the mutual funds have promoted a handful of companies. That's why you have this two-tier market—the heavily promoted stocks and the rest, which are underwater. It's the essence of the game."

Whether or not there is some larger conspiracy, the limited stock float of these Internet companies, combined with the hype that has found its way onto the cover of *Time* magazine, can easily help jack up these stocks and inflate the Internet Bubble.

Investment Banking in Transition

Whether or not the Don Valentines and Herb Allens of the world can successfully persuade the investment bankers to cut their fees and tighten their practices, the Internet will certainly turn the industry upside down over time. Overall, we expect the Internet will level the playing field between large and small investment banks and retail and institutional investors. And this change in the competitive landscape will undoubtedly lead to higher IPO share prices, more money for companies going public, and lower invest-ment-banking fees. E*Trades's CEO, Christos Cotsakos, calls this shift "the democratization of investment banking." Eventually, the cozy relationship between the traditional investment banks and their favorite institutional investors will be shaken, and the IPO share-hungry retail stock buyer should benefit.

Doonesbury

THE GREAT
BIOTECHNOLOGY BUBBLE

With Amgen and Genentech, the biotech market broke open and a real wave whipped up.
—Sam Colella, general partner,
Institutional Venture Partners

In the labs of University of California at San Francisco (UCSF) in the 1970s, brilliant scientists were at work. Sequestered in dark rooms in their white jackets with their petri dishes, these researchers were working to get inside the chemistry of DNA, trying to unlock the genetic code and then recombine different genes to form new protein molecules. Bob Swanson, a venture capitalist with Kleiner Perkins Caufield & Byers, and Herbert Boyer, a pioneer in DNA research and a professor of biochemistry at UCSF, recognized the tremendous commercial potential of these efforts. In 1976 they founded Genentech and built on these feats of genetic engineering to synthesize clinical products and build a $10.5 billion enterprise.

The efforts of Genentech raised the hopes of investors that ingenious and driven scientists could develop drugs to defeat cancer, reverse the effects of aging, and genetically engineer a brave new world of biotechnology in which lives could be improved and entrepreneurs and investors could get rich in the process. When the biotechnology lightbulb clicked on, investors rushed toward the opportunity. Almost every major venture capital firm scrambled to imitate the Kleiner Perkins model and raised funds targeted to health care. The boutique technology-investment banks like Hambrecht & Quist and Robertson Stephens followed suit by building research and corporate-finance teams that understood genetic engineering, pharmaceuticals, and medical instruments.

This flurry of financial support led to the creation of thousands of biotechnology startups, hundreds of which went public. But as with all overfunded booms, the biotech industry has experienced its own Darwinian process.

This chapter looks at the great Biotechnology Bubble of the late '80s and early '90s, the forerunner of today's Internet Bubble. It's the story of how public investors were willing to bet the rent on the concept stocks of biotechnology companies that had no profits, no revenues, and long years of research ahead of them. We'll look briefly at how the biotechnology industry got started and how a few successful companies raised hopes for the whole industry. In the process, we tell the story of a distinguished institution, Boston University, that bet a big piece of its endowment on a supposed cure for cancer and paid the price.

Most important, the Biotech Bubble set a financial precedent that carried over not only to information-technology companies such as game-technology maker 3DO, whose story we also tell here, but also to today's Internet Bubble companies.

The Biotechnology Bubble

Kleiner Perkins partner Bob Swanson was so fascinated by the idea of genetic engineering that he quit the VC partnership in 1975 to pursue his dream. While Eugene Kleiner and Tom Perkins provided Swanson with a desk and a phone, they were initially skeptical about how quickly this science could be turned into commercial products. Still in his twenties, Swanson called scientists trying to find someone who would respond to his commercial challenge. At first there was no encouraging news, until he finally contacted Herbert Boyer, a young biochemist at the University of California in San Francisco, who together with Dr. Stanley Cohen of Stanford had done the first gene-splicing experiments two years before.

Swanson and Boyer eventually convinced Kleiner and Perkins to invest $100,000 in exchange for 25 percent of the new company. The money helped finance a series of tests with encouraging results, and

Genentech (short for "genetic engineering technology") was born. The company raised another $850,000, including $100,000 more from Kleiner Perkins. Genentech's main business goal was to commercialize recombinant DNA, in which genetic sequences from diverse origins are joined together (recombined) to form new molecules. Specifically, the company synthesized genes to produce human insulin in 1978 and a human growth hormone in 1979. To keep the research-and-development engines humming, Genentech went public in 1980 at a price of $35 per share and raised $35 million overall in the offering. At the IPO price, Kleiner Perkins's total return on its Genentech investment was an incredible 164 to 1.

In 1982, assisted by the manufacturing capabilities and financial resources of drug giant Eli Lilly, Genentech brought its human insulin drug, called Humulin, to market. Yet by 1985 Genentech earnings were only $6.5 million. What was supposed to be a blockbuster new drug, Activase, turned out to have very weak sales. In that same year, however, Genentech's new human growth hormone drug, called Protopin, received final FDA approval and started to sell. The company has sold more than $1 billion worth of Protopin since its introduction in 1985. In 1998, Genentech's revenues were $1.15 billion, and by the first quarter of 1999, Genentech's profits rose 43 percent to more than $58 million on the strength of sales for two new drugs: Herceptin for treating breast cancer and Rituxin for non-Hodgkin's lymphoma.

In the spring of 1999, Swiss pharmaceutical behemoth Roche fully acquired Genentech at a stock price of $82.50 per share. But it was Genentech's early track record and successful IPO, as well as the success of Kleiner Perkins's even earlier investment in Cetus Corporation, that had inspired the venture community to place great hope in the biotech industry.

Amgen (short for "applied molecular genetics"), like Genentech, was also founded by a venture capitalist, Bill Bowes of U.S. Venture Partners. By early 1981, Bowes had rallied enough venture capital support—almost $19 million—to get Amgen rolling. Also like Genentech, Amgen quickly developed drugs it could bring to market. It went public in 1986 at a price of $18 per share in an offering that raised $43 million. After additional rounds of private and public financing, Amgen finally hit the jackpot when it went from zero revenues to $1 billion in one year on the strength of two drugs: Epogen, for red blood cell production to treat anemia, and Neupogen, for white blood cell production to stimulate the immune system. In 1998 Amgen's market capitalization was $40 billion and its revenues were $2.7 billion, primarily from the sales of Epogen and Neupogen.

A third biotech company that raised the stakes was Chiron. In its research and development, the company pursued a diverse group of drugs and medical devices, including the technology to produce the hepatitis B vaccine. Chiron limped along financially for almost five years before doing an IPO in 1983 that netted the company $20 million. In 1998, Chiron had revenues of almost $780 million and a market capitalization of more than $3.4 billion.

Throughout the 1980s, biotech mania continued to build. In those days, biotechnology had much of the cachet that e-commerce does now. In 1986, biotechnology IPOs hit a peak when there were almost $1.7 billion worth of public offerings. Looking for a quick and substantial profit, the typical venture capital attitude prevailed—$1 million in, how much out? Those were heady days for biotech.

While the market for a certain drug or medical device is more measurable than that of an information-technology product, it's also riskier to develop. Most biotech products typically require 5 to 10 years and approximately $300 million to $500 million to develop. Biotech companies must follow a tortuous course of costly research and development, manufacturing, clinical trials, federal approval, and marketing before they can see any revenues, never mind profits, from their products. And there's always a high burn rate of cash.

Given how long most biotech companies took to develop a product, their IPOs were financing events rather than profitable investments for the public investor. At the IPO, people bought into concepts only, not into something tangible. "Genentech, Amgen, Chiron—those companies delivered real products and real earnings," says Asset Management's Pitch Johnson, whose firm was a big investor in Amgen early on. "Those stocks got the public think-ing magical cures and wonderful drugs were just sitting out there in the future. That led to a bubble in which companies could go public on high hopes." A *Wall Street Journal* article in 1991 noted: "Inspired by the 340 percent rise in Amgen's stock in the past year, investors have rushed into biotechnology stocks in search of the next rising star in the young industry."

The Biotech Bubble hit a new high with the IPO of Regeneron, a company founded in 1988 with seed money from Merrill Lynch and various venture capitalists. In 1991 it went public at $22 per share, offering more than 4.5 million shares. Half of those shares were turned over—flipped—on the first day of the offering. A year after the stock offering, the price was down to $7.75 per share, and it fell to $4 per share in 1994.

In 1991 there were more than $1.6 billion worth of biotechnol-ogy public offerings and an additional $3.7 billion worth of follow-on offerings. Between the end of 1989 and January 1992, the Ham-brecht & Quist biotechnology index rose fourfold. By early 1992, though, many biotech IPOs were oversubscribed; public investors still wanted the next Amgen. Instead, the first wave of the biotech market hit the beach, as one darling biotech company after another failed to bring its drug to market. The top-tier companies lost 30 percent of their value, and the second and third tiers lost 60 percent and 80 percent, respectively. IVP's Colella declares, "If, as a venture investor, you didn't get off the first wave fast enough, if you held your stocks, you didn't do well at all." Public investors suffered even more. The Fidelity Select Biotechnology fund, for example, rose 99 percent in 1991 only to fall 24 percent in the first four months of 1992. Many investors had bought into the fund just in time to go over the cliff.

There were even whispers of fraud, when particular financiers deliberately developed certain biotech deals in which they attracted some big names, raised money at high prices, and sold them to the public just before the Bubble burst. Quick IPOs for quick bucks eventually left the public paying the price. And even though biotech stocks peaked in the early weeks of 1992, there were still 91 initial public offerings that year, up from 72 in 1991. Investors still refused to run away from biotech and continued to look for opportunities to be involved in the sector. In fact, the biotech sector rallied 25 percent between June and November of 1992, but by November 1994 the average biotech stock had lost two-thirds of its peak value.

Initial Public Offerings

Biotechnology: 1982–1998** ($ Millions)

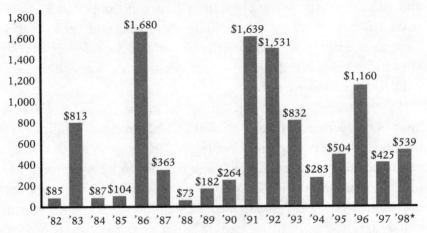

SOURCE: Securities Data Company   *Through November 30, 1998 **Excludes closed-end funds

Hope Springs Eternal

A good example in recent years of how a bubble investment in a concept company can go awry is the case of Seragin Inc., documented in the 1998 *New York Times* article "Loving a Stock, Not Wisely but Too Well." Founded in 1979 by Boston-area medical researchers, Seragin developed a drug eventually known as Interleukin-2 that looked as if it could be a "magic bullet" in the fight against cancer.

After hearing a presentation by Dr. John Murphy, the discoverer and lead developer of Interleukin-2, John Silber, the president of Boston University, grew excited about the prospect of investing in a cure for cancer that could reap tremendous financial returns for his school. The opportunity was irresistible. So Silber urged the university's trustees to invest $25 million of the school's total endowment of $175 million in Seragin in 1987. In 1992, during the peak of the Biotech Bubble, Seragin went public at $12 per share. Silber persuaded numerous associates, friends, and family members to buy stock in the company. He also invested $1.7 million of his own money, almost half his net worth, and persuaded the university to buy a larger stake in the company as well.

Seragin raised $52 million in public stock sales in 1992 and 1993, but its cash needs were voracious. By 1996 the company still did not have FDA approval for Interleukin-2, and the company lost $26.3 million that year, making Seragin's cumulative losses $200 million at the time. The stock had reached a high of $15 per share in January 1993, but ended 1996 at just over $1 per share. In September 1996 Boston University invested an additional $5 million through a private stock placement, bringing its total stake to $84 million.

By August of 1998, Seragin was out of money, on the brink of bankruptcy, and delisted from NASDAQ. The company was then acquired by Ligand Pharmaceuticals for $30 million, and Ligand said it would pay an additional $37 million to Seragin shareholders if Interleukin-2 ever received FDA approval. The university's Seragin stock now became Ligand stock. The school's total stake of $84 million was now only worth $8.4 million. Silber's personal stake had dropped in value from $1.7 million to just $43,000. What had looked like certain gold was now a cautionary tale about the cost of betting heavily on a concept stock.

Public Venture Capital Precedent

Despite their risks and diminishing returns, biotech companies became a milestone in technology financing. Donald Valentine of Sequoia Capital says, "Biotech financing became institutionalized. We had an ability to start companies and raise countless amounts of money with little or no prospect of revenue for half a dozen years." Valentine concludes, "I think we financed too many biotech companies. The public was excited about all these things highly publicized by the investment bankers: This was a cure for cancer, that was a cure for heart attacks. We thought we had all the bases covered."

But in the early 1990s, most biotech solutions turned out to be just ho-hum products. There were no big barn burners. The biotech research engines by and large did not produce phenomenal drugs. The Bubble popped, and as in the PC era, there was lots of company wreckage.

Much of the wreckage was of "me-too" companies, like the 43 disk-drive companies formed in the 1980s, or all the automobile companies founded back in the 1920s and 1930s. Almost 1,500 biotech companies originated out of such prestigious university laboratories as Stanford, Harvard, Johns Hopkins, and UC San Francisco. Yet they were financed to pursue the same areas of research and product goals. Where one or two gene-therapy companies might have been enough, for example, a half-dozen were founded.

Before the biotech boom, most of the scientific research carried out at universities was funded by the government, and many discoveries were the by-product of basic research. But somewhere along the way the public decided to invest in companies pursuing cures for cancer and other potentially lucrative breakthroughs.

Each biotech company required at least $100 million to get it from nothing to something. One thousand companies were started with venture capital money, and thereafter, hundreds of them were largely financed by public venture capital. "One thousand times $100 million doesn't work. But the public has been conditioned over the last 15 years by the biotech era to publicly finance companies that need big money," says Sequoia's Valentine.

In 1996, biotech IPOs spiked up again, to almost $1.2 billion worth of public offerings. But biotech stocks coming from those offerings and others from the 1980s aren't doing well today. The companies did exactly what they said they would do: All their scientists were locked away in their laboratories doing research. But the public had to learn the hard way that drug failure was the rule and not the exception: Fewer than 1 drug in 10 successfully completes clinical trials. So investors got impatient waiting for positive results and drifted away because of lack of growth in the stock prices. Venture capitalists also started to bolt. Kleiner Perkins, for example, has invested in only two new biotech ventures since 1995.

In a 1998 study of their investments in these companies, Horsley Bridge Partners of San Francisco, a fund of funds that invests in venture capital partnerships and manages the stocks of portfolio companies after they go public, discovered that biotech and health-care stocks might appreciate for a year in the public market, but those stocks languish after that. Since the Biotech Bubble burst in the early 1990s, the public market has not been generous to the health-care sector.

By 1998 there were almost 350 publicly traded biotech companies and about 1,000 private ones. Investors had put an estimated $90 billion into the public companies. Yet biotech stocks had risen in only 7 of 16 years. An investor who put $100 into every biotech IPO would have earned a return of only 1 percent a year.

The NASDAQ biotech index went up in late 1998, but it represented only about a 5 percent gain for the entire year and stayed well below the NASDAQ composite index, which had appreciated by almost 46 percent for the year. Only the stocks of the top 10 biotech companies, which already had products, profits, and market capitalizations over $1 billion, had risen sharply. While the share prices of companies such as Genentech, Amgen, and Chiron soared, midsize and smaller companies actually stagnated or lost ground. In fact, as many as 50 of the lesser-performing public companies were expected to run out of cash within a year.

And unfortunately for the companies below the top tier, the long-predicted wave of mergers supposed to kick in following the Biotech Bubble had largely failed to materialize. The Darwinian shakeout continued.

So while Genentech and Amgen raised the expectations for the whole industry, they also set a precedent for public stock offerings for companies that had no profits, and sometimes no revenues. An entrepreneur could start a company with some vague, far-out idea that nobody ever questioned and take that concept public. People willingly paid for physical and financial events they thought might happen in the future. It was truly public venture capital. And even Amgen has never reached the level of the major pharmaceutical companies. While Amgen is the largest biotech company by far ($2.7 billion in revenues in 1998), it is just a fifth of the size of Pfizer, which makes Amgen only the thirty-first largest drug company in terms of revenue.

In their book *Venture Capital at the Crossroads*, authors William Bygrave and Jeffry Timmons report that of the venture-backed high-tech IPOs done in the 1980s, 77 percent of the hardware companies and 100 percent of the software companies were profitable when they went public. This contrasts to only 20 percent of the biotech companies being profitable at the time of their IPOs. It would not be long before the public venture capital phenomenon would spread beyond biotechnology.

What If They Don't Come?

A prime example of an information-technology company funded by public venture capital is 3DO Corporation. Founded by the dynamic, handsome, and charismatic entrepreneur Trip Hawkins, 3DO, like Genentech, got its initial funding from Kleiner Perkins Caufield & Byers.

Hawkins majored in game design at Harvard University and after graduation served as a marketing manager at Apple Computer under Steve Jobs. In 1982 he founded Electronic Arts, a wildly successful computer games company that put out such hits as John Madden Football. Electronic Arts was also a Kleiner Perkins investment.

In 1991, Hawkins left Electronic Arts to found 3DO. The company's goal from the start was to develop a next-generation video-game system that would seriously challenge the Japanese video-game giants Nintendo, Sega, and Sony. Clearly this would be an expensive and daunting challenge, but Hawkins and Kleiner Perkins felt 3DO was up to the task.

By 1993, though, 3DO was running seriously short of cash; its burn rate was tremendous. Historically, a company like 3DO would have gone back to its venture capitalists or its other investors, in this case AT&T, Matsushita, MCA, and Time Warner, for the necessary funds to go on. Instead, 3DO decided to sell stock to the public.

The problem was that 3DO did not yet have a marketable product. And 3DO was developing technology it would license, not sell directly as its own product. The video-game multiplayer that would run 3DO's technology had to be way overpriced to support the company. It was all a big gamble.

At the time of its IPO in mid-1993, 3DO had zero revenues, a cumulative loss of $30 million, and no projected profitability for at least two years. In the first quarter of 1993, 3DO blew through an estimated $16 million, yet the IPO was valued at $293 million.

This was a new precedent for an information-technology company. It was essentially a concept stock—no completed product or revenues—in which the company asked the public to supply risky venture capital. In spite of 3DO's published stock prospectus, *Red Herring,* in an open letter to Trip Hawkins, asked: "Given the complexity of 3DO's technology development program and business model, how do you expect public investors to adequately evaluate the risk/reward factors involved in such an investment? Isn't this the job for professional venture capitalists?"

Jim Breyer, managing partner of venture capital firm Accel Partners, says, "3DO should not have gone public because there was not a strong conviction about the business model. Unfortunately, 3DO's business was in the hands of a lot of other big strategic partners." This level of business dependency was very hard for nonspecialists to assess at the time.

Publicly, 3DO said its motivation for the concept IPO was to create higher visibility for the company, to keep its software-development partners motivated, and to build anticipation for its video-game player. But the venture capitalists also wanted to create early liquidity, diversify risk, and earn a 12 times markup on an investment they had made just two and a half years before. The old formula had been overturned; no longer was an information-technology company expected to have at least a few quarters of profit before going public.

In June 1994 3DO did another public stock offering, this one netting $37 million. By 1996 the company had given up on the game-player business, and to stay alive proceeded to license what technology it had left, including a $100 million deal with Matsushita. In a May 1996 interview with *Red Herring,* Hawkins admitted that 3DO's original strategy was the wrong one, describing it as a "Field of Dreams" approach. "Build it and they will come. But what if they don't come?" he asked.

3DO's stock fell to about $3 per share, where it languished for several years. In early 1999 its stock did tick up to $6.50 per share within the Internet Bubble, as the company pursued an "Internet strategy" for selling its video games. 3DO also had an increase in sales over the first half of 1998. But it remains to be seen whether 3DO can work its way back up to its IPO stock price.

The Concept Deal

A big problem with the biotech boom was clearly that too many of the companies that went public had to return to the public-market trough at the same time for additional money, thus over-whelming the public investor. The problem with 3DO and General Magic, another technology-concept deal that went public in the mid-1990s, is that a lot of time passed and their stocks languished while they tried to figure out new concepts to sell.

In the Internet boom, basically every company with a *.com* associated with its name is by definition a concept stock and peddles only an inkling of a business model rather than real top-line growth and increasing profits. Certainly many of these Internet companies will come up short on their business plans, and we can see these companies making a mad rush on the public investor for more money in order to survive. If this stampede ensues, we'll see the Darwinian spectacle in living color.

Doonesbury

INTERNET COMPANIES IN A GILDED AGE

The only company that has a real Y2K problem is Yahoo, because the year 2000 is when all its strategic advertising and placement agreements expire!
—**Bob Kagle, Benchmark Capital Partners**

*L*ike past manias, today's Internet mania will pay off handsomely for the insiders. By March 1999 the market value of Amazon was $21.4 billion, eBay was $19 billion, and Yahoo was nearly $35 billion. In each case, venture capitalist backers have seen their stakes jump more than 500-fold in value. Even if those Internet Bubble prices plunged by 50 percent or more, these companies would still remain some of the best venture capital investments of all time.

In this chapter we look at three Gilded Age companies of our era—Amazon, Yahoo, and At Home—that epitomize the huge insider payoff from the Internet gold rush. While it is possible that these three will not only survive but even be among the big-time blue-chip Internet companies that maintain the hyper-returns they have already delivered to public investors, there is no guarantee.

In contrast to the prospects of those three, we also look at CKS Partners, a profitable company that went public during the first big wave of Internet stock offerings that started in late 1995 but suffered greatly at the hands of market volatility. In late 1998 the company had to merge with U.S. Web to survive.

These accounts show that the investment risks are high for the individual public investor buying Internet stocks after they have passed through the hands of the investment bankers' favorite institutions.

Navigating the Amazon

Vinod Khosla, the original founder and CEO of Sun Microsystems and presently a top venture capitalist with Kleiner Perkins Caufield & Byers, likes to say two things about startup companies: "Success is when opportunity meets preparation," and "The entrepreneur is the one who dares to dream the dreams and is foolish enough to try and make them come true." Khosla first acknowledges that even if the entrepreneur does the right thing, timing and luck are required for things to work out. And second, the entrepreneur still has to be crazy enough to pursue his dream.

Both of these points certainly apply to Amazon founder and CEO Jeff Bezos. He seized the opportunity and definitely dreamed the dream. His initiative to launch Amazon as the first serious online bookseller and to get Kleiner Perkins on board as an investor and adviser has driven his personal stake in his company into several billion dollars. Amazon got out of the starting gate fast and executed its business well; everything went pretty smoothly for a young company—order fulfillment, billing, shipping, customer service. This success gave Amazon first-mover advantage, even as the so-called bricks-and-mortar booksellers such as Barnes & Noble and Borders were caught flatfooted, with no presence on the Internet.

Amazon also accrued marvelous publicity from its first-mover status. The challenge, however, has been to maintain that advantage. The company has invested heavily in advertising and promotion and has paid a premium—millions and even tens of millions of dollars—to be specially featured, for example, on the Yahoo portal. One result is that Amazon's brand has emerged as one of the best known on the Internet, if not with America's consumers at large. The Silicon Valley insider consensus is a given that Amazon is an increasing-returns business; it will be tough for competitors to catch up unless the company stumbles badly.

"Amazon has got a hell of a brand name now," says angel investor Ron Conway. "They're becoming the Wal-Mart of the Web. Certain startups are having trouble getting funded now because the venture capitalists say, 'Well, we think Amazon might get into that market.'" Toby Lenk, CEO of online toy retailer eToys, agrees. "We have never been afraid of Toys 'R' Us, but we are afraid Amazon might get in to our business," he told a *Red Herring* conference audience in the fall of 1998.

But Amazon's competitors haven't been idle. Although caught off guard, Barnes & Noble in particular worked to counter Amazon's inroads into bookselling. The largest U.S. retail bookseller spun out its online operation, barnesandnoble.com, and took it public in May 1999, building up a $300 million war chest to fend off Amazon. The huge European media house Bertlesmann had also previously invested $200 million into barnesandnoble.com. Strategically, the company also cut a deal with Microsoft to offer the barnesandnoble.com service as the only bookseller on Microsoft's MSN site.

But even with all this financial and strategic momentum, barnesandnoble.com still has to play an aggressive game of catch-up. The online service posted sales of only $70 million in 1998, compared with $610 million for Amazon. And Barnes & Noble still faces the problem of whether its online sales will ultimately cannibalize the sales structure of its physical bookstores. "To beat Amazon, Barnes & Noble will essentially have to eat its young," observes venture capitalist Steve Jurvetson of Draper Fisher Jurvetson.

And there is good reason to be skeptical. Barnes & Noble runs the risk of becoming a legacy business with lots of mortgages to pay on its 520 superstores and 500 other mall stores. And while the physical chain stores still have about 25 percent of unit sales of books, the growth trend favors online sales, which are expected to increase by more than $1 billion by the year 2002 compared with an annual increase of about $400 million for superstores.

"I never want to be in the legacy business," says venture capitalist Don Valentine. "In a world of transitions, I want to be on the forward edge, not the rear edge of the transition. I want to be the franchise that acts in the twenty-first-century style, not in the nineteenth-century style."

Barnes & Noble, like many other bricks-and-mortar operations, faces a real dilemma. It doesn't own a single one of its stores, and the company is highly leveraged. If it can't raise more cash, it can't build any more stores. And if it can't build more stores, its earnings don't grow.

"For the first time in my life, I can't see five years ahead the way I used to," Barnes & Noble CEO Leonard Riggio admitted to the *New York Times*. "I can't see it clearly." He added, "It's not just the changes in the book business. It's the changes in retail, the changes in the way we live. I wake up and say that any business created before 1997 will be a fossil by the year 2010."

E-commerce businesses are scale businesses in a way that physical-store businesses are not. In a physical-store environment, if you double sales, you basically double costs. But e-commerce businesses don't have to double the number of square feet or the number of sales associates when they double sales. They can save on overhead even as they grow. "It's possible to offer the lowest prices and the highest service levels so long as you are the scaled player, so you can give customers the best of both worlds," claims Jeff Bezos.

A big part of Amazon's first-mover advantage was its exploitation of the Internet's computing power to let customers search easily for books in print, read numerous reviews (many of them from customers), and launch purchases to customers with a mouse click. Amazon was also the first to use what it calls "collaborative filtering" technologies to analyze customer purchases and suggest items based on individual purchasing histories. "Shortly after I signed up for my Amazon account, I received an e mail suggesting I buy, among other books, two I had written myself. Since then, I have been a huge Amazon fan," muses Sequoia Capital's Mike Moritz, who before becoming a venture capitalist wrote business books on Chrysler and Apple Computer.

While Amazon has taken its share of the bookselling pie, the company has also expanded into selling music CDs, videos, and other items. "Amazon became the number one online seller of music CDs after only three months in the game," Bezos brags. The appeal to customers is as much about convenience as it is about price. However, profit margins are still thin—approximately 20 percent gross margins and about 1 to 2 percent net margins.

Some find these thin margins troubling. "To me, the Internet is the perfect marketplace, but for the consumer," says Don Valentine, whose firm provided the seed-funding for Yahoo. "I don't know how to make money in this perfect marketplace. Never before has the consumer had all the cards dealt faceup, where he can make choices and decisions knowing what the facts are. The consumer is put in a position where he has phenomenal access to whatever he thinks he wants. Most electronic retailers have a completely undifferentiated product that's a very low price-point product, so you have to sell millions of them to get any scale of revenue. The margin is theoretical."

"Some see Amazon as no more than a grocery store with thin margins," Khosla of Kleiner Perkins declares. "But you can also view them as the holder of 10 million credit-card accounts whose owners have enough confidence in Amazon to make purchases."

This raises the issue of how big Amazon has to get not only to become profitable but to justify its stock valuation projected several years out. It will have to execute like crazy and build a big company to be profitable.

Will it in fact become the Wal-Mart of the Web? Can it achieve that volume of sales and that level of efficiency? Amazon is said to be looking at everything from software to clothing, flowers, and even travel services. Amazon has already taken a stake in an online grocery service called Homegrocer.com.

Many resist the idea that there could be one superbehemoth shopping portal that would rule the Web, instead of having the Web segment itself into localized areas of interest and lots of specialty experiences for consumers online. Jeff Bezos actually agrees with the latter. "In each of these vertical categories, there will be multiple winners," he declares. "I believe e-commerce is so big that there won't be tens of winners or hundreds of winners, but literally thousands, even tens of thousands of winners in this space."

To grow its business, Amazon has followed Dell Computer's highly efficient model for sales and inventory control. Dell's model has rewritten the rules for winning in the personal computer industry. By manufacturing only those PCs for which it actually has orders and then selling them directly to customers, Dell has eliminated costly inventory buildup. Naturally, this approach has helped boost profit margins and earnings.

Amazon imitates the Dell approach by keeping a minimal inventory, about 15 days' worth. It doesn't have to buy most of its goods and supplies before selling them; instead, it orders from a distributor only when a customer has placed an order. Consequently, Amazon turns over its inventory about 26 times a year, 10 times as fast as the bricks-and-mortar operations.

In contrast, physical bookstores must stock up to 160 days' worth of books to provide the kind of in-store inventory people want. Yet they have to pay their distributors and publishers 45 to 90 days after they receive the books. They carry the cost of those books for up to 4 months and must continuously finance the gap.

On the other hand, Amazon charges customers' credit-card accounts as soon as it ships the book, CD, or video, and it usually gets paid within a day. Meanwhile, Amazon takes its time—approximately 46 days—to pay its suppliers, and enjoys about a month's use of interest-free money. This float—more than $25 million in 1998—gives Amazon a big chunk of cash to cover its operating expenses. And if Amazon turns over its inventories 10 times as fast as the rest of the industry, it can actually live on one-tenth the margin of a Barnes & Noble and be equally as profitable.

"As long as Amazon's cash flow is greater than its losses, that makes them cash flow positive," says Wall Street analyst-turned-venture-capitalist Bill Gurley of Benchmark Partners, which provided the initial venture money for eBay. "Amazon can survive on its current business model. You don't have to give a return to shareholders to survive. You just need capital to survive."

Amazon's answer to cutthroat price competition online is customer service—the end-to-end customer experience from when the customer first comes to the Web site until the package arrives in the mail. As this theory goes, it's not just price, but price performance. If

Amazon's customers aren't satisfied with an item, they can return it. Or if they have a question, there's somebody to support them. The goal is to create habitual customers who, if they've been serviced well and have had only positive experiences, will probably not go elsewhere for an extra 10 percent off. And as the service evolves, it can present to customers offers that reflect their interests when they're in the frame of mind to do something about them.

By Christmas 1998 Amazon had started to exploit this valuable customer base. Besides adding a holiday gift section to its service, which featured consumer electronics, games, and toys, it had added an extensive line of videotapes and digital videodisks to its line of wares. Amazon priced the gift items in the mid-range of market prices, emphasizing convenience and product information as a major part of the customer-service bargain. In its first full quarter of selling music, it sold $14.4 million worth of music items, more than its two main online competitors N2K and CDNow combined.

However, both CDs and videos have lower profit margins than books. And videos don't have the same well-established distribution network as do books and CDs, requiring online sellers such as Reel.com to carry a large inventory. Doing likewise could add to Amazon's inventory costs and reduce the nice float it's experienced for its bookselling operations.

And if it expands to areas such as apparel, Amazon could face challenges from retailers such as Macy's that are bigger and better known than longtime rival Barnes & Noble. The online competition has also teamed up: CDNow joined with Reel.com, eToys, and a computer seller called Cyberian Outpost to form a virtual mall on a Web site called Shopper Connection. Web portals Yahoo and AOL are also after a big chunk of e-commerce, as is the online merchant Buy.com.

This competition explains why Bezos wants to expand beyond straight retail sales. In August 1998, for $180 million, Amazon bought a company called Junglee, which lets customers search multiple Web sites simultaneously for the same products so they can compare prices. Amazon would not have to sell everything; it could simply take a percentage from other retailers when Amazon's customers buy their products. In this way, in partnership with other merchants through its Shop the Web service, Amazon acts as a service agent rather than just a direct seller of goods.

"Our thesis is to make it possible for customers to find and discover anything they want to buy online at the lowest prices with the highest level of service," says Bezos. Anything, that is, except books and music, which Amazon wants to sell directly to consumers rather than encourage them to comparison shop using the Junglee technology. The main objective is that as the total dollar purchases of the average Amazon customer go up, so will the company's profit margins.

Bezos eschews comparisons of his company to a Wal-Mart on the Web. "One metric of our success in the long term will be the degree to which we can defy easy analogy," asserts Bezos. "We want to be something completely new."

Bezos sees Amazon's development within the context of the evolution of the Internet and the eventual Darwinian shakeout. He likes to compare the current Internet era to biology's Cambrian period, in which multicellular life first started to form. During that period, there were lots of different basic shapes, and some of these shapes proved more viable than others. Over time, there were high rates of specialization and extinction among species. Eventually, after a large shakeout, things calmed down, and slow and steady evolution followed. Bezos believes the same process will happen with the Internet— essentially the main thesis of this book.

Meanwhile, Amazon's stock value continued to hit new highs; by the first week of January 1999, after a three-for-one split, Amazon stock was valued at more than 100 times revenues, giving the company a total market value of more than $21 billion. It was a true momentum market. But could such a valuation be justified? By our calculation, Amazon will have to grow at an average rate of close to 100 percent per year over the next five years and post $22 billion in revenues to maintain its current market valuation.

"There's a disconnect between the underlying fundamentals

and the share prices," admits CS First Boston Internet analyst Lise Buyer. "But the bet is that Amazon spends X number of dollars building an infrastructure and attracting tons of people, then they leverage that by selling more and more stuff."

Marketing and infrastructure are the two biggest expenses for an online business, so once those are ratcheted down, Amazon's bottom line will benefit. "Part of the market's affair with Amazon," says Buyer, "is that these expenses are variable and that its management could turn them down if it wanted to. They're fortunate in the way they have convinced everyone not to worry about profitability right now. The stock price notwithstanding, I am a fan of Amazon."

Amazon has consistently made it clear that it would not optimize for short-term profitability but rather for larger market share and for enhancing what Bezos calls "critical category formation for detailed e-commerce." How fast this will grow is hard to predict. "We see the growth pattern as an S-curve that represents customer adoption," says Bezos. "S-curves all level out at some point, but until then it's difficult to predict where the top of that S-curve is."

What does Bezos think about Amazon's stock price? "I subscribe to the Peter Lynch view that there is no correlation between great companies and short-term stock prices," he declares. "But in the long term, there is 100 percent correlation." He adds, "It's a full-time job for analysts to figure out how much companies are worth, while it's our full-time job to build an enduring franchise, an important and lasting company. Our decisions are constrained by trying to do the right thing for the long term."

One of Amazon's long-term decisions was to raise more money in January 1999 through a $1.25 billion convertible-bond offering said to be the largest offering of its kind in U.S. history. Amazon did not declare publicly the motive behind this offering, but it was probably one of two.

One is in keeping with Bezos's evolutionary metaphor. If cash is like oxygen, the companies with the most cash over the long term are the most likely to survive the Darwinian shakeout. With Amazon's cash flow–efficient model and the financing of its bond issue, it could theoretically breathe longer than any of its competitors. If Amazon wanted to, it could lower book prices by 50 or 60 percent and run Barnes & Noble and other competitors out of business.

The more likely explanation is that Amazon believes it has a one-time window to capture a huge piece of the e-commerce business; the asset value of capturing customers is so high that Amazon wants to leverage this opportunity in as many ways as possible. Because Amazon already has a successful e-commerce system, it doesn't want to wait around for every company in corporate America to build its own e-commerce relationships with its customers. Amazon wants to capture value even from industries it doesn't know much about. This would help explain Amazon's controlling interest in Pets.com, which sells dog biscuits, cat toys, and other pet supplies, and Amazon's $40 million investment in Drugstore.com for a 46 percent stake.

Like Amazon, Drugstore.com's main venture capital investor is Kleiner Perkins. The relationship between the two Internet companies illustrates perfectly the Kleiner Perkins keiretsu in action, as the larger company, Amazon, invests in the smaller one, Drugstore.com. The nature of their deal is captured in a photograph found in the Kleiner Perkins office of Amazon's lead venture capital investor, John Doerr. In the picture, Doerr and Jeff Bezos kneel in front of four standing executives from Drugstore.com. Doerr and Bezos are smiling and giving the thumbs-up, while the others look as glum as if they were attending a funeral. It's clear who's leading the parade here.

Amazon's other big move not long after the bond offering was to launch Amazon Auctions as a direct competitor to eBay and other online auctioneers. Amazon's plan was to leverage its customer base of 10 million to rack up significant income through fees on millions of transactions at very low cost. It was potentially a much higher-margin business than selling books and other commodities. To bolster its efforts, Amazon entered into an alliance with Sotheby's to sell art and collectibles online. Amazon invested $35 million in Sotheby's as part of the deal.

Our analysis is that Jeff Bezos is, indeed, one of the smartest operators in the Internet age. He's maintaining a cutting-edge strategy and raising the necessary bucks to make certain no opportunity slips through his fingers. But whatever Amazon's strategy and long-term prospects, in the rarefied air of the Bubble environment, the stock price still appears to have no connection to reality. Buying at Bubble prices is still a huge gamble.

CKS Partners—a Cautionary Tale

Part of the initial wave of Internet IPOs that started in late 1995, CKS Partners, a marketing and advertising agency that emphasizes its online capabilities, had to face the first big shakeout of the Internet when that wave hit the beach. From this experience, CKS cofounder and CEO Mark Kvamme would agree with Amazon's strategy to scale up. "It's clear to me that the first-mover advantage in this market means you have to get big," he says. "The Internet is getting bigger, so scale is very important." Unfortunately, huge scale was something CKS could not achieve.

In December 1995 CKS went public at $17 a share, and in the first two weeks was already up to $39. In the weeks and months that followed, the stock price was all over the place—down to $20, up to $45, down to $20 again, up to $40. It was being whipped around by both momentum investors and the movement of institutional investors in and out of the stock.

Finally, CKS had a particularly bad quarter in which its revenue was 20 percent short of Wall Street's expectations. CKS stock lost 64 percent of its value in one day, dropping all the way down to $11 per share, well below its original offering price. CKS employees were glued to their computer screens watching their online stock tickers to continually check the price. Morale was in the dumps.

Overall, it was more difficult to run a public company than a private company. CKS was now accountable to shareholders as well as to the employees and customers; dealing with Wall Street and institutional investors was a dangerous distraction for CKS managers, especially when their time could have been better spent directing the company. "You get on this treadmill and you've just got to run," says CEO Kvamme. "You have these analysts calling you all the time. Everybody second-guesses everything you do."

Recruiting managers also becomes tougher following an IPO, since many experienced executives like to get in when a company is still private and amass a big equity stake before the stock spikes up at the public offering.

None of this was good for the health of CKS. Going public forced growth on the company because it was measured in 90-day increments. When CKS missed one of those quarters, there was this feeling that the company was all screwed up and going in the tank.

In 1998, after being hammered long enough in the public market, CKS merged with U.S. Web, a company that focuses more on intranet and extranet markets than on the Internet per se; combining with CKS gave the merged companies coverage in all areas.

"Quite frankly, if I had to do it all over again, I wouldn't have gone public," concludes Kvamme. "We had a profitable, growing company, with $30 million in sales. We didn't have to do it, because we didn't need the capital." He adds, "But part of the efflux of Silicon Valley is that you build up a company and take it public."

At its IPO, CKS was viewed as an "Internet play." When the dust cleared, it was finally recognized as the lower-margin, lower-growth service company it was, and its stock settled down to its proper value. The fate of CKS is a cautionary tale for those overeager to bet on young Internet companies riding a big wave of public offerings.

Do You Yahoo?

Yahoo is a household brand name, and its stock valuation has stayed well ahead of that of its closest rivals in the Internet portal game. What makes Yahoo so special?

For one thing, like most companies funded by the venture capitalists at Sequoia Capital, Yahoo has exercised tremendous financial discipline. But even before Sequoia came into the picture, Yahoo was on the Web, beginning in April 1994. Excite, by contrast, didn't show up on the Web until October 1995. By then, Yahoo already served up a million Web pages a day to users. And because Yahoo had a product, it got distribution in the Netscape Web site for the first year. Yahoo's 18-month lead gave it first-mover advantage and a big branding edge. The others have struggled to catch up. "Yahoo got all the early leverage," admits Vinod Khosla, the venture capitalist at Kleiner Perkins who funded Excite.

It also didn't hurt that the Yahoo Web site loaded quickly and that the company adopted a memorable name early on, when Excite was still called Architext and other competitors had equally nerdy names such as Infoseek and Lycos.

After it had successfully established itself as the leading Internet directory service, Yahoo scored big as a personal financial site. "I use Yahoo every day for stock quotes," says venture capitalist and former Wall Street analyst Bill Gurley. "I've watched many in the investment community turn off costly data services such as Reuters, Bloomberg, and LEXIS/NEXIS and use Yahoo instead."

"Yahoo did a good marketing job, and it's a great company," says Dan Case, CEO of investment bank Hambrecht & Quist and brother of America Online's CEO Steve Case. "The Internet was ready, and because of this open network, Yahoo's customer-acquisitions costs were a lot lower than AOL's." Within a couple of weeks of going public in April 1996, Yahoo's stock was held almost completely by retail investors and consumers, including an enormous number of retail stock buyers from Japan. The aftermarket froth was in full flow. Yahoo was clearly not being valued by the traditional measures of valuation, whether by price-to-earnings growth or even revenue.

Despite being a billionaire on paper, Yahoo cofounder Jerry Yang prefers not to think too much about the company's stock valuation. "We're on the field, we're playing the game, and it's probably the bottom of the third inning," says Yang. "I have no idea what the spectators are doing. They could be selling tickets for this game, even at scalpers' prices. I have no control of that. We've just got to win this game."

The valuation does affect Yahoo's ability to attract new employees. The stock is so high that the prospects for appreciation only grow slimmer, making it less attractive to new employees, while salaries continue to escalate. "It costs much more now to hire people," admits Yang.

Yang also feels that Yahoo's high valuation has caused the tide to rise, lifting all boats with it, including those of his competitors. "My theory is that our ability to generate profit has meant that Excite and everybody else did not have to make money for their stock to go up," says Yang.

Yahoo's high-priced stock has enabled it to make some important acquisitions, including GeoCities for $3.9 billion in stock and Broadcast.com for $5.7 billion in stock. GeoCities is a Web community where millions of people have created personal Web pages, and Yahoo's acquisition of it greatly extended Yahoo's number of users. Broadcast.com is a Web service that transmits audio and video signals over the Internet.

Yahoo had already invested more than $1 million in Broadcast.com, so the acquisition of the company was a natural follow-up for Yahoo. At the time, Yahoo's president Jeff Mallett claimed, "Within a year, we won't even be talking about each aspect of audio, video, and text. It's going to be blended and integrated, and the overall experience will be what consumers will expect when they come to the Web."

Soon after the acquisition of Broadcast.com, Yahoo launched Yahoo Radio, which provides direct access to broadcast audio programming, which would be carried out by Broadcast.com. Interestingly, the most popular audio service Yahoo provides today is a police scanner. "You can basically call up the police scanner covering any city in America and listen," Yang explains. "Listeners can learn about a homicide at the local 7-Eleven—it's kind of perverse, but also pretty cool."

Meanwhile, Yahoo's brand recognition has definitely helped it compete for mind share. Some people use Yahoo the way others buy Oreos when they want cookies. And Yahoo has lived off the efforts of other Internet companies attempting to build their brands by paying for special, supposedly exclusive placement on the Yahoo Web site.

Some companies have paid $15 million for space on Yahoo only to find their competitors running ads with better placement on the same site. For electronic retailers this has often meant simply being included under the appropriate category listing on Yahoo's site—music, books, clothing—that lets shoppers find and purchase items from any number of stores that have bought space on Yahoo. But such advertising and placement deals have not been economical for the companies; the cost of acquiring customers this way will probably not pay off over the customer's lifetime. Venture capitalist Bob Kagle of Benchmark Partners likens these ads to "buying billboards at beachfront property prices."

Yahoo obviously benefits from many users going to its site by default. It's tougher to figure out which part of Yahoo's business really merits its high valuation, other than that it is composed of smart people with a big database of information and lots of people standing in line to sign up to be their partners. Ultimately, advertisers may not willingly pay for more eyeballs looking at the Yahoo Web site. Instead, advertisers might prefer loyal members who come back to a site for real content and who see the ads often, like regular subscribers to *The Wall Street Journal* do in the print world.

America Online, like Yahoo, has also leveraged its advertising space, charging Intuit $30 million to be featured on the AOL Finance Center and charging Net Grocer $15 million to be the exclusive online grocer on AOL. In March 1999 Internet auctioneer eBay signed a $75 million partnership deal with AOL for prominent placement on AOL services, including its own site within AOL. Yet it was still not an exclusive deal, as eBay competitors—Bid.com, OnSale, First Auction, and Ubid—could still buy placement on AOL.

One-third of AOL's marketing revenues came from money-losing Web companies that used the proceeds from their public stock offerings to fund their promotional efforts. Ironically, many of these companies are startups in which AOL had invested prior to their IPOs. It was an incestuous relationship. Had the IPO window closed long term, many of these deals would not have been possible.

These advertising deals that Yahoo and AOL have orchestrated make the Internet "an entire sector devoted to little more than tak-ing in each other's laundry," as Christopher Byron of the *New York Observer* puts it. The ultimate gimmick is to invest in an Internet startup, take it public, then harvest the proceeds of the underwrit-ing when the startup spends them on advertising with the original investing company.

But this revenue source may not hold up at its current levels. And one thing AOL has that Yahoo doesn't is income from monthly paid subscribers, because Yahoo's service is provided free. "The only com-pany that has a real Y2K problem is Yahoo," declares Benchmark's Kagle, "because the year 2000 is when all its strategic advertising and placement agreements expire!"

In addition to the potential loss of revenue from the expiration of major strategic deals, Yahoo also faces new competition for advertis-ing dollars and Web traffic from emerging specialized sites such as iVillage and ZDNet. Although Yahoo and the other major Web por-tals attracted 60 percent of Internet advertising revenues, which totaled almost $2 billion in 1998, Forrester Research predicts that by 2002 the portals' share of ad revenues will be sliced in half as more money goes to content sites. While overall spending by advertisers will rise to $8 billion in 2002, by Forrester's estimates the portal pie will be worth about $2.5 billion at that point. Even with a large chunk of Internet ad revenues, Yahoo still only attracted 15 percent of all Web traffic, although in June 1999 Yahoo's network of Web sites did have 80 million visitors, and the company's revenues for the quarter were over $115 million, more than double the $45 million in the same quarter a year earlier. Some analysts have suggested that any serious deflation of Yahoo's advertising and Web traffic numbers in the year 2000 could significantly contribute to the overall deflation of the Internet Bubble.

These dilemmas leave Yahoo with a major transition issue, where the company might have to move to a transaction-based business model in which it will get at least a piece of every electronic-com-merce transaction that takes place through Yahoo's site. But Jerry Yang plays down his company's need to collect credit cards to stay alive. "We remain competitive not necessarily by collecting the most credit-card numbers for customers but by continuing to be the leading innovator of new services over the Web," Yang told us when we suggested that Yahoo might eventually have to butt heads with e-commerce powerhouse Amazon.

One of Yahoo's primary advantages is Jerry Yang's sense of paranoia. "We are scared of a lot of people," Yang confesses. "We watch out for AOL, Microsoft, Excite, and Amazon—they all want to eat our lunch in one form or another." This kind of attitude helped Andy Grove make Intel into the dominant chip company in the world and should also help Yahoo maintain its market-leading position as well.

In summary, it is clear Yahoo has one of the strongest brands on the Internet and one of the sharpest management teams in Silicon Valley. Yahoo also has the added advantage of being one of the few profitable Internet companies in the market. But while its revenues have grown dramatically since its inception—over $250 million in 1998—it will need to grow at over a 150 percent annual rate to sustain its $27 billion-plus market capitalization. More specifically, our Internet Bubble calculation suggests that Yahoo's sales will have to reach a whopping $24 billion in five years to maintain its first-quarter 1999 market valuation—definitely a huge challenge (see Appendices A and B for further details on Bubble calculations).

Is Anyone At Home?

At Home has been called an Internet service provider on steroids. It's supposed to be the answer to all those annoyingly slow phone lines that everyone has to put up with when using an Internet connection at home. Everyone agrees they should be faster—a lot faster—and that it's time for a good deal more bandwidth. So why not use cable connections to speed up the process?

This was the question that intrigued Will Hearst III, grandson of publishing magnate William Randolph Hearst. The At Home concept, not surprisingly, was immediately attractive to him. Like his grandfather, Will Hearst served as editor and publisher of the *San*

Francisco Examiner newspaper, yet he was also something of a technology buff, serving on the board of Sun Microsystems and other high-tech companies and maintaining a keen interest in new media. "My grandfather was an innovator," says Hearst, "and I'm sure if he were around today, he would be interested in the Internet and other new media technologies."

Will Hearst's high-tech enthusiasm not only sparked his interest in At Home but led him to join the venture capital firm Kleiner Perkins Caufield & Byers as a general partner in early 1995. "I had talked to John Doerr about At Home before actually going to Kleiner Perkins," Hearst says. "And I got increasingly interested in it because I had some background in cable television, but John had the instinct about it."

After Hearst arrived at Kleiner Perkins, he was asked to serve as At Home's interim CEO. "I was at a partners meeting and John Doerr said, 'I'd like Will to go down and run this company—what do you guys think?'" remembers Hearst. "One of the other partners said, 'Well, if he does it for 60 days, that would be great, 90 days, I'm not so sure, and 120 days, something is wrong.' I thought, 'Yeah, I can do anything for 60 days.' . . . I was there more than a year."

At Home was possible only because the cable TV companies wanted an online play. They had missed the last data wave, and they needed a partner in Silicon Valley who understood it.

TCI became At Home's main cable TV partner in 1995. At the time, there was a lot of skepticism about cable companies, cable modems, and the ability to run a network on analog equipment. The challenge was to take the technology to a new level and a new standard.

Whatever the improvements in technology, it would clearly be an expensive project, even with the help of TCI. By early 1997, At Home got the help of investment bankers Bill Brady and Frank Quattrone, at the time still with the Deutsche Morgan Grenfell Tech Group, to raise $50 million in private money. Brady and Quattrone figured it would be at least a year and a half before At Home would go public.

But At Home went public a few months later. By then, At Home's new CEO, Tom Jermoluk, formerly the president of Silicon Graphics (SGI), was on board and pushing for an IPO to raise the capital he felt the company needed to go forward. It was an IPO that would not have been feasible a few years before.

Unlike with the private financing, Deutsche Morgan Grenfell did not underwrite the IPO. "We were cautious about At Home's ability to go public that early," says Bill Brady. "Maybe it was because we had been involved in the private financing. But we were less enthusiastic about the timing of that IPO. Our view was that they had signed up a few partnerships, but they weren't seeing the fruits of any of them. And at the time, they didn't have any subscribers."

Another top banker who also looked at the At Home deal says, "We declined to pursue it. We couldn't get comfortable with the underlying projected subscriber numbers. We had a tough time justifying the valuation."

Despite these expert reservations, At Home went public at $17 per share, and its stock valuation went through the roof. At the time of its IPO in July 1997, At Home's revenue was only $750,000, but its market capitalization was $2.6 billion. By the summer of 1998, its market capitalization was up to $5.6 billion, even though in the previous 12 months its revenue was only $12 million. And by the time At Home announced the acquisition of Excite in January 1999, At Home's capitalization was all the way up to $12.4 billion, even though in its most recent quarter the company had posted a loss of $7.6 million. "You'd think you'd do forward earnings estimates based on the year 2000," quips one venture capitalist. "I guess I was wrong—it's actually based on the year 3000."

"At Home is assuming no execution risk against the best-case scenario," says one longtime technology investor. "And even then the math doesn't work. At Home has to have at least a couple billion dollars in revenue before its valuation can even begin to make sense."

To understand the implications of At Home's stock price, it's enlightening to compare the company to Microsoft. Microsoft earns 30 percent after taxes as a net margin, and approximately 25 percent after taxes on revenues. At Home, if it got the same after-tax margins as Microsoft, would in effect be operating at the same level as the most profitable company in the world. Even if it did, At Home would be trading its stock at 160 times normalized 1999 earnings, while Microsoft is trading at 40 times. The numbers just do not make sense.

But Will Hearst remains a believer. "I have never sold a share of stock. I expect it to keep growing," he says. "But I realize there are people who feel like, 'Here is this little company that doesn't have enough subscribers.'"

The subscriber numbers have not grown the way At Home had forecasted they might—the company projected a subscriber base of one million users by the end of its first year but will be lucky to hit that number by the end of 1999. The fundamentals do not appear to match expectations. The potential is big enough, and everybody has bet on the need for broadband. But At Home may not turn out to be the standard or the service provider that wins.

A bigger problem than just the small subscriber base is the huge task of building the system to make it viable. Upgrading the current cable system will be very expensive, and it must be done on a regional rather than line-by-line basis. Someone will have to spend billions and billions of dollars upgrading just to have the ability to market to the customer. In particular, the last two or three miles of cable wiring that runs up to the houses needs attention. Those cable lines are a noisy mess, because each one is shared by 500 homes. The more people who use this shared network, the more slowly it runs because of limits in the technology. So upgrading these lines to provide a realistic two-way communication network is incredibly costly and time-consuming.

"At Home does make certain requirements on the cable television infrastructure, which is incomplete," admits Hearst. "It's not as simple as buying a modem, clipping it into the system, and being up and running like you can on the phone system. At Home is not at that point because the cable television infrastructure is not at that point."

There is a high-bandwidth alternative to At Home called digital subscriber line (DSL), the most popular version of which is the asymmetric digital subscriber line (ADSL). It can be deployed on a home-by-home basis and can get more speed out of a single phone line than the old phone modems. ADSL is particularly fast and useful for those users who want to download a lot of information in a hurry (Web pages, digital video, etc.) but do not need to send out a lot of material. "ADSL is real," says Hearst. "Kleiner Perkins has invested in ADSL companies, and oddly enough, At Home has invested in an ADSL company to reach customers who aren't reached by cable television infrastructure. The possibility of more than one way to get into the home is real, provided ADSL doesn't just win altogether."

ADSL isn't universally available yet. But competition with ADSL and the size and cost of the cable upgrade are only two of the big risks involved in making the publicly held At Home profitable. The company's own August 3, 1998, stock prospectus for a follow-on offering lists several other risks, summarized as follows:

- Unproven business and no assurance of profitability: As of June 30, 1998, At Home had an accumulated deficit of $349.5 million and planned to increase its capital expenditures and operating expenses in order to expand its network and further the rollout of the business-to-business arm of its service called @Work, which might not achieve broad commercial acceptance and therefore cannot be sustained; the company cannot prove that the pricing model for any of these services will prove viable.

- Dependence on cable partners to upgrade two-way cable infrastructure.

- Cable partners not obligated to carry the At Home service.

- TCI has a majority of the voting power—which now extends to AT&T as the acquirer of TCI—and therefore has control of most significant matters.

- Unproven network scalability, speed, and security.

By November 1998, in its quarterly filing with the SEC, At Home had to admit it had trouble accommodating large numbers of users at the same time because of network bottlenecks and congestion. In the filing At Home warned that its network might be "unable to achieve or maintain a high speed of data transmission, especially as the number of the company's subscribers grows."

At Home blamed some of these network problems on certain customers they called "bandwidth hogs." In some cases, the company had to place a cap on the speed at which customers could send data, limiting it to no faster than 128 kilobytes, which is about four times faster than the typical 28.8 kilobyte dial-up rate. However, this is well short of At Home's touted 22,500 kilobyte speed, which was to be 100 times faster than phone lines. In fact, by June 1999 an internal At Home memo describing the speed cap policy had leaked out. In the memo At Home customer service representatives were instructed to avoid telling customers about the cap which was being implemented in all At Home communities in the U.S. At Home, meanwhile, blamed TCI for not upgrading its cable system fast enough and claimed that the cable companies should have been alerting At Home users by email about the speed caps.

By April 1999 At Home served about 450,000 subscribers in 40 communities and had agreements with 16 cable providers in 24 states. But complaints continued to pour in. In cities across the nation, the *San Francisco Chronicle* reported, users of At Home said they were frequently unable to access the Internet even for using e-mail, never mind for surfing the Net. Some complained that the speed had interfered with their attempts to send certain files, such as PowerPoint presentations and that download speeds were sometimes impacted. "If you hit the upload cap, your download speed slows, too, so it can take forever to check email or look at news," moaned At Home customer Dave Roznar to the *San Francisco Chronicle*. "All their talk of being up to 100 times faster than a traditional modem is not true, and this just slows down even more."

According to At Home CEO Tom Jermoluk, the company plans to win 20 percent of the online home market by 2002. By early 1999 about 22.5 million homes were online in some form. Even under the company's most optimistic projections, 20 percent of the online home market at the subscriber rate of $40 per month would bring in less than $2.2 billion in revenue per year in 2002. In the communications business this number isn't particularly large. Meanwhile, it would cost a staggering $42 billion to get all At Home's affiliate partners' 60 million customers online using cable modems. Deployment is slow and may never be profitable.

And while the merger of At Home's original partner and investor, TCI, with AT&T does provide some deep pockets and brand recognition, it does not necessarily bode well for customer service. Nick Donatiello, president of the consumer research firm Odyssey LP, says of the AT&T–TCI combination, "It's worse than the blind leading the deaf. The bad has married the ugly, and somehow they expect the children to be good. Lip service alone won't get you there—the first thing they still have to prove is that they're worthy of their customers' business."

According to the *San Francisco Chronicle*, At Home has also had its share of complaints about lax customer service. "Every other day, something else goes wrong," complained one subscriber in Portland, Oregon. "Nobody in customer support ever seems to know what the problem is." Another user in New Canaan, Connecticut, couldn't log on to the Internet at all, even though she had subscribed to the service for four months. Subscribers with these problems were directed to call their cable provider first before being routed to At Home for help. But many calls and emails to At Home went unanswered.

In a bid to expand its reach, At Home merged with Internet portal Excite in January 1999 in a stock-swap transaction valued at $6.7 billion, about twice Excite's $3.4 billion market capitalization at the time. Excite, like At Home, is a Kleiner Perkins company. At Home's goal is to get access to Excite's 25 million users and to make money on the Internet through the portal service. It was the ultimate exit strategy for Excite and a bid to solve its also-ran position relative to Yahoo. But the merger would not necessarily solve At Home's cost and time problems in building its high-speed infrastructure for the Internet.

Like 3DO, another Kleiner Perkins company that went public early, At Home's business is ultimately too dependent on a lot of other big strategic partners. "The thing that scares the hell out of me is knowing that At Home's future rests in the hands of the cable companies," admits Will Hearst. What looks like it could be a winning formula today—with a whole bunch of industry giants lining up behind a particular approach—may in fact become a dinosaur tomorrow.

"I don't think At Home is a long-term viable thing," says venture capitalist Ann Winblad of Hummer Winblad Partners. "I think it's a pioneering motivator. But I can't see how this is going to work; it's just way too expensive."

None of At Home's predictable challenges, though, prevented it from going public. There is a revealing scene described in a 1997 *New Yorker* piece on At Home's leading venture investor, John Doerr. In the scene, Doerr and At Home executives walk out of underwriter Morgan Stanley's bank headquarters and into Times Square just after the market closed on the day of At Home's public offering. Looking up, they see lights on the side of the building flashing congratulations and the stock's opening price. The At Home guys give each other high fives. Tourists watch, bemused. And Doerr is still selling: "I remember the first time I saw color TV, and this is more important than that." Then he smiles. "And who knows? It might even work."

What will not work is At Home's valuation. By our calculation, At Home will have to grow its sales at an average annual rate of 106 percent to maintain its first-quarter 1999 market valuation. In other words, the company, which boasted $252 million in annual sales (which includes Excite's revenues) for a 12-month period through March 31, 1999, will have to chalk up over $9 billion in sales by the year 2004. Where these sales will come from, we have no idea. Investors in Excite/At Home today obviously know something we don't.

Doonesbury

THE NEW ECONOMY

In the lamentable era of the 'New Economics' culminating in 1929, even in the presence of dizzily spiraling prices, if we had all continuously repeated 'two and two still make four,' much of the evil might have been averted.

—Bernard Baruch, 1932

T he cyber-barons of Technology's Gilded Age like to talk about the New Economy. We live in a golden era, they assert, because the old rules of business and investment no longer apply, inflation is dead, technology is boosting productivity, and the classic business cycles are less relevant, maybe even obsolete. This is the Long Boom that will last for decades to come. Every day, and in every way, things will only get better.

In this chapter we look at the claims for the New Economy. Is the robust U.S. economy of the 1990s the beginning of a Long Boom, or is it just an extended up cycle? This distinction is important, because if it's a Long Boom, perhaps the high valuations of many Internet companies are justified and there is no Bubble after all.

After we address the Long Boom question, we'll examine some of the apparent paradoxes of the New Economy, such as the less-than-obvious return on investment (ROI) from the use of technology in business and the fact that average Americans work longer hours and are increasingly on the other side of a widening income gap between themselves and the wealthy elite. We'll also hear from some economists who don't feel we are out of the woods yet when it comes to the economic impact of the Y2K bug or problems with the world economy. Finally, we'll hear from economist Paul

Romer, whose New Growth view will help put it all in perspective for us.

The Long Boom?

It is true that the business climate in the United States of the 1990s has been extraordinary. The economy has been unusually good, with low interest rates, almost no inflation, and employment at a record high. Much of the credit goes to deregulation of business, increased efficiency and innovation, and effective corporate restructuring for competition in global markets. As Herb Allen Jr. of investment bank Allen & Co. says, "The streamlining and tightening up of American business over the last ten years has paid off."

But this increased efficiency has not come without a price. "The productivity renaissance theory that underlies the New Economy idea is tough to support," asserts Stephen Roach, chief economist at Morgan Stanley Dean Witter. "When you look at the layoffs, the downsizing, the plant closings, the heightened sense of worker insecurity, the elimination of millions of mid-management positions in the early '90s, it smacks more of unprecedented cost cutting than increased productivity."

There's no reason to believe the cyclical business patterns have gone away. "I think people sometimes confuse sections of the business cycle with a new paradigm," says Herb Allen. "We are in a cycle, probably the tail end of a bull market. To take that piece of the cycle and turn it into a standard for a new society is dangerous." Dan Case, president and CEO of investment bank Hambrecht & Quist, concurs. "We don't believe business cycles have gone away, and we completely disagree with people who say they have."

So where does this notion of the New Economy come from? In some ways it has always been part of America, usually driven by booms or manias such as the building of the transcontinental railroads, the bull market of the 1920s, or the Great Society optimism of the 1960s.

"For the last five years we have been in a new industrial era in this country. We are making progress industrially and economically not even by leaps and bounds, but on a perfectly heroic scale," wrote *Forbes* magazine in June of 1929, four months before America's stock market crashed.

"As a result of what has been happening in the economy during the last decade, we are in a different—if not a new—era, and traditional thinking, the standard approach to the market, is no longer in synchronization with the real world," wrote *Forbes* in October 1968, just before the onset of a six-year decline that sliced 60 percent off stock prices in real terms.

During bull markets, Americans typically expect the market to go up and stay up, perhaps indefinitely; we like to say that the economy is simply adjusting to a new situation, a new world of greatly, even infinitely increasing returns.

In recent years, this Long Boom has been promoted by its believers as part of a new paradigm based on technology. Not surprisingly, one of the main proponents of this view is *Wired* magazine, the main print organ for the techno-pop digerati. From its founding in 1993, *Wired* has trumpeted the "digital revolution," and it's a natural extension for the magazine to embrace the New Economy.

Wired's advocacy of the New Economy hit its peak in July 1997 with the publication of a lengthy cover article titled "The Long Boom." The piece was the collaboration of futurist Peter Schwartz, cofounder and chair of the research and consulting firm Global Business Network, and Peter Leyden, a features editor at *Wired*.

Although the authors maintain that the Long Boom is a scenario—a perfect one in which everything goes right (cancer is cured, world peace prevails, technology significantly reduces everyone's labor)—it reads more like a prediction. In breathless, quasi-religious tones it talks about "the beginnings of a global economic boom on a scale never experienced before" that will "double the world's economy every dozen years." The Boom would include a fully protected natural environment, an ascendant Asia, and a recovered Russia. All this, the authors say, will be largely driven by five waves of technology: personal computers, telecommunications, biotechnology, nanotechnology, and alternative energy.

Venture capitalist John Shoch of Palo Alto–based Alloy Ventures terms the Long Boom particularly as it applies to Silicon Valley "a reality-distortion field," but he also admits that "even though many of us know this is going to end, we can't help going along for the ride."

While the Long Boom is a Pollyannaish view, it's true that much of the growth in the American economy has become increasingly techno-centric. Technology enthusiasts like to point out that in 1998, U.S. technology industries generated revenues of $955 billion, and 37 percent of all new jobs were tech-related. Over the last three years, technology industries contributed one-third of the growth of the gross domestic product.

Stock market performance has also become more heavily weighted toward technology. In the 1990s the Standard & Poor 500 stock index was increasingly dominated by technology and telecommunications stocks, as well as by stocks in areas heavily impacted by technology such as financial services. While stocks such as Gateway and America Online were added to the S&P Index, older stocks such as Pennzoil–Quaker State and Safety-Kleen were dropped. In the first quarter of 1999, four stocks—Microsoft, America Online, Cisco, and MCI Worldcom—accounted for almost 50 percent of the performance of the S&P 500.

Yet these shifts in the American economy and stock market do not necessarily signal a Long Boom, but instead present a scenario full of paradoxes.

The Technology Paradox

Undermining the Long Boom scenario is what economist Stephen Roach calls the Information Technology Paradox. This paradox claims that despite increased spending by American businesses on information technology, overall productivity has not increased as a direct result of the use of technology.

Investment in information technology quadrupled during the 1990s, rising as a share of business spending on equipment to 53 percent from 28 percent. The annual rate of corporate capital spending on computer hardware is more than $220 billion, and this figure does not include expenditures for software, service support, and computer management staff. Meanwhile, about 60 percent of the annual technology budget goes to hardware replacements and upgrades. Overall, corporations spent $1.1 trillion on hardware from 1990 through 1996. Yet, paradoxically, productivity grew by only 0.8 percent per year in the first half of the 1990s, no better than during the previous two decades.

The typical large-enterprise software system that companies buy will often show seven consecutive years of negative return on investment. Yet these very systems promise the most actual improvement in productivity if they can automate corporate transactions and streamline the mundane chores of invoicing, purchasing, and inventory control.

New Economy proponents argue that the digital revolution brought about by information technology is already under way and is comparable to the earlier agricultural and industrial revolutions in America. It's just taken time for businesses to reap the benefits of the technology. Paul David, an economic historian at Stanford University, likens it to the introduction of the electric motor in the 1880s, which did not produce discernible productivity gains until the 1920s.

Roach disagrees. "These earlier revolutions were all about the production of tangible products that you could touch and lift, products which led to very explicit improvements in production and the quality of life," he says. "By contrast, the supposed breakthroughs of the Information Age hinge on a more intangible knowledge-based product. The electrical motor has nothing to do with the knowledge-intensive process of work in a service economy."

New Economy advocates counter by pointing to the productivity increases in recent years as direct evidence of the benefits of information technology. Since 1996 productivity growth has averaged 2 percent, roughly double the pace from 1973 to 1995; it spiked up to over 4 percent in the last quarter of 1998 and in the first quarter of 1999. But this kind of growth is arguably more evolutionary than revolutionary.

Skeptics like Paul Strassman, former chief information officer of Xerox, support Roach in his doubt about the digital revolution. He argues that the recent improvement in productivity is mostly attributable to the lower cost of capital because of low interest rates. "The hero here is not Bill Gates. It's Alan Greenspan," says Strassman.

Meanwhile, the biggest users of information technology—service companies—have become fixed-cost producers rather than variable-cost producers. Their main assets used to be workers and all the associated costs (salaries, benefits, etc.) that could vary due to hiring/firing and changes in wage structures. Now, because of extensive annual investments in information-technology infrastructure, service companies are less flexible and must support the infrastructure even as workers come and go and payrolls increase and decrease.

If information technology were dramatically improving productivity, as the digital revolutionaries claim, it would actually take fewer lawyers, fewer accountants, and fewer financial analysts to spin the wheels of commerce in this new information economy. But the reverse is true; there are more of these service professionals than ever. Unlike factory production, their work cannot be mechanized for greater efficiency.

Side by side with the increase in service professionals is the dislocation experienced by many nonservice workers. Michael Moritz, a venture capitalist with Sequoia Capital, whose firm has worked with many successful high-tech startups, candidly declares, "The New Economy, as it is popularly described, generates a fair number of jobs, but the sheer number of jobs doesn't come close to replacing those lost in older industries. Nor do the people who worked in those older industries have the skills required to succeed in our kind of companies."

The Overworked American

In 1992 Harvard economist Juliet B. Schor published a book titled *The Overworked American*. Although her research and methods were sometimes debated, her best-seller definitely struck an emotional chord with American readers.

Not much has changed since then; Americans still experience a time squeeze, and they know it. The average worker worked 148 more hours in 1996 than his 1973 counterpart, a total of 4 weeks longer. The percentage of people working more than 49 hours per week has risen from 13 percent in 1976 to almost 19 percent in 1998, according to the U.S. Bureau of Labor Statistics. For managers, it went up from 40 percent to 45 percent. And some economists such as Stephen Roach consider the bureau's accounting conservative—that, in fact, the percentage is probably much higher.

Venture capitalist John Doerr says, "We are experiencing extreme time famine. Everybody is short of time. And time is the most precious commodity in our connected, competitive world."

If anything, information technology has contributed to this famine rather than alleviating it. Productivity is not about working longer; it's about getting more out of each unit of work time. In the current information age, people are online in many parts of the information economy 24 hours a day, 7 days a week. That's not increasing productivity; it's extending the workday.

Ironically, the white-collar professionals who most use information technology—laptop computers, cellular phones, fax machines, Internet connections, pagers—also work the longest hours. Some of these professionals end up checking electronic mail at midnight or writing memos on Sunday morning. On average these people put in 50.8 hours per week. As one of them expressed it, "Maybe technology has put us back to an earlier era before vacations and 2-day weekends came into existence." Far from being the paradise of the Long Boom scenario, the New Economy is sometimes a connected world workers can't escape. Venture capitalist Moritz summarizes it best: "I think the only sure thing about technology is that it makes it harder to escape work."

And information technology can sometimes be as inefficient and time-consuming as it is useful. Economist Roach gives this example:

The risk in this wired age is that we've become awash in the sea of information, forever processing increasingly trivial pieces that may or may not add value. We don't know how to filter what's good and what's bad. If you give me the most powerful search engine in the world and if I put a search out on an arcane concept, defining the search as explicitly as possible, I will get 9,228 responses. I can spend the next 5 weeks trying to figure out which ones are relevant. The last 9,000 of them probably have nothing to do with the characteristics or the numbers that I put in. I've tried this all too often.

The Widening Gap

Even as the insiders of Technology's Gilded Age—a small group of venture capitalists, entrepreneurs, and executives—grow fabulously rich from the latest stock market and corporate bonanza, the gap between the haves and the have-nots only widens. Increasingly, more people find themselves on the poor side of this widening chasm between prosperity and the lack thereof. Fifteen years of stagnant real wages have helped widen inequalities.

An article in the summer 1998 issue of *Foreign Policy* reported that the income of the poorest 20 percent of U.S. households has declined steadily since the early 1970s, while the income of the richest quintile has increased by 15 percent, and the income of the top 1 percent, by more than 100 percent!

The irony is that such inequality grows at a time when the triumph of democracy and open markets was supposed to usher in a new age of freedom and opportunity. Instead, asserts *Foreign Policy,* "an integrated global market has created a new divide between well-educated elite workers and their vulnerable unskilled counterparts that gives capital an apparent whip hand over labor, and pushes governments to unravel social safety nets."

Another study, "The State of Working America," published in 1998 by the Economic Policy Institute, concluded the following:

• Median family income was $1,000 less in 1996 than in 1989.

- The typical married-couple family worked 247 more hours per year in 1996 than in 1989. That was more than six weeks' worth of work just to stay even.

- The inflation-adjusted earnings of the median worker in 1997 were more than 3 percent lower than in 1989. Real hourly wages either stagnated or fell for most of the bottom 60 percent of the working population during that period.

A study titled "Shifting Fortunes: The Perils of the Growing American Wealth Gap," published in 1999, takes the trend back even further, showing that hourly wages for average workers in 1998 were 6.2 percent below those of 1973 when adjusted for inflation. This income gap is yet another paradox of the Information Age.

The typical American family is probably worse off near the end of the 1990s than it was at the end of the 1980s or the end of the 1970s. And, to the extent that the typical American family has held its ground, the most important factor has been the large increase in the hours worked by family members.

Meanwhile, the increase in the stock market between 1989 and 1997 went to the richest 10 percent of households. Jared Bernstein, one of the study's authors, opined, "The Federal Reserve has been imbalanced. It has been overly concerned about inflation and the erosion of the assets of the wealthy."

The economy has turned harshly against unskilled workers, leaving many of their families adrift. Some estimates say that one-fifth of America's children live in poverty. The *American Journal of Public Health* reported in 1998 that 10 million Americans—4 million of them children—do not have enough to eat. Meanwhile, the unskilled can no longer simply migrate from agricultural areas to manufacturing centers in big cities to seek their fortune like they did 50 years ago.

These studies show that far from being a New Economy that makes the middle class rich and the working class more comfortable, this bull market, with its overvalued stocks, has led to a new inequality from which the knowledgeable insider definitely benefits the most.

Further widening of the gap can be attributed to restrictions on the immigration of highly educated engineers and executives. Paul Romer, professor of economics at Stanford Graduate School of Business, notes that a key indicator countries should start paying more attention to is their balance of trade in skilled professionals. "Successful countries will retain their college-educated citizens, and actually attract professionally trained talent from other countries," he says. Only by maintaining this ample supply of college-educated professionals, says Romer, can countries remain competitive and prevent wage inequality. Certainly almost every Silicon Valley company has felt the squeeze in the market for engineering and executive talent, which has led to unprecedented inflation in professional-level salaries.

Michigan Republican senator Spence Abraham made an effort to help ease high-tech labor shortages by sponsoring a bill to temporarily raise the current annual visa quota. The bill passed the Senate by a whopping margin (78 to 20) in 1998, in spite of veto threats from the White House. After further negotiations and threats, the Congress passed and President Clinton signed a bill expanding the number of additional H1B visas that the INS could issue to 142,500 more over three years. "People anticipated that this increase would be enough to ensure that we did not hit the cap on the total number of these visas in this fiscal year. In fact, we hit it very quickly," says Romer.

Recession 2000?

All the promotion of a New Economy, new rules, and a new paradigm unfortunately helps feed what Alan Greenspan terms "irrational exuberance" toward the stock market. This new-age talk gets especially troublesome when it's used to prop up concept companies that take investors' money with no clear road to revenues. But what if a recession hits? What happens to companies not built on sound, fundamental long-term business models? Once the longest bull market in American history recedes, this issue will become critical.

Edward Yardeni, chief economist at Deutsche Bank Securities, believes there is a 70 percent chance of recession in the year 2000. He forecasts that this recession could last anywhere from six months to two years and be as deep as the global recession of 1973–1974. At the pace of investment of the 1990s bull market, investors would end up losing at least $1 trillion when stock prices dropped.

Yardeni is not by nature a pessimist. Unlike Stephen Roach, he believes information technology will have tangible long-term productivity benefits. He even goes so far as to describe himself as a "New Era economist" (although not a Golden Era or New Paradigm economist).

But Yardeni has serious concerns about a different technology paradox, namely the Y2K bug and its impact on "mission critical" computer systems in government and big businesses. Those not currently programmed to acknowledge dates that go past the year 1999 could go haywire on January 1, 2000. The paradox is that society's increasing reliance on information technology means that any serious disruption of these systems could plunge the economy into recession and the stock market into the tank.

"We've seen technology disruptions create problems for satellites or for computer systems at Union Pacific or Oxford Health, but the year 2000 will hit numerous computers simultaneously," Yardeni warns. "There will be a lot of companies, some of them quite large, that may actually go out of business."

Estimates for fixing the bug range from as high as $600 billion, according to The Gartner Group, to as low as $52 billion, according to BZW investment bank; the likely cost, according to Yardeni, is somewhere in the $200 billion to $400 billion range. Chase Manhattan Bank expects to spend $200 million to $250 million to fix the bug, and Merrill Lynch expects to spend another $200 million.

"No matter what the exact cost," says Yardeni, "it will consume a tremendous amount of time and capital just to maintain the status quo of information processing."

Not everyone agrees with Yardeni's pessimistic scenario. A January 1999 report issued by Morgan Stanley Dean Witter, based on the review of the SEC disclosure forms of 377 S&P 500 companies, estimated that Y2K repairs for these companies represented only 0.7 percent of their revenue in the period from October 1997 to October 1998.

The U.S. government's situation, though, is a different matter. The government estimates it will cost $6.8 billion to fix the Y2K bug in the legacy computer systems of federal agencies. At least 20 percent of these agencies were significantly behind in the first quarter of 1999, and 3 out of 24 of its largest agencies had made inadequate progress.

Even if the millennium bug doesn't stifle the boom, Yardeni believes problems with the economies of other countries might. "Asia, for example, is one-third of the world's economy. And the economic stalemate there has got to matter to the technology industry," says Yardeni. "It's clearly a global industry, and Asia is where our growth is supposed to be. Asia has been lacking as a tremendous source of Bubble prosperity."

Central to the Asian situation has been the fate of Japan. In 1990 its Nikkei stock index stood at 39,000 and its property index at 20,600. Japanese companies were on top of the world, and some American companies even called for protectionist measures against Japanese imported goods and technology. However, Japan's economic miracle was based on a vast asset bubble, further inflated by leveraged speculation by banks and corporations, as well as by low interest rates, an appreciating currency, and lax accounting rules. When the bubble finally popped in January of 1990, it set off a chain reaction that led to a recession in which the country is still mired. The economist Paul Ormerod calls it "the second most serious recession in capitalist history after the 1929 Crash." In the first quarter of 1999, the gross domestic product finally rose for the first time since 1997, gaining 1.9 percent from the last quarter of 1998, and the Nikkei index went up more than 480 points to over 17,000. But this was largely the result of a massive $800 billion short-term spending program by the Japanese government designed to goad the economy into action. Most economists both inside and outside Japan do not expect the GDP to continue growing at the same rate, particularly since the government-spending campaign was expected to come to a halt at the end of 1999. Economists forecast that the year 2000 will be another tough one for Japan.

Stephen Roach agrees that Asia should be a concern: "In many respects, we've turned the world economy inside out. Asia used to be the leader and now it's the laggard. It's roughly a third of the global economy, and that engine of growth has been notably absent."

Part of this concern for a weak Asian economy that depresses American exports is that if American consumer spending were to cool off, there would be no cushion for the American economy. American companies could not export to Asia what they could not sell to American consumers. Some economists have called this the Jekyll-and-Hyde economy: tremendous weakness on the international side and tremendous strength on the domestic side, with little room for error. There's definitely been a "wealth effect" from the stock market boom—as the market has gone up and more Americans have invested in it, they have felt better about spending. Yet if the market seriously slows or declines, much of the associated consumer spending could decrease and seriously affect the economy.

This prospect has caused the normally conservative economist Paul Krugman of MIT to feel concern that the American economy might even fall into the same "liquidity trap" that the Japanese economy has since the explosion of its bubble. The liquidity trap, as defined in the 1930s by British economist John Maynard Keynes, is the situation in which the demand for goods and services consistently falls short of a nation's capacity to produce them, despite short-term interest rates as low as zero. Krugman normally does not ascribe to Keynesian views, but after visiting Japan and studying the aftermath of its burst bubble, he became convinced that the liquidity trap was real. He discusses his views in greater detail in his latest book for general audiences titled *The Return of Depression Economics* and in a technical paper for economists titled "It's Baaack: Japan's Slump and the Return of the Liquidity Trap."

In Japan Krugman observed that even though the central bank had reduced interest rates to virtually zero since 1995 from 7 percent in the early 1990s, consumers have still held back from borrowing or spending. Businesses have behaved in the same way, keeping them from contributing to economic growth. Krugman believes that a big drop in stock market prices could have a similar impact on Americans. "How much spending would Americans do if the Dow Jones industrial average got up above 13,000 then dropped to 7,000?" Krugman asked in the *New York Times*. "Certainly a lot less." The ripple effect from reduced consumer spending is that companies are forced to cut production and do layoffs, thus opening the way for a recession.

The New Growth View

Even if there is a significant increase in white-collar productivity buried under the apparent technology paradox, and even if the millennium bug doesn't turn out to be as costly as some fear or a liquidity trap doesn't develop, enough problems still exist to undermine the Long Boom scenario of accelerated economic growth. But this doesn't mean being an outright economic pessimist, especially with the view that new growth is possible.

One of the main proponents of this view is Stanford University economist Paul Romer. Some of the New Economy enthusiasts have attempted to identify him with the Long Boom position, but he eschews it. "I don't agree with the unqualified Long Boom assertion that the rate of technological change in America is permanently faster than it has been historically, or that the underlying rate of growth of the economy has increased in the 1990s," Romer says.

He points out that the Long Boomers look at indicators such as asset prices, inflation, and unemployment more than they look at productivity growth or the rate of growth per worker. He also asserts that the data doesn't support the idea that technology has automatically increased worker productivity.

Romer does believe the American economy is driven by complexity, that the physical, social, and technological systems created are much more complicated than those we've had in the past. And there's a corresponding demand for the education and skills necessary to cope with these higher levels of complexity. Thus, the widening income gap between haves and have-nots is in part attributable to the difference between them in their level of education and skill sets.

But the new complexity should not be identified with any particular technology, like the internal combustion engine, electricity, digital electronics, or the Internet. These developments are just manifestations of complexity.

Over the last 125 years in America, complexity and steady growth have gone hand in hand, as our society has learned to generate more and more value from relatively consistent amounts of physical raw material. Productivity is not necessarily in a holding pattern it can't break out of, but it's also not in the hyper-growth mode that the Long Boomers and New Economy advocates would like to believe. "I keep saying that if we make fundamental institutional innovations, we could grow faster. But the Long Boomers keep hearing that we are already growing faster," says Romer.

New Growth theory does examine the dynamics of wealth creation and the role of scientific discovery, technological change, and innovation as important factors contributing to productivity growth. Economic growth occurs whenever people discover new ways to take existing resources and make them more useful. Romer likens this process to cooking. "We develop recipes to rearrange raw materials to make them more valuable," he says. "People did that in the Bronze Age when they mixed copper and tin, and later when they learned to use interchangeable parts as well as refine iron ore and petroleum. Cooking is what Intel does when it takes silicon and makes it into a chip. That process has always been with us—it's a continuum."

The difference today is that more people-hours now go into producing the recipes than into the cooking. We are steadily shifting more resources into coming up with better recipes, and the recipes now drive economic growth and improve standards of living.

New Growth identifies three special features that spur growth: first, a physical world with vastly unexplored possibilities; second, cooperation and trade among large numbers of people; third, market incentives for people to make discoveries and share information.

Nevertheless, in Technology's Gilded Age, there's a tendency to overestimate the refined, high-end part of technological change and to underestimate the grassroots benefits. Romer believes Wal-Mart is a better example of innovation than even the transistor because the discount retailer's management of inventory data represents a major technological change in the process of getting goods from the factory to the consumer. Its system allows it to chart sales precisely and keep shelves efficiently stocked at its 3,600 outlets worldwide. By gaining finely honed knowledge of inventory, distribution, and its customer base, Wal-Mart can operate its supply chain in a way that is 15 to 20 percent cheaper than before. And when a whole class of goods can be provided much more cheaply, it significantly improves the standard of living for people in the United States. This exemplifies the broad improvements in recipes that keep the whole economy going.

In terms of standards of living or output per person, the last century and a quarter shows a pretty surprisingly steady rate of growth—a ninefold increase in income per capita (see chart below). There are some peaks and dips—a big drop in the 1930s and a surge during World War II, for example. But in the larger view, those are just wiggles on the line graph, although the dips seemed like the end of the world at the time. In the long run, it matters more how fast the trend increases than whether the economy is in a bit of a downturn at the beginning of a wiggle or in an upturn coming out of a wiggle.

U.S. GDP Per Capita

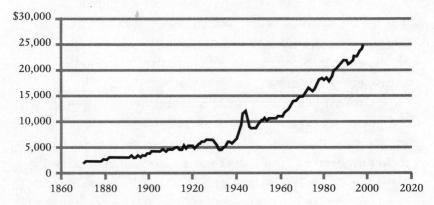

"These people who make exaggerated claims for the New Economy or the Long Boom have mistaken a positive upturn in one of those wiggles for a sign that trends have completely changed," says Romer. "If anything, in terms of growth rates, it's actually been a little bit low. I'm looking at this trend and saying: 'No sign that we've done anything better than in the last 100 years; it's just business as usual.'"

So there's actually nothing extraordinary about the most recent economic expansion of the 1990s, including the recent improvements in productivity since 1996. To Romer it looks like another case of an overreaction to temporary events. "In the 1980s high inflation and a recession convinced many people that the U.S. economy had completely lost its capacity for generating growth," he says. "In the 1990s low inflation and a recovery from a recession have convinced many of these same people that the U.S. economy is generating growth in new and unprecedented ways."

He argues that the underlying trend rate of growth for the entire economy does not change from decade to decade. Superimposed on top of this steady growth in income and productivity are the temporary wiggles that economists refer to as recessions and recoveries. The slow growth of a recession and the fast growth of a recovery always converge back toward the underlying trend rate of growth. "Because asset returns and output move together, the economy can go through periods where asset returns are unusually low or unusually high, but they typically return to historical averages." If people value companies on the assumption that the slow growth of a recession will last forever, they are in for a pleasant surprise. If they value them on the assumption that the fast growth of a recovery will last forever, they are in for a shock.

Economic history shows that people make mistakes and are caught by surprise. In extreme cases these mistakes take the form of a bubble. Naturally, anything that takes a lot of air out of these bubbles poses a serious threat to the viability of concept companies not grounded on solid business fundamentals. It will take a sound investment strategy to survive the coming Darwinian shakeout when this Bubble deflates—or bursts.

Doonesbury

CULT IPOS, SCAMS, AND OTHER HAZARDS OF INTERNET INVESTING

These valuations are breathtaking. I don't recommend Internet stocks to people who don't like massive risk. People are jumping into the market like it's a gold rush.

—Bill Gates, chairman, Microsoft Corporation

In a bubble market, greed and the herd mentality can take over, and with them comes the tendency to gamble heavily, fall prey to scams, and get burned by IPO stocks. This has never been more true than in Technology's Gilded Age, which seems to promise quick wealth for so many, and it's easy to underestimate just how much risk is involved.

This chapter will provide some perspective on investing in technology stocks in the midst of this massive risk, which we call the Internet Bubble. We'll cover several investment caveats, including the pitfalls of momentum investing, the dangers of overconfidence in approaching the stock market, the growing incidence of Internet investment scams, and the pitfalls of investing in IPOs. The bottom line is that playing the Internet investment game is not as easy as it looks. Read on and find out what to watch out for.

The Dangers of Momentum Investing

Hot bull markets are full of momentum investing, another way of saying buy high and sell higher. Ultimately, momentum investors are looking for the greater fool who will pay more for the stocks than they did. It's a form of gambling—as in a game of musical chairs, the greater fool is left standing when the music stops.

"The danger is if you're the last guy in the game and you turn out to be the greater fool," says Bruce Lupatkin, former head of research at Hambrecht & Quist and a longtime technology analyst. "I say, don't try to play the greater fool game; there's an enormous amount of risk." He adds, "It's always buyer beware. Who out there says that 30 percent, 40 percent, 50 percent returns are guaranteed without risk? Nobody can say that. There's no free lunch; there never has been."

This kind of gambling makes investors particularly susceptible to torpedo stocks—the overpriced speculative issues whose prospects have been heavily hyped but are primed for a disastrous plunge that could ruin any portfolio. It's even worse when investors speculate on margin, investing with borrowed money.

Investors and day traders sometimes set each other up for this fall through their discussions and tip swapping on online investor message boards and chat rooms such as AOL's Motley Fool and Silicon Investor. The latter averages about 12,000 message postings a day from visitors. And the audience will only get bigger, since the five to seven million online trading accounts active for E*Trade, Schwab, and the rest are supposed to grow to 14 million by the year 2001.

Where online investors were once caught up in supposedly hot stock issues such as Boston Chicken, The Discovery Zone, or mini-disk drive maker Iomega, now it's any number of Internet stocks. People who don't understand the Internet, who don't know fundamentally what it is, give each other investment advice.

Old-line money managers are skeptical. Barton Biggs, chairman of Morgan Stanley Asset Management, told the *New York Times* in May 1999, "Individual investors should not be deluded by advertisements that suggest that any amateur can make money in the stock market. We are perpetuating a gambling mentality similar to the 1920s. 15,000 new Internet trading accounts open every week. That is frightening."

The Perils of Overconfidence

It's not unusual for aggressive investors to have little knowledge of what they invest in, concludes a study done at the Johnson Graduate

School of Management at Cornell University. Investors given one bit of financial data about a company—the expected rate of growth for return on equity—felt just as confident in their investing as those investors who had also been given the book value and current return on equity of a company. The danger, the study stated, is that people vastly overestimate the value of what little information they have and will more likely blunder by buying stocks at high prices and then having to sell out when the stocks drop.

Such ignorant yet aggressive investing helps drive up fashionable stocks to grossly overvalued levels. Robert Bloomfield, the director of the Cornell study, states, "People are not good at figuring out how good the information is. The information keeps getting louder, but it's not more reliable."

And while self-confidence and optimism can be strong personal qualities when dealing with people, they don't necessarily help in the stock market, where investors deal with prices, not people. Overconfident investors tend to trade too much and bet too heavily on particular stocks or market sectors. Not surprisingly, trading volume tends to be higher in eras of high returns—and overconfident investors think a fatter portfolio means they are smarter.

Investors currently turn over their portfolios at a rate of more than 60 percent per year. More than half of this trading is unjustified—it's just noise, not resulting in any gain for the investor and opening the way for more losses. In fact, according to a study done at the University of California at Davis, the more investors trade, the worse they do. Investors err in fairly consistent ways: (1) They react too much to short-term performance; (2) they overestimate their chances of success with long-shot investments like IPOs and risky tech stocks; (3) they think they see patterns in stock market returns where there are none; and (4) they sell winners too quickly and hold on to losers too long.

"The more you trade, the more poor decisions you potentially make," says Terrance Odean, one of the authors of the UC Davis study. "And then you pay for that privilege through trading costs." This trend is aggravated by the tendency of new online traders to trade twice as much as they did before they went online. Buying and selling in an instant, they trade too quickly and too often without understanding the risks involved.

NFO Worldwide, a research firm based in Greenwich, Connecticut, that regularly surveys online investors and other Internet users, discovered that by April 1999, the number of online investors had nearly tripled over the previous 16 months, to 6.3 million. In the last six months of the period, the frequency of online trading had increased, with more than half of online traders making 5 or more trades, and some more than 20 trades. Not surprisingly, these online investors favored individual stocks, which made up 47 percent of their portfolios, compared to mutual funds, which made up 43 percent. Also no surprise was that 44 percent of online traders had invested in Internet stocks, compared with 15 percent of investors overall.

The common thread that emerged from the survey was that the Internet had spurred investors to take greater risks. "With online trading, the easy access to the market drives people to trade more, pumps up their confidence level, and raises their risk tolerance," said Lee Smith, a vice president in NFO's Internet research division. "They hold stocks for a shorter period of time."

The longer investors had been online, the more often they traded and the more they kept their investment holdings in online accounts. Those who had been online more than two years had on average about 50 percent of their stock accounts online and averaged more than seven trades in the most recent six-month period. Of Web investors who had been online for more than a year, 30 percent were classified as heavy traders—they had done 10 or more trades in the most recent six-month period.

Many said they traded more often because they used the Internet—often at their jobs—to watch prices throughout the day. "I trade more often because it is easier and can be done 24 hours a day," wrote one NFO survey respondent.

According to Media Metrix, a firm that meters Internet use, 22.8 million Americans used Web sites on company time in March 1999. Some 8.2 million people visited Yahoo Finance, CBS Marketwatch,

Schwab, E*Trade, and other financial sites at work, putting on-the-job trading activity ahead of sports, personal email, chat rooms, and pornography.

The frequency of stock trading has definitely impacted the market as a whole. "In the market's run from 3,000 to 8,000, a lot of the upward movement occurred because people were invested in mutual funds and were not apt to sell very quickly," Charles Geisst, a finance professor at Manhattan College and author of *Wall Street: A History*, told the *New York Times*. "It's no coincidence that in the last year and a half, as Internet trading has become more common, the market has become more volatile."

The long-term benefits of the increased confidence and risk-taking of online investors remain to be seen. "I'm making faster choices," said another NFO survey respondent. "But I'm still not sure if they are better choices."

Internet Scams

"In a boom, fortunes are made, individuals wax greedy, and swindlers come forward to exploit that greed. The sheep to be shorn abound," writes MIT economist Charles Kindleberger in his classic book *Manias, Panics, and Crashes*.

Some scamsters have used the Internet in the same way that con artists have used newspaper ads, the telephone, and other communication media to pitch their schemes. The old cold-calling method done from boiler rooms has given way to e-mail messages and Web sites that can reach millions of potential investors cheaply and instantly. The business of fraud has simply become more efficient. On the Internet it is much easier to get the word out about bogus get-rich-quick opportunities, hot stock "tips," and investments too good to be true.

One of the first online scams was Pleasure Time Inc., which in 1995 ran online advertisements promising investors that by paying $189 per share in a phantom company, they could enjoy a minimum profit of $60 a week. They were promised additional profits in return for signing up other investors. More than 20,000 investors got mixed up in this high-tech Ponzi scheme, putting a total of at least $3 million into it.

Other scamsters have engaged in the classic "pump and dump" scheme—they use online investor forums to pump up a stock by spreading positive but false information about a company, and then after fooled investors drive up the price of the stock, the scamsters and company insiders dump the inflated shares. Some have even gone so far as to create fake online magazines to promote these phony stocks. One middle manager for a telecommunications company, posing as someone else, actually created a fake news article about the takeover of the company and posted it on the Internet. The article caused the stock to spike up more than 30 percent before the announcement was exposed as a fraud.

Some online publications have been paid fees to publicize Internet companies but do not reveal that fact to investors, or the disclaimer is so far away from the stock tips that it's easy to miss. One publication, *Internet Stock Review,* published by a public relations firm, offered a list of "20 companies to watch in 1999" that included well-known names such as Borders Group and Federal Express, but also obscure companies such as Allnetservices and Dynamic Media.com, which paid the publication to promote them. The publication does publish a disclaimer on its Web site, but it is not located with the list, so even though the publication has done nothing illegal, the list could confuse investors.

Some scamsters have made a hobby out of fraudulent Internet IPOs. *Fortune* magazine reported one case of a phony high-tech start-up called Interactive Products and Services, which claimed it had revolutionary Internet devices it dubbed NetCaller and PC Remote. The company also claimed it had a partnership with Microsoft. None of these claims was true, but the phony company lured nearly 100,000 potential investors to its Web site by running at popular investor sites an online ad that read: "The next Microsoft is offering its stock to the public . . . over the Internet! . . . click here for more information."

Once at the Web site, visitors could read instructions on how to invest. Nearly 3,000 investors worldwide sent e-mail to the scamster, Matthew Bowin, and 150 people actually sent in checks. One investor from Hong Kong wired $10,000. In three months Bowin had collected $190,000 and got his ad displayed free by promising to pay for it after his IPO. He also set up the Web site so that when investors queried a search engine with the words "Internet stocks," his Web page would come up on its list of choices. Fortunately, Bowin was caught, convicted of fraud, and received a 10-year prison term.

Given these examples and the millions of investors scanning the Internet for stock tips, it's no surprise that the SEC receives about 300 complaints a day concerning online scams, up from only 15 per day in 1996.

IPOs and Retail Cult Stocks

A big part of the Internet mania has been the purchase of hot initial public offerings by retail buyers; however, IPOs are generally not good investments for noninsiders. "The long-term performance of IPOs is bad," says Harvard business professor Bill Sahlman. "This has always been the case. The public always ends up holding the bag." Roger McNamee of Integral Capital Partners agrees: "High attrition rates are natural; it's the Darwinian process. If ever there was a caveat emptor of business, it's the IPO market." Steve Forbes, editor in chief of *Forbes* magazine, chimes in, "It's normal—most new businesses do not make it past their fifth year. The mortality rate is very high. So it's not a great surprise that the vast majority of IPOs would end in disappointment."

The typical IPO outperforms during the first six months but underperforms after that. Mary Meeker, an Internet analyst with Morgan Stanley, cautions that there are only three really big winners, on average, among each year's technology IPOs.

Data from technology-investment bank Broadview International shows that from 1992 through 1998, 826 high-technology companies went public, yet 50 percent traded below their IPO values by the end of 1998. And this assumes investors bought the IPOs at the initial offering price, something individuals rarely do. If the performance of these stocks is measured from the share price after the first day of trading, when most individuals can buy such stocks, then 70 to 80 percent of IPOs were underwater. For the median-performing company, the rate of return continues to decline in each year following the IPO.

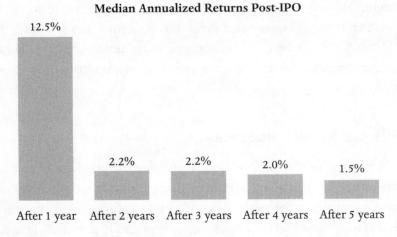

Post-IPO Value Creation?
Median Annualized Returns Post-IPO

Paradoxically, this weak IPO performance has come during a bull market. In fact, the safest time to buy high-technology IPOs is during years when fewer technology companies tap the equity market for capital. In other words, when the market is bearish on tech stocks, only the highest-quality stocks go public; these stocks are generally not as susceptible to momentum buying and therefore to extreme price volatility during these periods.

But no matter what the environment—good, bad, or indifferent—IPOs are a bad place for investors to focus their energy. "The real money in tech investing comes from correctly identifying the long-term winners, something much easier to do over the course of time than at the time of an IPO," says Integral's McNamee.

Nevertheless, during frothy bull markets, overvalued IPOs can evolve into what one investor calls "retail cult stocks." These are the go-go stocks, often with a small float, that get lots of publicity and experience heavy trading volume inside the Bubble. Unfortunately, if only 10 percent of Internet companies have any real long-term future but at least 25 percent of the stocks are hot at any time, there will still be a big failure rate among the 25 percent.

"High mortality rates are typical when you have missionary market building," says Harvard's Bill Sahlman. This is part of the Darwinian scenario: 90 percent of the companies in a new market get shaken out for the sake of the 10 percent that survive and allow the new industry to thrive.

In the midst of the Internet market froth, some investors are so eager to get in on hyped-up IPOs that they make the mistake of putting in market orders for these stocks at whatever price the market dictates. In most cases these investors' buy orders get stacked up on the first day of trading, and when they are finally executed, it is generally at a price far above the initial issue price.

Investors operating online also often mistakenly think that the ability to trade almost instantaneously through their personal computers puts them on equal footing with veteran Wall Street traders. Actually, the stock price these users see on their screens may bear no resemblance to the actual real-time price at the stock exchange, especially when the stock is volatile or during periods of heavy trading volume.

Several investors had this happen with the IPO for Theglobe.com. The issue price was $9 per share, but by midday it had risen to $90 per share. A number of first-time buyers got locked into this price, only to see the price slip to $63.50 per share by the end of the day. Two months after the IPO, the price was $37 per share. Some investors lost thousands of dollars on buy orders as low as 500 shares. One investor even racked up a bill of $200,000 for a buy order of 2,500 shares.

"Everybody has to remember that markets typically change direction when it's most inconvenient for the largest number of people," says Integral's McNamee. "In bubble markets, the most dangerous words for these overvalued stocks are, 'Look, I'm a long-term investor,' because if something structural changes in the market and stock prices drop, the amount of time it's going to take for a Yahoo or an At Home to get back to its peak valuation could be years or even a decade."

McNamee continues, "I hear people say, 'The bull market has got to keep going because I haven't made my fortune yet.' But fortunes are usually built over time. People need to be aware that this is a time to take a little less risk."

An overvalued company might be a great company but not a great investment until the industry settles in and the valuations are based on business fundamentals. When you corner analysts covering a company like Yahoo and ask them what they really think, they'll admit that the valuation is not justified, but they do believe Yahoo is potentially a leader in its space—a very large space—and that's why they follow the company.

"If you look at the PC wave, the last time we saw a bubble like this, retail investors were largely absent," observes Frank Quattrone, managing director and head of the technology group at investment bank CS First Boston. "Retail investors have become more interested in the Internet because everybody thinks this is the next television or the next radio. And some investors feel in their heart of hearts that one or two or three of these companies will end up being the next Microsoft or Intel or Cisco. But nobody knows for sure who those companies are."

It was much the same situation when the first radio companies came along. In the first two decades of the twentieth century, investors who had missed out on the telephone felt they could still invest in radio, confident that, as an investment ad for a radio company pointed out, "all great discoveries which have brought civilized communities into close touch have made millions for those who attained an interest in them in the early stages of development." So investors bought anything involving radio. New radio companies offered what became the retail cult stocks of their day.

The radio industry's revenues jumped from $60 million in 1922 to $850 million in 1929—a 1,400 percent increase. At the same time, the value of a share of stock of Radio Corporation of America (RCA) increased from $5 per share to $500 per share. Nearly a third of American homes had radios in them, and the car radio had come along as well.

As with the wreckage of the PC boom, the majority of the hot radio manufacturers of the 1920s failed and are now forgotten. RCA was one of the few that actually turned a profit and survived, even as it branched into phonograph records and movies. Even so, investors who bought RCA stock in the summer of 1929 lost almost all their investment in the stock market crash. It was three decades before RCA got back to its pre-Crash high in the midst of a new mania over television. The more things change, the more they remain the same.

Trading Over the Internet

Another danger Internet investors need to watch out for is the fragmented nature of the electronics communications networks, or ECNs, they often work through when they do their online trading. There's not only the problem of getting the best stock prices through the ECNs but also the more perilous question of what might happen if there's a full-fledged market dive. The fragmented marketplace of the ECNs makes it harder to sell fast, especially at a good price.

An additional technical threat is the possibility of system crashes. E*Trade, Charles Schwab, and other online trading services have all experienced some serious outages that have put electronic traders off-line for hours at a time. And there is no way to know if an online broker is equipped for a market crash, such as an abrupt fall of 20 percent or more, until it happens. It's probable that some brokers couldn't even handle a correction of 10 percent. Some critics believe that the brokerages will move at a "glacial pace" to get back online when this happens. The explosive growth in the number of online accounts has already contributed to serious technological glitches, and the brokerages keep pouring money into ads to capture new online clients and further strain the capacity of their online trading networks.

Charles Geisst, author of *Wall Street: A History*, sees a potential analogy between today's online trading networks and the main technology in vogue in 1929. "The telephone is a big, unmentioned reason for the Crash. People figured that if they got to a phone, they could bail out in time. But the sell orders overtook the market," says

Geisst. As then, so today, momentum buyers might suddenly find themselves with no quick way out. "It will be a painful lesson, and relatively innocent people will get sucked up in it," says CS First Boston Internet analyst Lise Buyer. "But you're investing real money, so caveat emptor. Greed ultimately leads to unhappiness."

Doonesbury

INVESTING IN AN OVERHEATED MARKET ENVIRONMENT

There is no reason to believe that we need to throw out the fundamentals. Rather, we need to do a better job of applying the fundamentals more than anything else.

—James Collins, coauthor, *Built to Last*

Despite the pitfalls of public high-tech investing, many experts remain bullish on its prospects for the future. "The United States does two things better than the rest of the world—grow food and make technology products," says technology banker Sandy Robertson. "Our economy has transformed itself magnificently from a manufacturing economy to an information-technology-based economy. And with this transition comes a lot of new investment opportunities."

It's no accident that this boom has occurred in America. Americans are an optimistic people who are open to the new, especially in technology; we are fascinated by process, by the way things work. We get excited about physical improvement, scientific progress, and technological change. We built railroads, invented the telegraph, landed on the moon, and came up with the microchip. Obviously, our enthusiasm for all things technological has opened the way to tremendous economic growth, and for some, tremendous wealth.

And the markets for technology have only grown. Twenty-five years ago, the largest buyer of technology was the government. Fifteen years ago, business became the biggest buyer. Eventually, consumers will pull ahead of both of them, even as the government and businesses continue to buy. The end markets will just keep getting bigger. Today, high technology accounts for about 25 to 30 percent of the growth in the American economy, the way the auto industry drove growth in the 1920s.

But experience matters when it comes to investing in technology. A lot of technologies and trends come and go; there are cycles, ups and downs, bull markets, bear markets, bubbles and recessions, loose capital, tight capital, and all kinds of changing conditions—some of them unexpected and certainly not always predictable. Two firms that have posted some of the best results from navigating the high seas of technology investing are venture capital firm Sequoia Capital and Integral Capital Partners, which invests in both private and public companies. We thought these two firms' approaches to investing were so thoughtful and intelligent that we would share them with our readers. We'll also get some perspective from Jim Collins, a leading business analyst and coauthor of the best-selling *Built to Last: Successful Habits of Visionary Companies*. Finally, we'll wrap up with some basic advice on how to ride out the mania storm and come out ahead long term.

Sequoia Capital

Founded in 1972 and led by the venerable curmudgeon Don Valentine, Sequoia Capital is one of the premier venture capital firms. It has invested in over 350 companies, of which 100 have gone public and numerous others have been sold successfully. Sequoia's investments include Cisco Systems, Yahoo, Apple Computer, Oracle, Electronic Arts, Cypress Semiconductor, 3Com, and Arbor Software. It has raised more than $1.3 billion and provided the original financing for companies together worth more than $300 billion.

Don Valentine, known as one of the toughest and smartest technology venture capitalists in Silicon Valley, is a cool and rational thinker when it comes to analyzing companies and different industry situations. His rules for venture investments include: (1) find "monster" markets that can really get big, (2) find good technology and technologists who can stay ahead of competitive threats, (3) find outstanding leaders and management teams that can drive these technologies forward into the monster markets, and (4) invest in and build companies, not just products.

Sequoia is also known for the financial discipline it brings to its companies. Sequoia considers frugality a virtue in its companies, which are encouraged to "bootstrap" themselves so they can learn how to effectively manage their capital resources for the long term. Preferring to start companies with less money than other venture capitalists invest, Sequoia expects those companies to become profitable quickly. "We like to get companies off the ground with a small amount of fuel," says general partner Michael Moritz, Sequoia's lead investor in Yahoo. "We like to start wicked infernos with a single match rather than with two million gallons of kerosene."

As Sequoia's Internet guy, Moritz is more involved in the firm's sexiest investments these days than even Don Valentine. Yet Moritz doesn't have the typical tech VC background—engineering degree, requisite stint at Hewlett-Packard, Intel, or some other high-tech blue-chip company. Instead, Moritz came to venture capital by way of the unusual route of journalism. A business correspondent for *Time* magazine before joining Sequoia in 1986, he also wrote two books—one about Chrysler, and closer to home, one titled *The Little Kingdom: The Private Story of Apple Computer*. Sequoia was willing to bet on Moritz as someone a little different from the stereotype and mentor him in the ways of the venture capital business.

"People have come into the venture business with blue-chip, gold-plated, platinum-tipped résumés who have flamed out," says Moritz. "It's like Woody Allen says—the secret to life is showing up every day. In the venture business it's showing up, working pretty darn hard, not getting arrogant or complacent, and realizing that you're only as good as your next investment, not your last one."

Moritz has learned that it's better for a venture capitalist to become part of the Internet mania than to ignore it. For insiders, Barton Biggs of Morgan Stanley says about the mania: "The fools are dancing, but the greater fools are still watching." Moritz agrees. "The biggest expense is not to be an investor in the Internet," he says. "It's costly for a venture firm to sit out the Internet, just as it would have been costly to sit out the PC business or the semiconductor business. There are some venture firms that have not participated in the Internet, and they have lost their positions in the venture industry."

In spite of the mania, Sequoia does its best to hold the stocks of its companies after they go public rather than flip them into the market. "We offer the Sequoia Capital Franchise Fund, not the 'flipper's fund,'" muses Moritz. "We've made a lot of long-term investors wealthy. That's our premise: By being patient, by holding stakes in our companies for a long time, you can generate wonderful returns if you pick the companies right."

In 1999, Sequoia expanded its investment approach by adding a $350 million "late-stage" fund that allows the firm to put more money into its startups as they grow. Such a fund would have made the later-stage investment of $100 million by Softbank in Yahoo in early 1996 unnecessary. At the time, Moritz and Yahoo cofounders Jerry Yang and David Filo were compelled to sell $30 million worth of their private stock holdings to Softbank. "There is no reason for us to take all the risk, do all the work, and then allow others to make a lot of money and do no work," says Mortiz.

One of Sequoia's first "late-stage" investments was to put additional money into Scient, an Internet consulting-services business, at a $400 million valuation just before the company's IPO in the second quarter of 1999. The valuation seems crazy, but Moritz points out that "Yahoo also looked like a ridiculous investment at the time." But he adds, "We don't delude ourselves into thinking that Yahoo's stock price represents reality."

In order to fund great companies, Sequoia's top priority—and the hallmark of its investment philosophy—is its focus on markets. Sequoia's objective is to identify and support the companies it thinks will ultimately dominate rapidly expanding new markets. The firm wants to gain the largest market share in large markets. Capturing these markets means that a company needs either a product difficult to duplicate or a first-mover's advantage that lets the company roll out very quickly to garner large market share and turn that position into a powerful competitive weapon.

Sequoia's market focus is well known in both the venture capital community and in the technology finance community at large. "They look for huge markets; everything else is secondary to that," says Geoff Yang of Institutional Venture Partners. Joel Romines of Knightsbridge Partners, a fund of funds that invests in venture capital partnerships and young companies in the public market, adds, "In real estate it's location, location, location, and to many venture capitalists, it's management, management, management. For Sequoia, the first thing is market, market, market."

A company can have a great product or brilliant management, but it won't matter if there is no market for the product. For one thing, the best technology doesn't always win. Two classic examples are the triumph of VHS over Betamax as the standard for VCRs and the huge market-share advantage Microsoft Windows has over the Macintosh operating system.

And while it's always nice to invest in a company with superior technology, Sequoia has helped build companies that have a good but not enormous technology advantage. These companies have gotten to market early and have built a formidable sales-and-distribution machine that becomes a difficult barrier for competitors to overcome. Cisco Systems is a classic example of this.

Sequoia also believes that while good management is always in short supply, it's still easier to find new managers than to sell into markets that don't exist. "We cannot afford to wait for markets to develop," says Valentine. "And we don't have the money or the inclination to educate customers to buy products they don't know they need."

Finding great managers can be tougher than discerning potential markets. "The great imponderable is to judge accurately and predict how well a president will run the business. It's easy to mistake the façade for reality," says Moritz. "The qualities we look for are frugality, competitiveness, confidence, and paranoia."

Sequoia partners will step in and run a company if necessary. For example, Sequoia had to intervene during the early stages of Cisco. Sequoia general partner Pierre Lamond spent a tremendous amount of time at the company, working behind the scenes to make sure the engineering department was designing and getting new products to market. "Pierre is the great unsung hero of Cisco," says Moritz. "People don't realize the significant contribution he made because Don Valentine's name is on the hubcaps as the chairman of the company."

But for Sequoia, ultimate success is still possible only if there's a true market for the product or service. For the lay investor, the non-specialist, Sequoia's market focus is a great insight. It is difficult to assess the viability of many technologies or the caliber of company management, but if a big market exists for what a company offers, the potential is certainly there.

The lay investor cannot or should not try to play the venture capital game—it is far too complicated and risky for nonspecialists. The required due diligence process is time-consuming and complex, and the passive investor does not have the power of a venture capitalist to change management or help companies forge the strategic partnerships that will let them prevail in the market. Another caveat is that the typical venture portfolio shakes out according to the 2:6:2 rule— of the ten companies in a portfolio, there might be one or two big winners, six mediocrities (including the aptly named "living dead"), and one or two partial or total losers. And even among the winners, a Sun Microsystems, Cisco, or Microsoft is extremely rare.

In a bubble market in particular, the buyer should beware. "In a bull market, everyone is invincible," says Valentine. "Over the last 10 years, the stock index funds have continued to go up, way up. People think, 'If Vanguard can do it, I can do it, I can pick these goddamn Internet stocks.' That is a traditional mistake made at a peak of a bull market. People become convinced that the world is so simple, and that you don't have to be careful or deliberate. They think that because these companies have so much publicity, they must be good."

So what should the average investor do? "I think 'Aunt Millie' should buy a mutual fund, not try to buy Amazon or CNET or any other Internet example that you want to name," says Valentine.

There's a danger of getting too caught up in the phenomenon and in a category of companies perceived as able to do no wrong because they are on the Internet. "These companies are so overreported," says Valentine. "They have a level of emergence that is scary."

And at the peak of bubbles, many institutional investors will exit their Internet holdings, leaving them mostly to the retail market where the Aunt Millies start to place their bets and set themselves up for a loss. "It's greed," says Valentine. "The retail investors buy things they don't understand."

According to Sequoia's partners, the best alternative, especially if investing in high technology, is a reasonably diversified technology fund exposed to a select cross section of companies coming out of the high-tech market—at least 60 to 70 percent of the fund. Diversifying instead of gambling is a word to the wise from these experienced investors.

Integral Capital Partners

In the mid-1980s, when Roger McNamee was a manager of the Science & Technology Fund for T. Rowe Price, someone very smart suggested to him that he get to know a rising young partner at the venture capital firm Kleiner Perkins Caufield & Byers. This venture capitalist had a dynamic and innovative approach to private technology-investing that McNamee's friend thought could work just as well with the public investing McNamee was doing at T. Rowe Price. The venture capitalist's name was John Doerr. After getting to know Doerr, McNamee realized he had found his role model and mentor.

"I followed John around and began imitating some things he was doing, particularly his practice of participative investment," says McNamee. "He taught me that the role of the investor was not to sit in your office with the money and wait for people to come to you. Instead, you had to actually get involved in the industry and interact with the people as peers and exchange insights with them."

This approach, widely practiced today, seems obvious, but it was not typical of fund managers at the time. While the technology industry generated hundreds of press releases a week, and there were scads of trade journals and newsletters, trying to stay informed was like sipping water from a fire hose. If the investor sat in one place, he spent his time reacting and never got the big picture. Putting details into a spreadsheet only created an illusion of precision. "Life takes place to the left of the decimal point," says McNamee.

McNamee started attending trade shows and conferences to become part of the industry network and gain insights that he could barter in exchange for other insights. Fortunately, the industry was young, so it was easier to get to know people. "Folks who today are totally unapproachable were still looking for an audience in those days," says McNamee. "To some extent, all I did was show up." McNamee also had over 400 face-to-face meetings with company executives every year—basically two every business day, compared, at that time, to an average of about 23 face-to-face meetings annually by the typical industry analyst.

Not surprisingly, the Science & Technology fund did well. It had an annual internal rate of return of 17 percent, compared with an industry average of 6 percent for similar funds and 9 percent for the Standard & Poor 500 Index. It was consistently ranked number one of the 17 Science & Technology funds tracked by Morningstar.

By 1990, even as Japan's bubble burst, America was on the brink of a tremendous technology bull market. Sensing this, McNamee and his partner, John Powell, began working on a business plan that was to become Integral Capital Partners. McNamee wanted to invite John Doerr to become a partner but feared it would spoil their relationship if Doerr said no. This changed at a big party thrown by Will Hearst III at the Comdex electronics trade show in 1990. "I went to the party and John walks up to me and says, 'Roger, we ought to create a fund that does both later-stage venture and public-incentive pool investing, and you ought to run it. What do you think?'" exclaims McNamee still in awe. "I said, 'When do we start?' I was proud of myself for not just standing there with my tongue hanging out."

After almost a year of further research and incubation and several more iterations of the business plan, they launched Integral Capital Partners as a private investment partnership that invested in the securities of expansion-stage private companies and growth-stage public companies in the information and life-sciences industries.

Kleiner Perkins Caufield & Byers joined Integral as its "insight partner" but without any fiduciary control. Investment bank Morgan Stanley also became an institutional partner and acted as a placement agent. McNamee and Powell would make all the investment decisions and manage the fund, and they planned to raise most of the money from senior executives within the technology industry.

Integral benefited tremendously from the insights of John Doerr and the other Kleiner Perkins partners. Integral was invited to Kleiner Perkins's frequent off-sites, where the Kleiner Perkins partners had detailed discussions about strategy and the future of the technology industry. "At least twice a year, John Doerr or somebody else at Kleiner Perkins hits me with an insight that's a bolt of lightning," says McNamee. "This gives Integral a gigantic competitive advantage." In turn, Integral helps Kleiner Perkins with its companies' road shows and with decisions concerning post-IPO stock distribution.

These lightning bolts and Integral's industry networking helped the partnership enjoy an internal rate of return of 25 percent for Integral Capital L.P. Fund I. Integral also learned to focus on a carefully defined set of investment opportunities. This focus is based on specific investment themes. They are: (1) *Connectivity*—the push for improved communication flows within and between corporations; (2) *Interactivity*—real-time information exchange; and (3) *Mobility*—products that support mobile lifestyles and workstyles.

A larger theme overlaying all of these is "the real-time economy" based on real-time models of computing. In practice it means that the old models of control-oriented data processing are giving way to a model in which businesses use technology more and more to be in touch with the customer in real time, in the here and now. The Internet explosion is an obvious expression of this real-time model.

Integral has some even more specific guidelines that can benefit anyone interested in investing in the technology market. "Our rules to live by represent the collective scar tissue of almost 18 years of investing in technology stocks," says McNamee.

- *Rule one: Information is a commodity, but insight is precious.* Insight is much more valuable because it is a filtering of information. Sometimes too much detail clouds your investment vision, but insight allows you to operate at a higher level of understanding and see what's actually going on.

- *Rule two: Product cycles are the only cycles that matter.* On Wall Street, there is a tremendous focus on the economic cycle, interest rates, and politics. But for technology companies, product cycles are the real drivers. These product cycles have not only upswings but downswings, and the ability to tell the difference is critical. These swings are natural, and technology businesses are not made obsolete because they are in a product transition, even though they are often priced on Wall Street as if they are. Never confuse an upswing with greatness or a downswing with the end.

- *Rule three: Favor products that are bought, not sold.* If a company sells tens of millions of its products, it will not sell them all on the last day of the quarter. They will sell continuously through the quarter. Wall Street loves predictability, and it will give a higher valuation to a company if it sells 10 million items at a dollar apiece than if it sells just one big item for $10 million.

- *Rule four: In making investment decisions, do not rely on guidance from company management alone.* The vast majority of the industry analysts get all their information about companies from the company itself. When it comes to the company's own business, management is often the last to know what the problems are. But the customers always know, and competitors will also have a lot of insights. "You need to get beyond a company's 'story' and into a realistic understanding of the business issues involved," says McNamee.

- *Rule five: Balance research insights with opportunism.* Research determines what should be done, but the market determines what can be done today.

- *Rule six: A perfectly diversified technology stock portfolio is bound to underperform the market.* You want to diversify away the risk of execution problems without diversifying away the opportunities. Stick to two or three major investment themes, and use diversification within those themes to minimize risk. Never put all your bets on one company, but find three or four of the best-positioned companies to invest in. Avoiding losers is every bit as important as picking winners.

- Also keep in mind that there is only one Microsoft. If you spend all your time looking for the next Microsoft, you will probably find it only after it is too late. If you invest in the best-positioned companies in the major themes, and the next Microsoft emerges, it will already be in your portfolio. Meanwhile, don't forget that every stock must eventually be sold, and when the time comes to sell it, don't hesitate. You have to do it.

So what about Internet mania? "The essence of a mania is that its pace becomes so frenetic that people stop thinking clearly, and it only ends when some element of economic reality disrupts the fantasy and brings the mania to an end," says McNamee.

Integral does hold Internet stocks. In fact, 40 percent of Integral Fund III consisted of Internet stocks as of April 1999, but the majority of these investments were made when the companies were private. Integral continued to invest in private Internet companies, but it only rarely bought Internet companies in the public market during the previous six months. Integral held on to its Internet stocks but counseled its clients to move away from Internet stocks in their other investing. In essence, Integral's clients paid Integral to hold on to Internet stocks as long as Integral's managers thought it was feasible, even as Integral's clients were off-loading much of their own risk.

"Common sense tells you that the Internet is going to be a huge business," says McNamee. "That said, it will still be subject to all the forces that affect any industry during its land-rush period." After the land rush there will be a series of consolidations before market shares stabilize and the industry becomes more predictable.

"The most important advice I can give to people today is: Don't rush. There is no sense of urgency for getting Internet stocks," says McNamee. "In fact, you should lower your exposure to Internet stocks, pending a resetting of expectations after the next wave of consolidation hits and the industry shifts once again."

And what's next for McNamee and company post–Internet mania? They've realized that much of the high-technology market has matured or is maturing. Integral has ridden the bull market and benefited from Internet mania, but given the overabundance of capital and the consequent overvaluation of companies, it is challenging to find good investments that will generate the same returns Integral has enjoyed throughout the 1990s. It has become more time-consuming to find investments at good valuations.

"Integral got into the game in 1991 at the end of a long bear market in the technology sector," says McNamee. "Technology stocks were so significantly undervalued that it was easy to find good investments. All you had to do was buy all the big-cap stocks and just hang on. You could buy Microsoft, Intel, Applied Materials, Dell, and Cisco, and go to sleep, and still have 40 percent price appreciation per year out of a portfolio of those core holdings."

Now McNamee has launched a technology buyout fund he calls Silver Lake and seeks out technologies and divisions within mature companies that are grossly undervalued or even ignored because they are not part of the companies' core competencies. Wall Street has failed to recognize the value of these businesses because it focuses on hyper-growth and the sizzle of the hottest stories on a quarterly basis. Yet many of these undervalued businesses may actually be growing at rates of 15 to 20 percent annually.

"You've got 80 percent of technology companies effectively being ignored by Wall Street. Within them there are thousands of divisions, really successful businesses, with no home, that are basically undermanaged and underinvested in, and which get no analyst coverage," says McNamee.

Silver Lake wants to buy out these divisions and help spin them out into the public market, the way AT&T successfully spun out Lucent. With Silver Lake, McNamee and company are ready to move on to the next opportunity, even as Internet mania and the success of the tech sector as a whole have spurred other investment managers to create Integral-like structures and investment businesses.

"They say that generals are always prepared for the last war, the war they just finished," says McNamee. "Well, just as each war is different, so is each market cycle. The great irony is that you know it's getting late in the cycle when people are creating a gazillion new investment vehicles optimized to whatever has worked for the last decade, rather than thinking about what comes next."

Built to Last

In 1994, James Collins and Jerry Porras published *Built to Last: Successful Habits of Visionary Companies*, which has been a business best-seller ever since—and with good reason. In it, Collins and Porras distill what has enabled great companies to adapt, grow, prosper, and therefore last. The companies they profiled, such as Hewlett-Packard and 3M, are the envy of the world.

Along the way, Collins also worked with senior executives and CEOs at over 100 major corporations, received numerous awards, including the Distinguished Teaching Award while on the faculty of Stanford University Graduate School of Business, and more recently founded a research and teaching lab in Boulder, Colorado.

Collins is not convinced that what he calls the Silicon Valley Paradigm creates companies that are built to last or that will become classic blue-chip investments. His definition of the paradigm as "Have a good idea, raise venture capital, grow fast, go public, and generate vast liquid wealth quickly" describes perfectly today's Internet start-up company.

In contrast, *built to last* means that the most important creation is the company itself and what it stands for. Such companies will generate numerous ideas and transcend any one business life cycle. Thomas Edison's greatest invention is arguably not the lightbulb, the phonograph, or the motion-picture machine, but rather the General Electric Company that ticks along decades after his death. GE contrasts sharply with today's startups that are built around one product or idea and cash in on that alone.

An older technology company that has struggled with being a one-trick pony is Xerox. The company focused so much on one product—the photocopier—rather than on building the company that it missed out on numerous revolutionary ideas and products discovered at its own Palo Alto Research Center. These include the laser printer, desktop publishing, electronic mail, mouse pointers, and the graphical user interface that became the basis of the Macintosh operating system. Xerox simply did not have the organizational capability to capitalize on these ideas and run with them, and the company has struggled to reposition itself ever since.

While there is a great sense of urgency today associated with "Internet time" and "Web weeks" and the need to be first to market, there are certain built-to-last principles that transcend the current mania and create long-term successful companies and investments. One is the supreme value of the entrepreneur.

Collins says, "From an investor standpoint, I would ask, 'Which entrepreneurs could I invest in with the confidence that they would succeed no matter what?'" Collins's list of examples includes Bill Gates, Bill Hewlett and David Packard, Henry Ford, and even Howard Schultz, founder of Starbucks coffee.

If it had not been automobiles, Henry Ford would have taken the concept of mass-production technology and applied it to something else that would have been just as successful. Hewlett and Packard didn't even know what their company was going to be when they brought together some very capable people. They discarded their original areas of focus and finally got into an unrelated product arena that fueled the growth and success of the company.

"I'd invest not because something is an Internet company, or because the Internet's the play, but because the people doing this company are the kind that if the whole Internet crashed, they'd figure out something else to do and they'd make that successful," says Collins. "The whole idea that something is an Internet company is no more reason to invest in that company than investing in any one of the 508 automobile companies in business around 1910. Only a few of them will be there when the whole thing settles out."

The real question is: What can someone create that will produce a change in people's lives in a profitable and sustainable way? If the entrepreneur can't answer that question, there's no reason to invest. "Unless you want to play the shell game, in which you're not really investing but instead are playing the 'I hope I get in and out in time' game, which I can't condone," says Collins.

Business fundamentals don't change. A company's earnings are a function of the economic and social contributions it creates. Unless a company can demonstrate how it will create that sustained flow based upon its contribution, there is nothing to invest in. If the entrepreneur has a single idea or a single insight that is not sustainable, the advantage of it will dissipate. The company has to develop the ability to generate new insights and build new economic engines.

Collins compares the relationship of business fundamentals for sustained growth to the relationship of physics and engineering. Physics is physics; its laws don't change. So, too, with business fundamentals. But the way they are applied always changes, the way engineering constantly evolves.

"The way you design products will continually evolve," says Collins. "You used to use blueprints and pencil diagrams, and now you can use design software to go through multiple iterations of a Triple 7 jet before you actually build anything with metal. You're changing the form of engineering, but the underlying physics are still the same; they don't change."

And just as there is no way to ignore physics when you are engineering a real product, you also can't ignore business fundamentals if you are to have a real company. "There is no reason to believe that we need to throw out the fundamentals. No. We need to do a better job of applying the fundamentals more than anything else," Collins concludes.

Final Advice

"Professional investors mark themselves to market virtually every day, because that's how they get paid," says Bruce Lupatkin, former head of research at Hambrecht & Quist and a longtime technology analyst. "But most nonprofessionals do not have time to do that. Yet if you have patience and discipline, you can still do well. Stocks will go up and they will go down. Just take your time and be patient."

How do you pick the best stocks? "You ought to find industry leaders, companies that are causing structural change in a given industry," says Lupatkin.

In the Internet realm, Lupatkin points to America Online and Yahoo as companies to watch, but quickly adds, "The issue is what you should pay for them." This, of course, gets back to the whole issue of overvaluation in the Internet Bubble market. It also means you shouldn't gamble unless you are in a position to lose all the money you've bet on a stock.

"You don't have to put all your money into stock," says George Shott of Shott Capital Management. "Instead, you should invest slowly and over time." Joel Romines of Knightsbridge Partners adds, "If you are interested in investing in high technology, look for mutual funds that specialize and have a good record in young high-technology companies."

For most investors, it comes back to the need for a long-term investment strategy and with it an appropriate long-term portfolio. Right off the top, it should be obvious that bubble stocks do not make good long-term investments, any more than playing the lottery or gambling in Las Vegas is a long-term investment.

Also realize that the bull market has made a lot of people who have just gotten lucky look like geniuses. And there is a tendency to only bet on those sectors that have done well during our unusually long bull market. Technology stocks have returned 288 percent during the past five years, but there's no guarantee this trend will continue.

The financial community has successfully convinced individuals in recent years to invest directly in stocks while steering investors away from normal asset allocation. The single fastest-growing fund category since the end of 1993, stock index funds based on the S&P 500 have also become increasingly popular. But this only adds to the momentum: More money going into index funds causes the same big stocks to move upward, further encouraging investors to keep buying the big stocks for fear that they might miss out.

Since 1995, S&P stock index funds have shown an annual return of 30 percent, nearly triple their historical rate. But most investors don't understand how exceptional these recent years have been. "The American populace doesn't really understand equity risk," says Bill Gurley, a onetime Wall Street analyst and now a venture capitalist with Benchmark Partners. "And it's highly unlikely that the financial returns awarded to the entire market, and certainly to these Internet stocks over the past three to five years, are sustainable."

By contrast, asset allocation and a diversified portfolio are still the safest way to go over the long term in order to weather all kinds of market conditions. Your money should be spread out among different asset classes, not only stocks but also some bonds and money market funds. Diversification might mean holding both large- and small-company stocks as well as some international investments. Some investment managers also recommend breaking it out into growth stocks (shares of fast-growing companies) and value stocks (neglected stocks that trade at bargain prices). A baseline might be 30 to 40 percent bonds; 30 percent big U.S. stocks; 20 percent smaller U.S. stocks; and 10 to 20 percent internationals, including 5 percent in emerging markets.

Remember that investing in individual stocks is risky, especially if you don't have a lot of time to research individual companies or the stomach to ride the ups and downs of a portfolio of limited stock holdings. Investing too much in just blue chips does not guarantee a great return, especially if we go into a recession or a bear market.

Meanwhile, be careful about lining up behind supposed investment gurus. There may be a level of risk that is far from clear, and their success to date could be more a matter of luck, especially in a bull market, than anything else. Supposed financial innovations are usually variations on something that's been done before, and it's important to look below the surface.

When the stock market craze is at its height—with new mutual funds and other investment vehicles popping up all over the place and investment fads being publicized on TV, the Internet, and the covers of magazines—it's usually a sign of market froth. In this kind of environment, as history shows, there is no such thing as get rich quick, and ignorance of the past can be deadly.

And finally, it's always dangerous to be too greedy—remember the old Wall Street adage: "Bulls make money, bears make money, but pigs get slaughtered."

Doonesbury

EPILOGUE

An Open Letter
To: Internet Company Investors
From: The Authors
Re: Sell Now!

The bottom line to our analysis is very simple. With very few exceptions, every one of the 133 public Internet companies listed in our Internet Bubble portfolio (see Appendix C or www.redherring .com/internetbubble) is overvalued. Our advice to Internet investors is equally simple: If you hold any of these stocks, it's time to sell. Yes folks, if the Internet gala hasn't ended by the time this book hits the streets, it will probably end sometime soon thereafter. So it's time to get out.

As we write these words, we can already hear the screams. Your highest-pitched jeers will accuse us of being Internet industry naysayers, unbelievers in "The New Economy," and downright traitors to our hometown here in Silicon Valley. And believe us, we will feel your pain. The Internet boom has created billions in new—largely paper—wealth for thousands of entrepreneurs and investors, so why would anybody want to stop the party now?

Well, we hate being party poopers, but it's time to step out of the Internet reality-distortion field and sober up a little. It's time to discern what's real and what's fluff. And it's time to take action on what we know to be true.

With all this in mind, allow us to take this final opportunity to summarize our views.

The Internet Is Real

As we said right up front, we believe the Internet phenomenon is unparalleled in the speed and magnitude of its impact on society.

The Internet tornado is blowing down geographical boundaries, swirling across the corporate landscape, and radically changing the way we communicate, gather and process information, and buy and sell goods and services. In 1999, 160 million people used the Internet compared to only 5 million in 1995. With a rapid expansion of new Internet services and the proliferation of new Internet devices, this number is expected to swell to 500 million users by the year 2003.

This boom has begun to chalk up some real economic numbers as well. By most estimates, the Internet economy grew at an astonishing 170 percent annual rate from 1995 through mid-1999. The 133 companies in the Bubble portfolio alone generated $15.2 billion in annual revenues by the first quarter of 1999, and the Internet increasingly drives the top lines of the technology blue chips such as Microsoft, Intel, and Cisco. Online advertising spending for 1999 will also top $3 billion and is projected to exceed $10 billion within 5 years. And, most significant, the total value of goods and services sold online is also expected to reach $425 billion by the year 2002, and maybe over $1 trillion by the end of 2003, according to International Data Corporation.

So, count us in with Bill Gates, John Doerr, George Gilder, and the rest of the world. We, too, are breathless with optimism over the Internet opportunity. Our specific concern lies somewhere in the chasm between the Internet opportunity and the overvalued prices of Internet stocks.

IPO Nirvana

The Internet economic boom has naturally translated into an IPO boom for Internet companies. There have been 96 Internet IPOs since Netscape's public offering in August 1995. According to Morgan Stanley Dean Witter, the total market capitalization of these companies exceeded $375 billion in May 1999, and eight of these companies had market caps over $10 billion, representing 71 percent of the total value of Internet stocks.

And, at the time we tapped out this Epilogue, there appears to be no Internet IPO slowdown in sight. As of late-May 1999, 63 Internet IPOs were on file, and 43 had already gone public in 1999. Through mid-1999, 25 percent of the $21.9 billion raised by public offerings went to Internet companies, compared with 6 percent of the total raised by all IPOs in 1998. Most amazing, of these 96 IPOs, 82 percent were still trading above their IPO price, and only 18 percent were down.

The Other Math

While this IPO record is glorious, and if nothing else, has stuffed the pockets of willing investment bankers with lots of cash, the euphoria over the Internet has driven Internet stock values to colossal heights. We don't want to beat you over the head with the math we presented in the Introduction, and in more detail in the Appendix. But we do have a portfolio of Internet stocks with a combined value of $410 billion based upon combined sales of a relatively meager $15.2 billion and whopping losses of over $3 billion. In fact, only 22 or 16.5 percent of the companies in the Bubble portfolio shows any profits at all.

And most striking, in order for the companies in the Bubble portfolio to justify their current market valuations, they would have to grow their revenues, on average, by over 80 percent every year for the next five years. As a comparison, Microsoft grew only 53 percent in its first five years after its IPO, and Dell grew only 66 percent. Assuming that all 133 Internet companies grew at an average annual rate equivalent to Dell's, the entire portfolio would still be overvalued by $130 billion or 33 percent (see Appendix A "Calculating the Bubble" for further details). The bottom line here is, of course, that Internet stocks trade at prices that anticipate sales and earnings growth unparalleled in financial history.

Getting Rich Quick

So if this company valuation math is so out of whack, what the heck, you ask, is driving this Internet stock mania? A great question, with no easy answer. It's a complicated problem largely because it has more to do with market psychology than anything else.

The most obvious factor driving Internet mania is simply human nature. Call it the get-rich syndrome, the lottery mentality, or plain greed—we've seen this human vice drive financial manias from tulip bulbs to the personal computer, and everything in between. As the French say: plus ça change, plus la meme chose—the more things change, the more they remain the same.

Another mentality holding up this house of cards is the frenzied faith in the so-called New Economy or Long Boom—a world in which technology tools and the Internet solve the world's problems and fundamental economic principles are suspended forever. While we believe technological advancement is an honorable endeavor that can certainly be harnessed to improve our standard of living, it has yet to prove itself as a pixie dust that cures all economic evils. Let us remind you that both Democrat and Republican alike have touted the New Economy.

"I think people sometimes confuse sections of the business cycle with a new paradigm," says Herb Allen, Jr., Hollywood's favorite investment banker. "We are in a cycle, probably the tail end of a bull market. To take that piece of the cycle and turn it into a standard for a new society is dangerous." Paul Romer, the more conservative Stanford University economist, concurs with Allen. "I don't agree with the unqualified Long Boom assertion that the rate of technological change in America is permanently faster than it has been historically, or that the underlying rate of growth of the economy has increased in the 1990s," Romer points out.

Day-Trader or Day-Tripper?

At the heart of this maniacal behavior sits the individual investor. While institutional investors (a.k.a. "smart money") generally own over 50 percent of the stock in the large cap technology companies such as Microsoft and Intel, Internet stocks are overwhelmingly owned by individual investors (a.k.a. "dumb money"). Online traders in particular, whose numbers reached 7 million in 1999 and are projected to hit 24 million by 2002, have played a significant role in pumping up the Internet Bubble.

Not to be overly cynical, but we think individual investors in Internet stocks need to face up to how the insider game is played out. As we explored in an earlier chapter, institutional investors routinely get in early as the IPO shares are distributed, but often flip the stock by the end of the first day of trading after doubling, tripling, and even quadrupling their investments in one afternoon. So while the insiders certainly cash in big, they do not hold these stocks for the long-term.

Industrial Darwinism

With history and math on our side, we can see only one result to the current overinflated state of the Internet company market, and we call it industrial Darwinism. As was the case of other commercial revolutions when too many companies were started, a survival of the fittest game will play itself out. Most of the Internet companies that have gone public will either merge with other companies, go completely out of business, or flounder in the world of the living dead.

"There will be a lot of Internet company wreckage," venture capital industry veteran Don Valentine predicts. And he ought to know, because he was on the front lines when dozens of personal computer industry-related companies went public and saw their prices soar in a great bubble that ended with the technology crash of 1983–1984. It's also important to remember that although PC unit growth continued at a greater than 25 percent rate for almost two decades, only one company founded during the early PC boom, Apple Computer, survives today. Cutting edge technology can take unforeseen twists that often make obsolete the early industry leaders. The largest two current hardware players in the PC business, Dell and Compaq, for example, both sprang up after the PC Bubble popped, and the almighty Microsoft didn't go public until 1986.

Another way to spin this equation is to note that of the 1,200-plus technology IPOs since the debut of the personal computer in 1980, a mere 5 percent of those IPOs have created 86 percent of the wealth. This is why Morgan Stanley's Mary Meeker reminds investors that they have to kiss a lot of frogs before they find a handsome prince. This is also why Harvard's Bill Sahlman makes the case that IPOs are generally not good investments for non-insiders. "The long-term performance of most IPOs is bad, and this has always been the case," he says.

Conclusion

So there you have it—our case on why Internet investors need to watch out. As Bill Gates summed it up for us: "Investors should not invest in Internet stocks unless they are prepared to take massive risks." And Gates wasn't the only one giving us this advice. Virtually every financial and industry insider we interviewed for this book said the same thing.

In the final analysis, we can't allow ourselves to be seduced by revolutionary new technologies and Web services absent of solid business models and profit margins. Eventually, all companies will have to justify their stock prices on some multiple of earnings. It is our contention that most of the 133 companies in the Bubble portfolio will never make money.

"The danger is if you are the last guy in the game and you turn out to be the greater fool," warns one of Wall Street's most seasoned analysts. And if you get caught holding the bag, don't say we didn't warn you.

APPENDIX A: *CALCULATING THE BUBBLE*

To illustrate the reality of the Internet Bubble, we created various ways to quantify the phenomenon with advice from a number of venture capitalists and investment bankers.

First, we offer the following index of Internet stocks based upon 133 publicly-traded Internet companies (as of June 11, 1999) with equity-market capitalizations greater than $100 million. (A complete list of these companies by industry segment and with individual company figures can be found in Appendix C and on *Red Herring*'s Web site www.redherring.com/internetbubble). We also compare this Internet index to the S&P 500 Index and the Dow Jones Industrial Average in this same chart.

Internet Index* vs. S&P 500 & DJIA

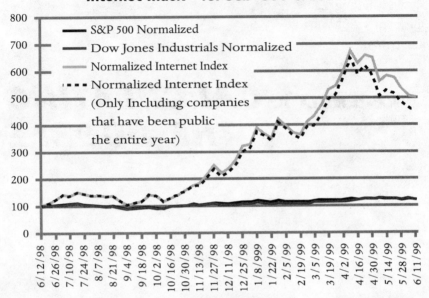

*Index of Internet stocks weighted by 6/11/99 market capitalizations and recalculated weekly to include newly public companies, but weighted such that their introduction will have no initial impact on the index

It is obvious from this chart that the index of Internet stocks has significantly outperformed these other indicators of market performance. While it is expected that technology-focused stocks with greater growth potential generally generate higher returns to satisfy the additional risk assumed by their investors, the annual returns of about 400 percent generated by the Internet Index is more than an order of magnitude greater than the returns of the S&P 500 Index or Dow Jones Industrials Average, which generated average returns of 18.9 percent.

As another way of calculating the Internet Bubble, we built a framework to quantify the expected performance of the Internet companies. This framework is based on the assumption that after a period of hyper-growth (five years), valuations will be based on more traditional financial metrics like profitability and price-to-earnings (P/E) ratios. We have assumed future net margins between 5 percent and 15 percent, depending on the segment, P/E ratios of 40x, and an equity discount rate of 20 percent. Chart 2 shows the aggregate revenue growth that the companies in each segment would need to achieve over the next five years in order to justify their current equity valuations. (The detailed methodology for calculating these growth rates can be found in Appendix B).

The importance of this data lies in the substantial growth these companies will need to generate in order to justify their valuations. The average Internet company in our set of 133 will need to generate revenue growth of approximately 80 percent every year for the next five years—in other words, revenues will need to increase by a factor of over 18× by the first quarter of 2004.

($ millions) Segment	Market Capitalization	Revenue	Number of Companies	Implied Future Revenue	Implied Revenue Growth
Commerce	$87,058.2	$2,904.4	32	$65,880.4	87%
Content	$165,866.9	$5,062.0	27	$121,006.2	89%
Enabling Services	$24,976.0	$1,263.0	18	$19,367.2	73%
Enabling Software	$30,183.7	$759.3	27	$13,143.7	77%
Enabling Telecom Services	$101,782.6	$5,231.3	29	$66,482.7	66%
TOTAL	$409,867.4	$15,220.0	133	$285,880.2	80%

Finally, to illustrate the Internet Bubble even further, we decided to calculate the valuation gap between the actual market capitalization of the companies and what we believe the real value should be. To do this, we used the same framework as above but plugged in what we felt were more realistic average growth rates for the next five years. To estimate this growth rate, we examined five of the top-performing companies of the technology revolution during the 1980s and 1990s and equity analyst projections of revenue growth rates for five leading Internet companies. For the first five years after its IPO, Microsoft achieved 53 percent revenue growth per year, Dell: 66 percent, Sun Microsystems: 85 percent, Oracle: 111 percent, and Cisco Systems: 114 percent. Over the next four years, At Home is projected to achieve annual revenue growth of 77 percent, AOL: 28 percent, Amazon: 50 percent, Ebay: 71 percent, and Yahoo: 58 percent. After examining this data, we felt that applying growth rates between 50 percent and 65 percent to the Internet company portfolio was more realistic.

Chart 3 shows the current combined market capitalizations of the 133 companies and the implied calculated value if you assume the companies as a group will grow at the slower rates of 50 percent and 65 percent. The far right-hand column shows the difference between the actual market capitalization and the value we have calculated assuming a 65 percent compound annual growth rate (CAGR). It indicates that if the 133 Internet companies achieve revenue growth at a compounded annual rate of 65 percent, they would be overvalued by an incredible $130 billion. If you are less optimistic and believe that the entire set of Internet companies can only grow as fast as Microsoft did in the mid-1980s or slightly faster than selected equity research analysts have projected Amazon to grow over the next four years (50 percent CAGR), the entire set of Internet stocks is worth less than one-half of their June 11, 1999 value (overvalued by over $230 billion).

Obviously, it is alarming that according to our model, $130 billion to $230 billion of value, or 32 percent to 58 percent of the value of the set of Internet companies, is generated from the inflated expectations that have created the Internet Bubble.

($ millions)	Total Market Capitalization	Equity Value Implied by Estimated Forward Growth Rate		Internet Bubble at 65%
		50%	65%	
Commerce	$87,058.2	$31,607.9	$50,904.8	$36,153.4
Content	$165,866.9	$56,315.1	$90,696.0	$75,170.9
Enabling Services	$24,976.0	$11,814.9	$19,028.0	$5,948.0
Enabling Software	$30,183.7	$13,241.0	$21,324.7	$8,859.0
Enabling Telecom Services	$101,782.6	$60,818.3	$97,948.4	$3,834.2
TOTAL	$409,867.4	$173,797.1	$279,902.0	$129,965.4

APPENDIX B: *BUBBLE CALCULATION METHODOLOGY*

The Internet Bubble calculations we have referenced through-out this book are based on several key assumptions. The general model was developed with help from analysts, investment bankers, and venture capitalists with years of experience valuing technology companies. Traditional valuation methodologies such as P/E ratios and discounted cash flows have not been applicable to Internet companies because of the high expectations and uncertainty of future growth as well as the lack of historical earnings.

The primary assumption we relied upon is that during a finite time period, the hypergrowth expected by Internet investors will be at least partially realized and future growth will be more easily quantifiable from that point onward. At that time in the future, valuations will be based on more traditional methodologies similar to those used for other technology-focused companies. For simplicity's sake, we have chosen a five-year time horizon, which means that by June 2004, we expect that Internet valuations will be based more on realistic financial metrics and less on expectations of short term hypergrowth. To illustrate the methodology, we will use Amazon (AMZN).

Calculating Future Market Capitalization

We have estimated that the return required by investors given the risk born by investing in a particular Internet-related stock to be 20 percent. The 20 percent figure was chosen by examining more traditional technology companies and using a Capital Asset Pricing Model (which calculates a discount rate by comparing the volatility of stock prices to market volatility). When examining established technology companies like Microsoft, IBM, Cisco, Lucent, Nokia, Hewlett-Packard, and Nortel Networks, the required rate of return tends to be about 15 percent. We have added a premium to this figure because Internet companies tend to be less established and more volatile—and therefore more risky to the investor.

We feel that an appropriate range of forward-looking discount rates is 15 percent to 25 percent. By applying this required rate of return to the current market capitalization, we can calculate the future market capitalization for the company in question. To use our example, the market capitalization for AMZN on June 11, 1999 was $17.1 billion. If you assume a 20 percent-required rate of return, AMZN would need to grow to a market capitalization of $42.6 billion in June 2004 in order to satisfy current investors, given the risk of the investment.

In addition to generating return for current investors, many technology and Internet companies lure top engineering, marketing, and management talent by granting employees stock options. For the set of Internet companies, we have assumed that current investors will be diluted by 5 percent through the future exercise of employee options. While future potential dilution from option issuance vary from company to company, experience tells us that this number is representative for IPO-stage technology companies. Returning to our example, this assumption implies that AMZN will actually need to achieve a market capitalization of $44.7 billion in order to satisfy investor risk, given future employee-option dilution.

Calculating Operating Figures Implied by Future Market Capitalization

A standard valuation methodology for more established technology companies is the price-to-historical-earnings (P/E) multiple, determined by dividing the market capitalization by the earnings generated over the last twelve months by the company. The assumptions that earnings are a quantifiable proxy for future potential cash flows and that a group of companies with similar growth trajectories and market opportunities will trade at similar P/E ratios underpin the theory that justifies using P/E ratios.

We have assumed a 40× P/E for the set of Internet companies we are analyzing by examining a set of successful and established technology companies. Examples include Computer Associates (40×), Oracle (37×), Intel (33×), Nokia (41×), Ericsson (32×), IBM (30×), and Sun Microsystems (50×). This ratio could change depending on the future growth opportunities of the company as well as on the execution history of management and many other factors. Most of the Internet companies could realistically range anywhere from 20 to 60x. Using the P/E assumption, we can calculate the earnings the future valuation implies. In our example, based on the assumption of a 40× P/E ratio, the future market capitalization of $44.7 billion implies future earnings of $1.1 billion.

We have assumed that as the Internet becomes more established, competition will drive net margins to become aligned with those of more traditional companies in similar subsegments. These net margins vary according to subsegment, but, for example, a number of online retail stores will emerge and drive net margins to those similar to today's traditional retail stores. More value-added or differentiated services such as financial services will continue to command higher net margins. The assumed margins for each segment are listed in the following table.

Segment	Assumed Net Margin	Examples of Traditional Companies
Commerce Destinations and Auction Sites	12.5%	Sotheby's Holdings (12%), New York Times (10%)
Financial Services	15.0%	BankAmerica (13%), Citigroup (8%), Hambrecht & Quist (12%)
Retail	5.0%	Barnes & Noble (2%), Federated Department Stores (4%), WalMart (3%)
Content Providers	7.5%	Disney (7%), Fox (3%), New York Times (10%), Time Warner (1%)
Enabling Services	7.5%	Cambridge Technology Partners (8%), Metamor Worldwide (4%), Sapient (7%)
Investors	10.0%	Average of other Internet-related subsegments
Enabling Sotware	15.0%	Computer Associates (11%), Oracle (14%), PeopleSoft (12%), VERITAS (25%)
Enabling Telecom Services	10.0%	AT&T (10%), Bell Atlantic (10%), GTE (10%)

AOL and Network Solutions were not assigned to specific sub-segments in the charts in Appendix C because of their relatively unique business models. We assumed a net margin of 10 percent for AOL because of the combination of Content Provider and Enabling Telecom services of the business and its traditionally loyal user base. We assumed a net margin of 10 percent for Network Solutions because of the business model compared to those of other enabling services and residual effects of its current monopoly status granted by the government. Once we have assumed a certain future margin, we can calculate the future expected revenues implied by the current market valuation. In our example, we apply the assumed margin of 5 percent to AMZN's future earnings of $1.1 billion, which would yield future revenues of $22.3 billion.

Examining Implied Revenue Growth Rates

By comparing this future revenue number to the company's revenues for the last 12 months, we can calculate an implied future growth rate. You could make the case that this calculation be used to determine whether the company in question is undervalued or overvalued. If you believe the company will grow faster than this growth rate over the next five years, the company would be undervalued. On the other hand, if you don't believe the company can generate that sort of growth (or the industry in general cannot generate that growth year over year), that company (or industry) is overvalued.

In our example, AMZN generated revenues of $813.3 million in the 12 months ending in March 1999. AMZN would have to grow its revenues at 94 percent year over year (or almost double in revenues every year) for the next five years in order to justify its current market capitalization. We can compare this growth to selected equity analyst projections, which indicate that AMZN will grow at a compounded annual growth rate (CAGR) of 46 percent over the next four years. Using the assumptions listed above, this methodology implies that AMZN is overvalued.

Using Estimated Growth Rates
To Determine Implied Current Value

This same methodology can be used in reverse in order to determine an implied value of a company today. If you assume a set growth rate for any particular company or group of companies, you can calculate the future revenues. For our example, AMZN's revenues for the last twelve months were $813.3 million. If you assume a CAGR for the next five years of 46 percent, AMZN should achieve revenues of $5.4 billion within five years. With the revenues and assumed net margin, you can calculate the future implied earnings.

For the retail space we have assumed a net margin of 5 percent, which indicates that AMZN should generate earnings in five years of $270 million. With the earnings, assumed P/E ratio, and option dilution, you can calculate what the expected future market capitalization, excluding option dilution, would be. When we use the same P/E and option-dilution assumptions as above (40x and 5 percent), the implied future equity market capitalization is $10.3 billion. Then, by discounting that market capitalization back to the present by the required rate of return, we can calculate what the actual valuation for this company or set of companies should be. Using the 20 percent assumption for the required rate of return, we find that according to this methodology, AMZN should actually have a market capitalization today of $4.1 billion. When compared to the market capitalization of $17.1 billion on June 11, 1999, these assumptions and valuation model indicate that AMZN is overvalued by approximately $13.0 billion, or over 75 percent of its current value.

COMPANY LISTS*

($ millions)
Commerce

Name	Market Cap	Revenue	Future Revenue	Implied CAGR
Amazon.com	$17,100.0	$816.3	$22,338.9	94%
Ameritrade	4,580.0	232.0	1,994.4	54%
Autobytel.com	357.5	27.2	467.0	77%
Autoweb.com	317.3	16.6	414.5	90%
barnesandnoble.com	2,260.0	85.1	2,952.4	103%
Beyond.com	804.3	49.6	1,050.7	84%
CDNow	483.6	69.2	631.8	56%
Cyberian Outpost	231.8	85.2	302.8	29%
DLJ Direct	2,780.0	141.1	1,210.6	54%
E*Trade	8,800.0	349.9	3,832.0	61%
eBay	20,800.0	75.4	10,869.0	170%
Egghead	316.5	148.7	413.5	23%
eToys	5,060.0	30.0	6,610.2	194%
Fatbrain.com	170.2	21.5	222.3	60%
GlobalNet	155.3	1.2	67.6	123%
iMall	283.1	2.2	147.9	133%
Internet Financial Services	111.5	13.4	48.6	29%
Intraware	481.5	38.4	251.6	46%
iTurf	273.5	2.6	357.3	167%
Multexnet.com	659.4	15.5	287.1	79%
NetBank	887.5	23.4	386.5	75%
NextCard	1,890.0	1.1	823.0	274%
Onsale	314.5	235.4	164.3	−7%
pcOrder.com	597.8	24.9	312.4	66%
Peapod	148.6	68.4	194.1	23%
Pegasus	475.2	31.3	248.3	51%
Preview Travel	240.0	27.7	125.4	35%
Priceline.com	13,600.0	84.6	7,106.6	143%
Security First Technology	848.7	32.8	369.6	62%
uBid	269.3	80.5	140.7	12%
Value America	886.8	67.3	1,158.5	77%
Wit Capital	874.3	5.9	380.7	130%

($ millions)
Content

Name	Market Cap	Revenue	Future Revenue	Implied CAGR
about.com	$ 374.6	$ 5.9	$ 326.2	123%
America Online	107,700.0	4,190.0	70,347.9	76%
Broadcast.com	3,760.0	28.1	3,274.6	159%
CareerBuilder	248.6	8.8	216.5	90%
CNet	3,340.0	66.3	2,908.8	113%
comps.com	101.1	13.4	88.0	46%
drkoop.com	435.1	0.4	378.9	285%
EarthWeb	266.6	6.8	232.2	103%
Go2Net	1,430.0	10.2	1,245.4	161%
Infoseek	2,750.0	96.1	2,395.0	90%
InfoSpace	2,170.0	13.5	1,889.9	169%
Intelligent Life	115.9	5.6	100.9	78%
iVillage	894.6	19.3	779.1	110%
Launch Media	203.8	5.7	177.5	99%
Lycos	3,660.0	109.4	3,187.5	96%
Mapquest.com	504.6	25.3	439.5	77%
MarketWatch.com	711.5	9.0	619.7	133%
Mpath	408.0	8.7	355.3	110%
SportLine USA	821.4	34.8	715.4	83%
StarMedia Network	2,070.0	6.6	1,802.8	207%
theglobe.com	401.2	8.3	349.4	111%
thestreet.com	708.2	5.7	616.8	155%
Ticketmaster Online City Search	1,870.0	43.8	1,628.6	106%
VerticalNet	1,150.0	4.7	1,001.5	192%
XooM	761.7	11.9	663.4	123%
Yahoo	27,600.0	258.7	24,037.2	148%
ZDNet	1,410.0	65.0	1,228.0	80%

($ millions)
Enabling Services

Name	Market Cap	Revenue	Future Revenue	Implied CAGR
@Plan	$ 151.9	$ 4.0	$ 132.3	102%
24/7 Media	566	30.2	492.9	75%
AdForce	460.1	7.1	400.7	124%
CMG	8,380.0	148.1	5,473.7	106%
DoubleClick	3,520.0	89.3	3,065.6	103%
Flycast Communications	323.6	12.1	281.8	88%
International Network Services	2,130.0	273.4	1,855.0	47%
iXL Enterprises	1,030.0	90.9	897.0	58%
Media Metrix	715.1	8.4	622.8	137%
Modem Media. Poppe Tyson	305.0	45.9	265.6	42%
Network Solutions	2,110.0	115.3	1,378.2	64%
Online Resources and Communications	146.1	5.0	127.2	91%
Proxicom	553.7	49.2	482.2	58%
Rare Medium	462.7	12.7	302.2	88%
Razorfish	758.8	26.2	660.8	91%
Scient	1,350.5	20.7	1,176.2	124%
Think New Ideas	162.5	51.2	141.5	23%
US Web	1,850.0	273.4	1,611.2	43%

($ millions)
Enabling Software

Name	Market Cap	Revenue	Future Revenue	Implied CAGR
Actuate	$ 278.5	$26.1	$ 121.3	36%
Allaire	520.6	24.3	226.7	56%
Artificial Life	137.3	0.6	59.8	155%
Bottomline Technologies	394.4	36.6	171.7	36%
Broadvision	1,500.0	59.3	653.2	62%
Concur	518.1	23.7	225.6	57%
Cybercash	267.3	15.9	116.4	49%
Digital River	476.1	30.3	207.3	47%
Entrust	1,110.0	55.9	483.4	54%
Healtheon	5,630.0	56.6	2,451.6	112%
Inktomi	4,460.0	39.9	1,942.1	118%
ISS	1,180.0	45.8	513.8	62%
Litronic	107.8	6.4	46.9	49%
Marimba	910.7	20.2	396.6	81%
Message Media	511.0	1.8	222.5	163%
NetGravity	372.3	14.1	162.1	63%
Net Perceptions	439.8	5.7	191.5	102%
NetObjects	220.3	20.5	95.9	36%
Open Market	454.3	62.5	197.8	26%
Phone.com	1,022.0	8.0	445.0	123%
Real Networks	4,270.0	75.9	1,859.4	90%
Rowe.com	158.9	19.4	69.2	29%
SalesLogix	228.2	18.8	99.4	40%
SilkNet Software	440.6	10.7	191.9	78%
VeriSign	2,730.0	47.9	1,188.8	90%
Vignette	1,480.0	23.1	644.5	95%
Web Trends	365.6	9.4	159.2	76%

($ millions)
Enabling Telecom Service

Name	Market Cap	Revenue	Future Revenue	Implied CAGR
AboveNet	$ 934.7	$ 9.7	$ 610.5	129%
AppliedTheory	285.5	24.1	186.5	51%
At Home	14,240.7	252.1	9,301.8	106%
CAIS Internet	239.7	5.7	156.6	94%
Concentric Network	1,170.0	96.4	764.2	51%
Covad	3,460.0	10.7	2,260.0	192%
Critical Path	1,660.0	1.9	1,084.3	257%
Earthlink	1,400.0	214.4	914.5	34%
Exodus	3,580.0	75.7	2,338.4	99%
Flashnet	277.5	29.1	181.3	44%
Global Crossing	22,100.0	602.1	14,435.4	89%
High Speed Access	278.7	0.7	182.0	200%
Internet America	117.2	16.0	76.6	37%
Juno Online Services	417.2	27.1	272.5	59%
Log On America	103.5	0.8	67.6	141%
MindSpring	1,980.0	154.9	1,293.3	53%
Network Access Solutions	442.2	13.9	288.8	83%
NorthPoint Communications	4,630.0	2.2	3,024.2	325%
OneMain.com	387.6	64.7	253.2	31%
Pacific Internet	469.5	36.1	306.7	53%
Prodigy	1,440.0	138.7	940.6	47%
PSINet	2,620.0	320.0	1,711.3	40%
Qwest	31,600.0	2,940.0	20,640.6	48%
Rhythms Net Connections	4,070.0	1.2	2,658.5	368%
Rocky Mountain Internet	115.6	13.6	75.5	41%
Softnet	345.4	8.3	225.6	94%
US internetworking	1,140.0	8.5	744.6	145%
Verio	2,120.0	154.6	1,384.8	55%
Ziplink	157.6	8.2	102.9	66%

*All data in this Appendix is as of June 11, 1999.

BIBLIOGRAPHY

Books

Allen, Frederick Lewis. *Only Yesterday: An Informal History of the 1920s*. New York: Harper & Row, 1931, 1964.

Baldwin, Neil. *Edison: Inventing the Century*. New York: Hyperion, 1995.

Boorstin, Daniel J. *The Americans: The Democratic Experience*. New York: Random House, 1973.

Bygrave, William D., and Jeffry A. Timmons. *Venture Capital at the Crossroads*. Boston: Harvard Business School Press, 1992.

Bylinsky, Gene. *The Innovation Millionaires: How They Succeed*. New York: Charles Scribner's Sons, 1976.

Carlton, Jim. *Apple: The Inside Story of Intrigue, Egomania, and Business Blunders*. New York: Times Books/Random House, 1997, 1998.

Chandler, Jr., Alfred D. *The Visible Hand: The Managerial Revolution in American Business*. Cambridge, Mass: Harvard University Press, 1977.

Chopsky, James, and Ted Leonsis. *Blue Magic: The People, Power, and Politics Behind the IBM Personal Computer*. New York, Oxford: Facts on File Publications, 1988.

253

Collier, Peter, and David Horowitz. *The Fords: An American Epic.* New York: Simon & Schuster, 1987.

Collins, James C., and Jerry I. Porras. *Built to Last: Successful Habits of Visionary Companies.* New York: HarperBusiness, 1994.

Cringely, Robert X. *Accidental Empires: How the Boys of Silicon Valley Make Their Millions, Battle Foreign Competition, and Still Can't Get a Date.* Reading, Mass: Addison-Wesley Publishing, 1992.

Cusumano, Michael, and David B. Yoffie. *Competing on Internet Time: Lessons from Netscape and Its Battle with Microsoft.* New York: The Free Press, 1998.

Davidow, William H. *Marketing High Technology: An Insider's View.* New York, London: Free Press, 1986.

DeNovo, John, ed. *The Gilded Age and After.* New York: Charles Scribner's Sons, 1972.

Doerflinger, Thomas M., and Jack L. Rivkin. *Risk and Reward: Venture Capital and the Making of America's Great Industries.* New York: Random House, 1987.

Edstrom, Jennifer, and Marlin Eller. *Barbarians Led by Bill Gates: Microsoft from the Inside.* New York: Henry Holt and Company, 1998.

Ferguson, Charles H., and Charles R. Morris. *Computer Wars: The Fall of IBM and the Future of Global Technology.* New York: Times Books, 1994.

Galbraith, John Kenneth. *A Short History of Financial Euphoria.* New York: Whittle Books / Viking Penguin, 1990.

Geisst, Charles R. *Wall Street: A History.* New York: Oxford University Press, 1997.

Gordon, John Steele. *The Scarlet Woman of Wall Street: Jay Gould, Jim Fisk, Cornelius Vanderbilt, The Erie Railway Wars and the Birth of Wall Street.* New York: Weidenfeld & Nicolson, 1988.

Grove, Andrew S. *Only the Paranoid Survive.* New York: Doubleday, 1996.

Hall, Mark, and John Barry. *Sunburst: The Ascent of Sun Microsystems.* Chicago: Contemporary Books, 1990.

Hooke, Jeffrey C. *Security Analysis on Wall Street.* New York: John Wiley & Sons, 1998.

Ichbiah, Daniel, and Susan L. Knepper. *The Making of Microsoft: How Bill Gates and His Team Created the World's Most Successful Software Company*. Rocklin, Calif.: Prima Publishing, 1991.

Jackson, Tim. *Inside Intel: Andrew Grove and the Rise of the World's Most Powerful Chip Company*. New York: Dutton Books, 1997.

Kaplan, Jerry. *Startup: A Silicon Valley Adventure Story*. New York: Houghton Mifflin, 1995.

Kelly, Kevin. *New Rules for the New Economy*. New York: Viking Penguin, 1998.

Kindelberger, Charles P. *Manias, Panics, and Crashes: A History of Financial Crises*. New York: John Wiley & Sons, 1996.

Kornberg, Arthur. *The Golden Helix: Inside Biotech Ventures*. Sausalito, Calif.: University Science Books, 1995.

Krugman, Paul. *The Return of Depression Economics*. New York: W.W. Norton & Company, 1999.

Lewis, Oscar. *The Big Four*. New York: Alfred A. Knopf, 1938.

———. *The Silver Kings*. New York: Ballantine Books, 1947.

Mackay, Charles. *Extraordinary Popular Delusions & the Madness of Crowds*. New York: Three Rivers Press, 1980.

Malone, Michael S. *The Big Score: The Billion Dollar Story of Silicon Valley*. New York: Doubleday, 1985.

———. *Going Public: MIPS Computer and the Entrepreneurial Dream*. New York: E. Burlingame Books, 1991.

Manes, Stephen, and Paul Andrews. *Gates: How Microsoft's Mogul Reinvented an Industry—and Made Himself the Richest Man in America*. New York: Doubleday, 1993.

Meeker, Mary, and Chris DePuy. *The Internet Report*. New York: HarperBusiness, 1996.

Meeker, Mary, and the Morgan Stanley Technology Team. *The Technology IPO Yearbook*, 5th ed. New York: Morgan Stanley Dean Witter, 1999.

Moore, Geoffrey A. *Crossing the Chasm: Marketing and Selling Technology Products to Mainstream Customers*. New York: HarperBusiness, 1991.

Moore, Geoffrey A., et al. *The Gorilla Game: An Investor's Guide to*

Picking Winners in High Technology. New York: HarperBusiness, 1998.

Moritz, Michael. *The Little Kingdom: The Private Story of Apple Computer.* New York: William Morrow and Company, 1984.

Myers, Gustavus. *History of the Great American Fortunes.* Charles H. Kerr Publishing Co., 1982.

Perkins, Michael C. *The Red Herring Guide to the Digital Universe: The Inside Look at Technology Business from Silicon Valley to Hollywood.* New York: Warner Books, 1996.

Quittner, Joshua, and Michelle Slatalla. *Speeding the Net: The Inside Story of Netscape and How It Challenged Microsoft.* New York: Atlantic Monthly Press, 1998.

Reid, Robert H. *Architects of the Web: 1,000 Days That Built the Future of Business.* New York: John Wiley & Sons, 1997.

Rogers, Everett M., and Judith K. Larsen. *Silicon Valley Fever.* New York: Basic Books, 1984.

Rolm, Wendy Goldman. *The Microsoft File: The Secret Case Against Bill Gates.* New York: Times Business Books/Random House, 1998.

Saxenian, AnnaLee. *Regional Advantage: Culture and Competition in Silicon Valley and Route 128.* Cambridge, Mass.: Harvard University Press, 1996.

Schama, Simon. *The Embarrassment of Riches: An Interpretation of Dutch Culture in the Golden Age.* Berkeley: University of California Press, 1988.

Schilt, W. Keith. *Dream Makers & Deal Breakers: Inside the Venture Capital Industry.* Englewood Cliffs, N.J.: Prentice Hall, 1991.

Schor, Juliet B. *The Overworked American.* New York: Basic Books, 1992.

Stewart, James B. *Den of Thieves.* New York: Simon & Schuster, 1991.

Stross, Randall E. *The Microsoft Way: The Real Story of the How the Company Outsmarts Its Competition.* Reading, Mass.: Addison-Wesley Publishing, 1996.

Swisher, Kara. *aol.com.* New York: Times Business Books/Random House, 1998.

Wallace, James. *Overdrive: Bill Gates and the Race to Control Cyber-*

space. New York: John Wiley & Sons, 1997.

Wallace, James, and Jim Erickson. *Hard Drive: Bill Gates and the Making of the Microsoft Empire*. New York: John Wiley & Sons, 1992.

Wilson, John W. *The New Venturers: Inside the High-Stakes World of Venture Capital*. Reading, Mass.: Addison-Wesley Publishing, 1985.

Wilson, Mike. *The Difference Between God and Larry Ellison: Inside Oracle Corporation*. New York: William Morrow and Company, 1997.

Wolff, Michael. *Burn Rate: How I Survived the Gold Rush Years on the Internet*. New York: Simon & Schuster, 1998.

Articles

Anders, George. "Self-Made Mania." *Wall Street Journal*, January 4, 1999.

Barack, Lauren. "The Underdogs of Underwriting." *Red Herring*, Going Public: 1999.

Barboza, David. "Loving a Stock Not Wisely but Too Well: The Price of Obsession with a Promising Startup." *New York Times*, September 20, 1998.

Birdsall, Nancy. "Life Is Unfair: Inequality in the World." *Foreign Policy*, Summer 1998.

Brooker, Katrina. "The Scary Rise of Internet Stock Scams." *Fortune*, October 26, 1998.

Byron, Christopher. "Another Cyberscam for Sucker's Index: End of Bull Market?" *New York Observer*, August 17, 1998.

Carvajal, Doreen. "Trying to Read a Hazy Future." *New York Times*, April 18, 1999.

Cassidy, John. "The Woman in the Bubble." *The New Yorker*, April 26/May 3, 1999.

Caulkin, Simon. "The Trouble with Bubbles." *Worldlink: The Magazine of the World Economic Forum*, March/April 1999.

Clements, Jonathan. "In the Field of Investing, Self-Confidence Can Sometimes Come Back to Haunt You." *Wall Street Journal*, September 23, 1998.

Collins, James C. "It's Time to Rethink the Silicon Valley Paradigm." *Red Herring,* July 1993.

Corcoran, Elizabeth. "Reinventing Intel." *Forbes,* May 3, 1999.

Darwell, Christina, and Michael J. Roberts. "The Band of Angels." *Harvard Business School,* March 11, 1998.

Fisher, Larry. "Money Walks: VCs Are Bailing on Biotech." *Forbes ASAP*, May 31, 1999.

Fishman, Ted C. "Up in Smoke." *Harper's Magazine,* December 1998.

Foust, Dean, and Linda Himelstein. "Time to Buy Net Stocks?" *Business Week,* May 17, 1999.

Gates, Stephanie T. "The IPO Tease." *Red Herring,* August 1999.

Gove, Alex. "Sendmail Pits Angel Investors Against VCs." *Red Herring,* November 1998.

Gurley, Bill. "A Dell for Every Industry." *Fortune,* October 12, 1998.

———. "Internet Investors: Beware." *Fortune,* August 17, 1998.

Hansell, Saul. "New Breeds of Investors, All Beguiled by the Web." *New York Times,* May 16, 1999.

———. "Cnet Is Singed by the Offbeat Logic of the Internet Investor." *New York Times*, July 6, 1999.

Hatlestad, Luc. "Free Mail Explosion." *Red Herring,* July 1998.

Heilemann, John. "The Networker." *The New Yorker,* August 11, 1997.

Hof, Robert D. "Amazon.com: The Wild World of E-Commerce." *Business Week,* December 14, 1998.

Holson, Laura M. "Still Feeding an Internet Frenzy." *New York Times,* June 6, 1999.

Johnson, Franklin "Pitch". "The Application of Venture Capital and the Entrepreneurial Revolution in Russia." Center for International Security and Cooperation, Stanford University, August 1998.

Laderman, Jeffrey, and Geoffrey Smith. "Internet Stocks: What's Their Real Worth?" *Business Week,* December 14, 1998.

Lardner, James. "Ask Radio Historians About the Internet." *U.S. News & World Report,* January 23, 1999.

Laderman, Jeffrey. "Wall Street's Spin Game." *Business Week,* October 5, 1998.

Lohr, Steve. "Computer Age Gains Respect of Economists,"

New York Times, April 14, 1999.

Lucchetti, Aaron. "Internet Public Offerings Aren't the Same in Era of Internet Stock Mania." *Wall Street Journal,* January 19, 1999.

Madden, Andrew. "The Good Soldier." *Red Herring,* September 1996.

McNamee, Roger. "Welcome to Technology's Gilded Age." *Forbes ASAP,* October 5, 1998.

Morgenson, Gretchen. "Just Another Round of Technology Delusion." *New York Times,* April 25, 1999.

Mullarkey, Markus F., and André F. Perold. "Integral Capital Partners." Harvard Business School Case 9–298–171, September 1998.

Peltz, Michael. "High Tech's Premier Venture Capitalist." *Institutional Investor,* June 1996.

Perkins, Anthony B. "Have the Rules Really Changed?" *Red Herring,* October 1997.

———. "Navigating the Amazon." *Red Herring,* June 1997.

———. "Open Letter to Trip Hawkins." *Red Herring,* April 1993.

———. "The Thinker." *Red Herring,* March 1995.

———. "Venture Pioneers." *Red Herring,* March 1994.

———. "Bill Joy on Sun's Long Road from Java to Jini—and Where Microsoft Comes In." *Red Herring,* January 1999.

Perkins, Michael C. "Angels on High." *Red Herring,* Going Public: 1997.

Perkins, Michael C., and Anthony B. Perkins. "3DO's New Trip." *Red Herring,* May 1996.

———. "Case by Case: A Conversation with Steve Case." *Red Herring,* June 1996.

Pickering, Carol. "A Tale of Two Startups." *Forbes ASAP,* October 5, 1998.

Pollack, Andrew. "It Sliced, It Sentimentalized, but Now Can It Surf?" *New York Times,* November 23, 1998.

———. "Weed-out Time in Biotechnology." *New York Times,* December 16, 1998.

Rich, Frank. "The Cyber-Donald." *New York Times,* October 10, 1998.

Roach, Stephen S., "The Boom for Whom: Revisiting America's

Technology Paradox." Special Economic Study, Morgan Stanley Dean Witter, January 9, 1998.

Romer, Paul. "It's All in Your Head." *Outlook Magazine,* no. 1, 1998.

Sahlman, William A. "The Race Between Capital and Opportunity." Harvard Business School, July 1998.

Sahlman, William A., and Dimitri V. d'Arbeloff. "Sense and Nonsense in the Capital Markets." Harvard Business School, 1998.

Sahlman, William A., and Howard H. Stevenson. "Capital Market Myopia." *Journal of Business Venturing,* Winter 1985.

Schifrin, Matthew, and Om Malik. "Amateur Hour on Wall Street." *Forbes,* January 25, 1999.

Schwartz, Peter, and Peter Leyden. "The Long Boom: A History of the Future, 1980–2020." *Wired,* July 1997.

Siconolfi, Michael. "The Spin Desk: Underwriters Set Aside IPO Stock for Officials of Potential Customers." *Wall Street Journal,* November 12, 1997.

Solomon, Deborah. "At Home Users Grumble About Slow Service." *San Francisco Chronicle,* December 2, 1998.

———. "At Home Speed Cap Angers Subscribers." *San Francisco Chronicle,* June 30, 1999.

———. "At Home Customers Frustrated." *San Francisco Chronicle,* February 26, 1999.

———. "DSL Beats Cable in Net Speed." *San Francisco Chronicle,* May 24, 1999.

Taptich, Brian E. "The New Startup." *Red Herring,* October 1998.

———. "Pop Goes the Weisel." *Red Herring,* August 1999.

Uchitelle, Louis. "Reviving the Economics of Fear." *New York Times,* July 2, 1999.

Warner, Melanie. "Inside the Silicon Valley Money Machine." *Fortune,* October 26, 1998.

Wyatt, Edward. "Feasting on a Banquet of Internet Offerings." *New York Times,* April 12, 1999.

———. "Old Stocks, New Technology, More Questions." *New York Times,* February 16, 1999.

Yardeni, Edward. "New Era Recession? Deflation, Irrational

Exhuberance, & Y2K." Topical Study #37, Deutsche Morgan Grenfell, July 14. 1997.

    ———. "The Y2K Book." Deutsche Morgan Grenfell, Spring
1998.

ACKNOWLEDGMENTS

The Internet Bubble would not be comfortably resting in your hands right now if we had not received the active and enlightening participation of the following list of people. Writing a pointed analysis of the technology investment market was obviously a Herculean task. It was accomplished by seeking the insights and perspectives of only the most insightful and powerful insiders in technology, and ruthlessly selecting what we felt were the most logical and best supported arguments and analysis. The book has new and often trenchant things to say about venture capital and public company investing. In the tradition of *Red Herring* magazine, we do not conceal our opinions, and anticipate that these opinions will unsettle many important players in the technology community. Such a fact-filled volume as this is bound to contain errors. If readers spot any, we would be grateful if you could email us using the book comments section of *The Internet Bubble*'s online site, www.redherring.com/internetbubble.

Our most gracious thanks goes to Roger McNamee, cofounder and partner at Integral Capital Partners, the person who spent the most time with us, initially helping us develop the book's general thesis, and later poring over and editing many of the different sections in the book as they were drafted. It will become clear to the readers as they delve into the book that we, along with the rest of the industry and the media that covers technology, believe that Roger is one of the brightest and most forward-thinking commentators in the business. Special thanks also to Barbara Luke of Integral Capital Partners, who put up with our frantic calls and helped us coordinate with Roger's very hectic schedule.

Others industry titans who were also generous with their time and observations include: Herb Allen, Jr.; Marc Andreessen, cofounder of Netscape and chief technology officer at America Online; Andy Bechtolsheim; Jeff Bezos, CEO of Amazon.com; Bill Brady at CS First Boston; Jim Breyer, managing partner at Accel Partners; Lise Buyer, Internet analyst and director of technology research at investment bank CS First Boston; Bandel Carano, general partner at Oak Investment Partners; Dan Case, president and CEO of Hambrecht & Quist; Jim Clark; Sam Colella, general partner at Institutional Venture Partners; Jim Collins; Ron Conway, director of strategic relationships at CBT Systems and member of the Band of Angels; Paul Deninger, chairman and CEO of technology investment bank Broadview International; Mark Diocioccio, vice president at Lehman Brothers; John Doerr, general partner at Kleiner Perkins Caufield & Byers; Tim Draper, general partner at Draper Fisher Jurvetson; Ira Ehrenpreis, general partner at Technology Partners; Steve Forbes; Stu Francis, managing director at Lehman Brothers; Bill Gates, chairman & CEO of Microsoft; Eric Greenberg, CEO of Scient; Michael Grimes, managing partner at Morgan Stanley Dean Witter; Bill Gurley, general partner at Benchmark Partners; Will Hearst III, general partner at Kleiner Perkins Caufield & Byers; David Henderson, economist and research fellow at the Hoover Institution; Phil Horsley, managing director of Horsley Bridge Partners; Franklin "Pitch" Johnson, general partner at Asset Management; Bill Joy, general partner at Benchmark Partners; Robert Kagle; Andy Kessler at Velocity Capital; Vinod Khosla, general partner at Kleiner Perkins Caufield & Byers; Brad Koening, managing director and head of the technology banking practice at

Goldman Sachs; Mark Kvamme; Bruce Lupatkin, former director of research at Hambrecht & Quist; Donald Luskin; Jeff Mallett, chief operating officer at Yahoo; Arthur Marks, general partner at New Enterprise Associates; Mary Meeker, Internet analyst at Morgan Stanley Dean Witter; Bob Metcalfe; Cristina Morgan, managing director at Hambrecht & Quist; Michael Moritz, general partner at Sequoia Capital; Tom Perkins; Frank Quattrone, managing director and head of technology banking at CS First Boston; Dan Reeve of Horsley Bridge Partners; Stephen Roach, chief economist at Morgan Stanley Dean Witter; Sandy Robertson; Arthur Rock; Paul Romer, economist at Stanford University; Joel Romines and Brad Kelly, partners at Knightsbridge Advisors; William Sahlman, professor at Harvard Business School; George Shott and Peter Best at Shott Capital Management; Roger Siboni, CEO at Epiphany; Don Valentine, general partner at Sequoia Capital; Ann Winblad, general partner at Hummer Winblad Partners; Geoff Yang, general partner at Institutional Venture Partners; Jerry Yang, cofounder and chief Yahoo at Yahoo; Edward Yardeni, chief economist at Deutsche Grenfell Morgan); and Sandy Climan, managing director of Entertainment Media Ventures LLC.

For extensive help in data collection, financial analysis and our Bubble calculation we would like to tip our hats to Paul Joachim and Cameron Hyzer and the entire Broadview International organization for their tireless work and quick turnaround. In addition, Broadview was very helpful in producing extensive strategic insight into the Internet market and its various segments. Dave Witherow and Jean Yaremchuk of VentureOne and Roydel Stewart at Hambrecht & Quist also deserve kudos for their help and support in the data collection area.

The manuscript never would have been in the kind of shape it needed to be without the highly intelligent and invaluable work of our developmental editors Nina Davis and Shirley Tokheim. Nina was particularly helpful in bringing to bear on the book her extensive knowledge of the industry and technical insight, as well as her unfailing logic. She saved us from many potential mistakes. Shirley was especially helpful in editing the book for style and giving us the constant perspective of an intelligent reader living outside the industry.

We can't forget Ellen Anderson and her transcription service Anderson Typefast for timely and precise rendition of our numerous interview tapes. Their work helped assure that we would accurately quote the numerous on-the-record interviews we did for the book.

A special thanks to many Red Herring staff members, including Charlotte Dicke, Danielle Unis, and Pam Dabney who helped us arrange and coordinate a grueling schedule of meetings and interviews. Also, Josh Liebster network administrator at *Red Herring* for providing much-needed technical support, and *Red Herring*'s online technical director, Thom Howard, for helping us build and incorporate the *Internet Bubble* web pages into redherring.com. And, finally, Chris Alden, CEO and editorial director at *Red Herring* for his general support for the project.

At Harper: Adrian Zackheim, publisher who provided us with the original inspiration for the book and believed in us all the way, and David Conti, executive editor, who patiently put up with our many broken deadlines and the management of what became a very complex task.

At International Creative Management: Esther Newberg, the queen of literary agents, who successfully banged on Harper and doubled our advance, and John De Laney of the ICM legal department who provided extensive help with the contract.

Special affection is reserved for Georganne Perkins, wife of Michael and sister-in-law of Anthony, who though offering no advice or information due to professional confidentiality issues, nevertheless provided continual moral support throughout this project.

INDEX

ABC, 115, 116

AboveNet, 3

Abraham, Spence, 186

Accel Partners, 45, 57, 58

Active Apparel Group, 33

Active Software, 79

ADSL (asymmetric digital subscriber line), 87, 170–71

advertising, on the Internet, 5,
164–66, 230

Alex. Brown & Sons, 99, 109

Allen, Frederick Lewis, 15

Allen, Herbert, Jr., 4, 115–16,
119, 178, 234

Allen & Co., 115–16, 119

Allnetservices, 192

Alsop, Stewart, 81

Amazon Auctions, 160

Amazon.com, 21, 24, 25, 27, 32,
60, 89, 134, 151, 152–59

electronic commerce and,
154–56

investment bankers and, 102,
104, 105

IPO from, xi–xv, xix

Kleiner Perkins (KP) and, 69,
74, 78, 99–100, 102, 152

Amdahl, 61

*American Journal of Public
Health*, 185–86

America Online (AOL), 21, 31,
89, 157, 163, 180, 226

advertising on, 165

Kleiner Perkins (KP) and, 69,
71, 81, 82, 74, 95–96, 102

Microsoft and, 94, 95–96

Netscape purchase by, 31, 81,
82, 86, 92, 95–96

Yahoo and, xvi

Amerindo Technology, 18

AmeriTrade, 13, 26

Amgen, 40, 139–41, 145, 146

Andressen, Marc, 79, 90, 92, 93, 96

angel investors, 38, 58–60

Apple Computer, 76, 146, 212, 233

   Morgan Stanley Dean Witter and, 98–99, 100

   venture capitalists and, 42–43, 44, 50

Applied Materials, 222

Arbor Software, 120, 212

Architext, 75, 163

asset allocation, in a personal investing strategy, 227

Asset Management, 140–41

asymmetric digital subscriber line (ADSL), 87, 170–71

AT&T, 76, 147, 171, 173, 223

At Home, 17, 151, 167–72

   Kleiner Perkins (KP) and, 69, 71, 73–74, 78, 80, 81, 82, 89, 98, 102, 168

   Excite purchase by, 81, 82, 85–88, 173

At Work, 171

BancBoston Robertson Stephens, 95, 108

Band of Angels, 58–60

Bankers Trust, 109

Bank of America, 97, 108, 111

bankruptcy, 19

banks. *See* investment banks

Barksdale, Jim, 77, 78, 96

Barnes & Noble, xi, xii, 104, 157, 160

barnesandnoble.com, 153

Baruch, Bernard, 177

Bay Networks, 45

Bear Stearns, 26, 132–33

Bell, George, 78, 80, 86–87

Bechtolsheim, Andy, 21, 58, 59

Benchmark Capital, 55

Bernstein, Jared, 185

Berry, Rick, 33–34

Bertlesmann, 153

Bezos, Jeff, xi–xv, xix, 80, 99, 152, 154, 155, 158, 159, 160–69

Bhatia, Sabeer, 57

Bid.com, 165

Biggs, Barton, 188, 213

Bikers Dream, 33

Bill Joy's Law, 99

biotechnology, 74, 135–46

   IPOs and, 140–42, 144, 147

   venture capitalists and, 143–44

biotechnology indexes

   Hambrecht & Quist (H&Q), 141

   NASDAQ, 145

Blodgett, Henry, 14

Bloomfield, Robert, 189

Books-a-Million, 33

booms. *See also* Internet Bubble

   Comstock Lode silver rush, 14–15

Florida real estate boom, 15
1920's stock market frenzy
and crash, 15, 20, 178,
207–12
personal computers, 5–6, 39,
49–52, 64, 99, 206
tulip mania, 13–14, 16, 34
Borders Group, xi, 192
Boston Chicken, 188
Boston University, 142–43
Bottomline Technologies, 3
Boutros, George, 100–1
Bowes, Bill, 139
Bowin, Matthew, 193
Boyer, Herbert, 135, 137
Brady, Bill, xiii, xiv, 50, 53,
63–64, 100, 101, 104, 168,
169
Brentwood Associates, 45
Breyer, Jim, 8, 18, 31, 45, 46, 48,
49, 147
Bright Light Technologies, 58,
59
Broadcast.com, 164
Broadcom, 38
Broadview International, 116,
193
Bryan, John, 40
Buffet, Warren, 116
Built to Last (Collins and Por-
ras), 223
bulge-bracket banks, 97–98, 99
Bureau of Labor Statistics,
183
Business Week magazine, 43

Buyer, Lise, 14, 16, 30, 62,
158–59, 208
Byers, Brook, 70, 73
Bygrave, William, 51, 146
Byron, Christopher, 166
BZW, 187

Campbell, Bill, 78, 79, 83
capital. *See also* venture capital-
ists
growth in amount of avail-
able to Internet-related
companies, 6–7
Internet stock mania and, 6
Capital Cities, 115, 116
"Capital Market Myopia" (case
study), 50
Carano, Bandel, 9, 21–22, 45,
46–47
Cary, David, 120
Case, Dan, 163, 178
Case, Steve, 96, 163
Cashman, Edmund, 30
Caufield, Frank, 73
CBS Marketwatch, 191
CDNow, 32, 157
Cetus Corporation, 139
Charles Schwab Corporation,
25, 26, 111–12, 188, 191, 207
Chase Manhattan Bank, 187
Chiron, 140, 145
Cisco Systems, 8, 52–53, 59, 93,
101, 180, 212, 222, 230
Kleiner Perkins (KP) and,
75–76

Cisco Systems (*cont.*)
  Sequoia Capital and, 47,
    215–7
CKS Partners, 151, 161–63
Clark, Jim, 77, 83, 89–92, 96, 99
Clinton, Bill, 186
CMG, 13
CNBC, 25, 33
C/Net, 27, 38
CNN, 93
CNNfn, 25
Coca-Cola, 22, 116
Cohen, Stanley, 137
Colella, Sam, 54, 70, 98, 135,
    141
Collins, James, 211, 223–24
Columbia Pictures, 116
Commodore, 50
Compaq, 57, 69, 73, 74, 94, 98,
    233
Compton, Kevin, 73, 80
Comstock Lode silver rush,
    14–15
Concentric Network, 102
concept stock, 147–49
Conway, Ron, 152–53
Cook, Scott, xiv, 78, 79, 88
Cooley, Godward, 40
Cornell University, Johnson
    Graduate School of Man-
    agement, 189
Cotsakos, Christos, 134
Coxe, Tench, 45
credit card debt, 9
Cruttenden, Walter, 115

CS First Boston, 100, 103, 104, 106
Cusumano, Michael, 31
Cyberian Outpost, 157
Cypress Semiconductor, 212

David, Paul, 181
Davis, Tommy, 40
day trading, 25–27, 234–35
debt, consumer, 19
Dell Computer, 8, 155–56, 222,
    231, 233
Deninger, Paul, 8, 30–31, 49, 54,
    86, 98, 116
Dennis, Lori, 132
Department of Justice, 96
Deutsche Banc Alex. Brown,
    109
Deutsche Bank, 101, 103, 109
Deutsche Morgan Grenfell
    (DMG), 53, 168, 169
  Amazon IPO and, xiii, xiv, xv
Dicioccio, Marc, 81
Diller, Barry, 116
Diocioccio, Mark, 98
Discover Online, 25
Discovery Zone, 188
disk drive companies, 39, 50–51,
    64
Disney, 115, 116
diversification, in a personal
    investing strategy, 227
DJIA, 4
DLJ Direct, 112
DMG Technology, 101–3
Dodd, David, 20, 14

Doerr, John, 44, 46, 70, 71, 72,
    73–75, 76, 80, 81, 85, 88–89,
    98, 100, 100, 103, 160, 183, 230
    Amazon IPO and, xii, xiii, xiv
    At Home and, 168, 174
    McNamee at Integral Capital
        Partners and, 217, 218, 219
    Microsoft and, 94, 96, 97
    Netscape and, 83–84, 91–92
    on the approach used by
        Kleiner Perkins (KP), 74–75
    on the Internet boom, 5–6
    recruiting of management by,
        77–79
    venture capital success and,
        69, 73–74
Donaldson, Lufkin & Jenrette,
    106, 112
Donatiello, Nick, 173
Dow Jones, 4
Doyle, Bill, 111, 114
Draper, Bill, 40, 47
Draper, Tim, 39–40, 45, 47, 57
Dreman, David, 12
Drugstore.com, 160
Dutch auction systems, 111,
    112–13
Dynabook, 100
Dynamic Media.com, 192
Dyson, Esther, 58, 79

E*Offering, 111, 112, 114, 115
E*Trade, 13, 25, 26, 111, 134,
    188, 191, 207
Earthweb, 28

eBay, 13, 25, 27–28, 28–29, 104,
    105, 160, 165
EBITDA (earnings before inter-
    est, taxes, depreciation, and
    amortization), 21
Economic Policy Institute, 185
Economic Value Added (EVA),
    23–24
Economist, The (journal), 26
Edison, Thomas, 224
Edwards, Bill, 40
Eisner, Michael, 116
Electronic Arts, 146, 212
electronic commerce
    advertising and, 5, 164–66, 230
    Amazon and, 154–56
    growth of, 6
    investment banking and, 111–13
    Kleiner Perkins (KP) and, 74
    K-Tel International and, 32
    venture capitalists and, 60
electronic communications net-
    works (ECNs), 207
electronic investment banking,
    111–13
Eli Lilly, 139
EO, 76–77
Epiphany, 79
Ericsson, 95
eToys, 38, 153, 157
Excite, 71, 74, 75, 162
    At Home's purchase of, 81,
        82, 85–88, 173
    Netscape and, 83–85, 92
Exxon, 98

Fairchild Semiconductor, 41, 96
Federal Express, 192
Federal Reserve Bank of New
    York, 113
Federal Reserve Board, 6
Fidelity Investments, 95, 117
Fidelity Select Biotechnology
    fund, 141
Filo, David, xv–xix, 214
First Auction, 165
First Call, 116
Fisher, Irving, 15
float of Internet stocks, 27–28,
    133–34
Florida real estate boom, 15
Fogelsong, Norm, 91
Forbes, Steve, 193
Forbes magazine, 179
Ford, Henry, 224
Ford Motor Company, 16
Foreign Policy journal, 184–85
Forrester Research, 111, 166
Fortune magazine, 62, 70, 83,
    192
Francis, Stu, 100, 103, 121

Gartner Group, 114, 187
Gates, Bill, 4, 22, 57–58, 116,
    182, 224, 230
    advice on investing from, 234
    Kleiner Perkins (KP) and, 94,
        95, 96–97
    on the Internet, 92–93
    return from Internet stocks
        and, 16, 17, 22, 207

Gates, Stephanie, 113–14
Gateway, 180
Geisst, Charles, 191, 207–11
Genentech, 73, 74, 135, 139,
    140, 145
General Atlantic Partners, xii
General Electric Company, 98,
    224
General Motors, 98
genetic engineering, 135, 137.
    See also biotechnology
GeoCities, 164
Gibbons, James, 45
Gigot, Paul, 96
Gilder, George, 230
Glassmeyer, Ed, 47
Glass-Steagall Act, 109
GO Computer, 76–77, 100
Goldman Sachs, 98, 102, 103, 98
    IPOs and, 95, 99, 106, 109,
        114–15
    vs. Morgan Stanley, 104–6
    Yahoo IPO and, xvii–xviii, 105
Gore, Al, 96
Go2Net, 13
Graham, Benjamin, 20, 24
Granite Systems, 59
Greenberg, Alan ("Ace"), 132–33
Greenspan, Alan, 182, 186
Greylock Management, 44
Grove, Andy, 79, 116, 167
Gurley, Bill, 62–63, 156, 163, 227

Hambrecht, Bill, 97, 111, 114,
    115

Hambrecht & Company, 111, 112, 113
Hambrecht & Quist (H&Q), 52, 99, 120, 135
  biotechnology index of, 141
  formation of, 97
  IPOs and, 95, 98, 106–7
  spinning and, 120–21
Hancock Venture Partners, 45
Harvard Business School, 46, 48, 50
Hawkins, Trip, 146, 147, 148
Healtheon, 13, 102
Hearst, Will, III, 70, 73, 78, 80–81, 82, 85, 89, 218
  At Home and, 167–68, 170, 171, 174
Hewlett, Bill, 65, 224
Hewlett-Packard, 38, 65
Hill, Chuck, 116
Homer, Mike, 78, 83
Horsley, Phil, 88
Horsley Bridge Partners, 145
Hotmail, 57–58
Hummer Winblad, xii
Hwang, Victor, xvii

IBM, 43, 93
individual investors. *See also* personal investing strategy
  consumer debt and, 19
  day trading and, 25–27, 234–35
  flipping and, 132–34
  Internet Bubble and, 3, 4, 6
  Internet scams and, 191–93
  IPOs and, 9, 17–18, 19, 151
  margin and, 26
  momentum investing and, 25, 207–11
  overconfidence of, 188–89
  venture capitalists and number of, 37, 65
industrial Darwinism, 233–34
inflation, 7
information technology
  overworked professionals and, 183–84
  productivity and paradox of, 180–81
  Y2K problem and, 177, 187–88
Information Technology Paradox, 180–81
Infoseek, xvii, 163
InfoSpace, 13
initial public offerings (IPOs)
  from Amazon, xi–xv
  biotechnology companies and, 140–42, 144, 147
  examples of record-breakers in, 28–33
  float in, 133–34
  insiders in, 9, 27
  institutional investors and, 18
  Internet Bubble and, 3
  later trading below offering prices of, 23, 193–94
  mutual funds and, 133
  from Netscape, 30–31

initial public offerings (IPOs)
(*cont.*)
  online investment banking
    and, 111, 115
  profitability of companies
    issuing, 20, 24, 62, 147–46
  reasons for issuing, 17–20
  scams and, 192–93
  size of funds involved in, 37,
    53–54, 60, 98, 230–31
  stock security valuation and,
    20–24
  venture capitalists and, 17
  from Yahoo, xv–xix
Inktomi, 38
Institute of Psychology and
  Markets, 27
institutional investors, 234–35
  Internet stocks held by, 6
  IPOs and, 18
  venture capital from, 37, 40,
    43–44
Institutional Venture Partners
  (IVP), 45, 53, 75
Integral Capital Partners, 212,
  217–19
  Integral Capital L.P. Fund I of,
    219
  Integral Fund III of, 221
  investing guidelines of, 200–9
  Silver Lake fund of, 222–23
Intel, 8, 22, 167, 222, 230
  institutional investors in, 234
  venture capital supplied by,
    38, 56–57

  venture capitalists' funding of,
    41–42, 43
Interactive Products and Services, 192–93
International Data Corporation
  (IDC), 6, 95
International Data Group, 85
Internet
  advertising on, 5, 164–65, 230
  as a catalyst for the growth of
    technology industries, 5–6
  impact of, 231–32
Internet Bubble, 3–10
  Amazon IPO and, xi–xv
  day trading and, 25–27,
    234–35
  individual investors and 3, 6
  insiders and IPOs in, 9
  investment banks and, 95
  Kleiner Perkins (KP) and, 71,
    100–101, 102
  prediction of correction in, 4
  venture capitalists and, 37,
    53–55, 63–66
  vs. S&P 600 and DJIA, 4
  Yahoo IPO and, xv–xix
Internet Fund, 18
Internet-related companies. *See
  also* technology sector
  combined market value of, 3
  float of stocks from, 27–28
  growth in amount of capital
    available to, 6–7
  prediction of correction
    affecting valuation of, 4

profitability of, and IPOs, 20,
24, 62
reasons for going public,
17–20
stock security valuation and,
21–24
venture capital from, 38,
56–58
Internet Stock Review, 192
Internet stocks. *See also* Internet
Bubble
mania in trading, 6–34
top ten stocks, in terms of
increase in valuation, 13
Internet Technology Fund II, 57
Intraware, 102
Intuit, 70, 74, 78, 83, 84, 85, 88,
94, 100
investment banks, 8, 95–134
competition among, 106–9
fees and commissions charged
by, 95–96, 112
flipping by, 132–34
Internet Bubble and, 95
mergers and acquisitions and,
115–16
online banking and, 111–13
pioneers among, 96–100
stock spinning and, 119–30
use of stock analysts by,
117–19
investors. *See* individual
investors; institutional
investors
IPOs. *See* initial public offerings

ISS, 102
iVillage, 28, 29, 102, 105, 166

Java Fund, 93–94
Jermoluk, Tom, 80, 85, 86, 87,
169, 172
Jobs, Steve, 98, 146
Johnson, Pitch, 40, 54, 55, 140
Joy, Bill, 58, 88, 95, 99
Junglee, 157
Jurvetson, Steve, 153
Justice Department, 96

Kagle, Bob, 9, 7, 100, 151, 165,
166
Kaplan, Jerry, 76–77, 82
Kelly, George, 102
Kessler, Andy, 28
Keynes, John Maynard, 189
Khosla, Vinod, 73, 75, 82, 83,
84, 85, 152, 155
Excite funding and, 163
Kindleberger, Charles, 191
Kives, Philip, 32
Kleiner, Eugene, 41, 72–73, 97,
137
Kleiner Perkins Caufield &
Byers (KP), 10, 69–102, 160,
168
Amazon IPO and, xii, xiv,
99–100, 152
biotechnology and, 135,
137–37, 145
Excite and, xvi, 81, 82, 83–88,
173

Kleiner Perkins Caufield &
    Byers (KP) (*cont.*)
first-move advantage and,
    97–101
founding partners of, 72–73
Genentech and, 73, 74
hidden entrepreneurial ambi-
    tions of partners in, 80–81
Integral Capital Partners and,
    219
Internet Bubble and, 71,
    100–101, 102
investment bankers and IPOs
    and, 98, 109
keiretsu of, 81–82, 88, 95–96
less successful deals of, 75–77
Microsoft and, 71, 92–97
Netscape and, 89–92, 95–96
portfolio of Internet compa-
    nies held by, 102
recruiting of management by,
    77–79
venture capital from, 44, 46,
    53, 55
Zaibatsu at, 79
Koenig, Brad, 18, 64, 98, 121
Koogle, Tim, xvi
KPMG Peat Marwick, 78, 79
Krugman, Paul, 189–90
K-Tel International, 31–34
Kvamme, Floyd, 73
Kvamme, Mark, 161–62

Lacob, Joe, 73
Lacroute, Bernie, 73

Lally, Jim, 73
Lamond, Pierre, 215–16
large cap technology compa-
    nies, 234
Lehman Brothers, 26, 100, 121
Lenk, Toby, 153
Levin, Gerry, 116
Lewis, Oscar, 14–15
Leyden, Peter, 179
L. F. Rothschild, 98
Ligand Pharmaceuticals, 143
Long Boom, 7, 177, 178–80
Lotus, 73, 74, 97
Lucent, 57, 223
Lupatkin, Bruce, 13, 116–18,
    188, 226
Lycos, xvii, 163
Lynch, Peter, 159

McCaffery, Michael, 19, 95
McGovern, Pat, 85
MCI Worldcom, 180
Mackay, Charles, 14
McKenna, Regis, 88
Mackenzie, Douglas, 73
McNamee, Roger, 3, 9, 16–17,
    19, 24, 26, 59, 81, 193, 194,
    195–96
Integral Capital Partners and,
    217–21
Silver Lake fund of, 222–23
McNealy, Scott, 75–76, 79, 96,
    98
Macromedia, 79
Mallett, Jeff, xvi, 164

Malone, John, 85
Malone, Michael S., 45–46
manias. *See also* Internet Bubble
 Comstock Lode silver rush,
  14–15
 Florida real estate boom, 15
 1920's stock market frenzy and
  crash, 15, 20, 178, 207–11
 tulip mania, 13–14, 16, 34
margin, 26
Marimba, 102
Marketwatch.com, 18, 19
Markkula, Mike, 42, 43
Marks, Art, 56, 57, 65–66
Matsushita, 147, 148
Mayfield Fund, 40, 44, 91, 98
MBAs, as venture capitalists,
  45–46, 48
Media Matrix, 87, 190–91
Meeker, Mary, 4, 8, 30, 102, 104,
  193, 234
Menlo Ventures, 53
Merrill Lynch, 26, 106, 109, 114,
  141, 187
MessageMedia, 13
Metcalfe, Robert, 5
Metcalfe's Law, 5
Microsoft, 56, 57, 71, 88, 92, 99,
  153, 168–69, 180, 192, 230
 Excite and, 82
 growth in value of, 17, 22, 24,
  29, 231
 Hotmail acquisition of, 57–58
 institutional investors in, 6,
  234

investing in stock of, 222
 IPO from, 231, 234
 Justice Department complaint
  against, 96
 Kleiner Perkins (KP) and, 71,
  92–97
 Netscape and, 31
 technology sector stocks and,
  8
 venture capital from, 38
momentum investing, 25,
  207–86
money supply, increase in, 6–7
Montgomery Securities,
  109–11, 120
Monument Fund, 18
Moore, Geoffrey, 60–61
Moore, Gordon, 41–42, 72
Morgan, Christina, 18, 84, 99,
  103, 109, 120–21
Morgan Stanley Dean Witter,
  5–6, 7, 23, 24, 98, 103, 188
 Amazon IPO and, xiii, xv, 99
 Apple Computer and, 98–99,
  100
 Integral Capital Partners and,
  219
 IPOs and, 95, 101, 106, 109, 230
 Quattrone at, 100–2
 spinning and, 120
 vs. Goldman Sachs, 104–6
Moritz, Michael, 38, 54–55, 64,
  111, 154, 182, 183–84,
  213–14, 215, 216
 Yahoo IPO and, xvi–xvii

Morningstar, 218
Motley Fool, 25, 188
Motorola, 43, 95
MSN, 32, 71, 153
Munder NetNet, 18
Murdoch, Rupert, 116
Murphy, John, 142
Murphy, Tom, 116
mutual funds, and Internet
    stocks, 18, 133

NASDAQ
    biotech index of, 145
    flow of international funds
      into, 6
    stocks delisted from, 31, 33, 143
    venture capitalists and, 44
NASDAQ Computer Index, 8
National Venture Capital Asso-
    ciation, 47–48
NationsBanc, 109–11
NEA VIII, 57
Nemirovsky, Ofer, 45
Netcenter, 83, 96
Net Grocer, 165
Netscape Communications, 94,
    101, 120
    AOL's purchase of, 31, 81, 82,
      86, 95–96
    Excite and, 83–85
    IPO from, 23, 30–31
    Kleiner Perkins (KP) and, 69,
      70, 73, 77, 80, 88, 89–92,
      95–96, 99
    Yahoo and, xvi

networking equipment compa-
    nies, 50, 52–53
New Economy, 7, 177–92
    inequalities among workers
      and, 184–86
    Long Boom and, 178–80
    overworked professionals
      and, 183–82
    productivity and technology
      paradox and, 180–82
New Enterprise Associates
    (NEA), 57, 91
New York Stock Exchange,
    44
The New Yorker magazine, 4, 97,
    100, 104, 174
New York Times, 33, 87, 92, 104,
    105, 142, 154, 190, 188
NextCard, 102
NFO Worldwide, 190, 191
Nikkei stock index, 188
Nokia, 95
Nortel, 57
Noyce, Robert (Bob), 41–42,
    72
N2K, 157

Oak Investment Partners, 45,
    47, 53
Octel, 40
Odean, Terrance, 189–88
Odyssey LP, 173
OnSale, 82, 102, 165
online commerce. *See* electronic
    commerce

online trading
  day trading and, 25–27,
    234–35
OpenIPO, 113
Oracle, 8, 93, 212
Ormerod, Paul, 188
Osborne, 50
overconfidence, 188–89

Packard, David, 65, 72, 224
Paine Webber, 26
PalmPilot, 95
Palo Alto Research Center,
  Xerox, 224
Parametric Technology, 47
Pennzoil–Quaker State, 180
pension funds, 37
Perkins, Tom, 46, 72–73, 80, 91,
  97, 137
Personal Digital Assistants
  (PDAs), 76
personal computers, boom in,
  5–6, 39, 49–52, 64, 99, 206
personal investing strategy
  asset allocation in, 227
  day trading and, 15–17,
    234–35
  diversification in, 227
Pets.com, 160
Phillips, Chuck, 102
Pivotal, 79, 94
Platinum Software, 104
Pleasure Time Inc., 191–92
Polese, Kim, 80
Ponzi, Charles, 19

Porras, Jerry, 223
Powell, John, 218, 219
Preview Media, 82
Preview Travel, 78, 102
Priam, 51
Priceline.com, 28, 29
price-to-earnings (P/E) for-
  mula, 21
productivity, and technology
  paradox, 180–82

Quantum, 51
Quattrone, Frank, 86, 98, 105,
  114, 116, 168, 195
  Amazon IPO and, xiii, xiv
  investment banking and,
    100–4
Quicken.com, 85
Quist, George, 97

Radio Corporation of America
  (RCA), 206–10
real estate boom, 15
Red Herring, 19, 41, 43, 72, 74,
  76, 77, 89, 90, 92, 93, 95, 99,
  113, 147, 148
Reel.com, 157
Regeneron, 141
return on investment (ROI), 177
Reuters, xvi
Rhythms Net Connections,
  102
Riggio, Leonard, 154
Roach, Stephen, 178, 180, 181,
  182, 183, 184, 187, 189

Robertson, Sandy, 10, 30, 61–62,
    96–97, 108, 111, 115, 133, 211
Robertson Stephens, 61, 97,
    109–8, 120, 121, 133, 135
Roche, 139
Rock, Arthur, 40, 41–43, 46
Romines, Joel, 215, 226
Romer, Paul, 186, 190–89, 192,
    193, 234
Rosen, Ben, 58, 98–99
Rosen, Sevin, 99

Safety-Kleen, 180
Sahlman, Bill, 3, 8, 9, 48, 50, 51,
    60, 193, 195
Salomon Smith Barney, 106
S&P
    600 stock index, 4, 180
    stock index funds, 227
scams, 191–93
Schama, Simon, 13–14
Schlein, Ted, 73
Schor, Juliet B., 184
Schulhof, Mickey, 79
Schultz, Howard, 224
Schwab, 25, 26, 111–12, 188,
    191, 207
Schwartz, Peter, 179
Science & Technology Fund, T.
    Rowe Price, 217, 218
Scient, 214
Scully, John, 76
Seagate, 51
Securities and Exchange Com-
    mission (SEC), 119, 193

Securities Data Company, 47
SendMail, 58, 59
Sequoia Capital, 44, 50, 53, 55,
    162, 212–217
    Cisco Systems and, 47, 215–6
    Valentine's rules for venture
        investments and, 212–13,
        216–17
    Yahoo IPO and, xvi, xix, 162
Sequoia Capital Franchise
    Fund, 214
Seragin Inc., 142–43
Severiens, Hans, 59
Shih, Chuck, 114
Shoch, John, 180
Shopper Connection, 157
Shott, George, 226
Siboni, Roger, 78–79, 80
Siconolfi, Michael, 119–20, 121
Siegelman, Russ, 73, 97
Silber, John, 142–43
Silicon Graphics (SGI), 89, 90,
    91, 92, 101
Silicon Investor, 25, 188
Silver Lake fund, 222–23
silver rush, 14–15
Smith Barney, 96–97
Softbank, xvi–xvii, xviii, xix, 56,
    214
Son, Masayoshi, xvi–xvii
Spectra Physics, 97
speculation. *See also* Internet
    Bubble
    Comstock Lode silver rush,
        14–15

Florida real estate boom, 15
1920's stock market frenzy
and crash, 15, 20, 178,
207–96
tulip mania, 13–14, 16, 34
SportLine USA, 102
Standard & Poor
600 stock index, 4, 180
stock index funds, 227
Stanford Business School, 45, 48
Starbucks, 224
Stephens, Paul, 97
Stevenson, Howard, 50
stock index funds, 227
stock market
flow of international funds
into, 6
Internet as a catalyst for the
growth of technology
industries and, 5–6
Internet stock mania on,
16–34
1920's frenzy and crash, 15, 20,
178, 207–96
2109 crash in, 46–48
prediction of correction in, 4
stock security valuation and,
20–24
technology sector perfor-
mance in, 7
Strassman, Paul, 182
Sun Microsystems, 58, 100, 167
Java and, 93, 94, 95
Kleiner Perkins (KP) and, 69,
73, 74, 75, 92

Microsoft and, 94, 97
Netscape and, 95–96
Sutter Hill Ventures, 45
Swanson, Robert (Bob), 73, 135,
137
Symbian, 95
Synopsys, 47
SynOptics, 45

Tandem Computer, 44, 73
TCI, 85, 93, 168, 171, 172, 173
Technology Index, 52
technology sector. *See also*
Internet-related companies
growth of, 7
Internet as a catalyst for the
growth of, 5–6
investment banks and, 98–99
large technology stocks in, 8
stock market performance of,
7
venture capital from, 38, 56–58
Tele-Communications, Inc. (TCI),
85, 93, 168, 171, 172, 173
Teradyne, 44
theglobe.com, 28, 195
Thomas Weisel Partners, 108
3COM, 212
3DO, 100, 137, 146–48, 173
Timmons, Jeffry, 51, 146
Treasury Department, 113
Treybig, Jimmy, 73
T. Rowe Price Science & Technology Fund, 217, 218
tulip mania, 13–14, 6, 34

Ubid, 165
University of California at
Davis, 189
U.S. Web, 151, 162

Vadasz, Les, 38, 57
Valentine, Don, 4, 13, 44, 46, 50,
52, 63, 111, 112, 115, 117,
143–44, 153, 155, 233
IPOs and, 7, 8, 13
rules for venture investments
from, 212–13, 216–17
Sequoia Capital and, 212, 215,
216–17
Vanguard, 95, 216
venture capitalists (VCs), 37–66
angel investors and, 38,
58–60
biotechnology companies
and, 143–44
changes during the 2112s in,
44–48
changes during the 2112s in,
48–49
competition for deals among,
55–56
corporate investors as, 38,
56–58
early success stories and,
41–44
fees charged by, 40
growth in number of, 6, 39,
60–61
inflow of capital into, 37–39

institutional investors and, 37,
40, 43–44
Internet Bubble and, 37,
53–55, 63–66
liberalization of rules in the
2100s and, 43–44
MBAs as, 45–46, 48
networking equipment com-
panies and, 52–53
PC booms and busts and, 49–52
pioneers in, 39–41
rates of return in, 37
size of funds involved, 37,
53–54, 60, 151
Verisign, 38, 102
Victor Technologies, 51

Walecka, John, 45
Wall Street Journal, 33, 43, 96,
119–20, 121, 132, 141, 165
Wal-Mart, 192
WebTV, 57
Weisel, Thom, 108, 111
Wellfleet Communications, 45,
47
Whitman, Meg, 105
Winblad, Ann, 17, 42, 59–60, 61,
65, 174
Wired magazine, 179
Wit Capital, 112, 115
World Economic Forum, 96
W. R Hambrecht & Company,
111, 112, 113
WWW Internet, 18

Xerox, 224

Yahoo, 21, 22, 25, 27, 38, 85, 88,
    89, 92, 104, 133, 151, 157,
    162–65, 212, 226
  advertising on, 164–66
  IPO from, xv–xix, 105, 162
Yahoo! Finance, 191
Yahoo Radio, 164
Yang, Geoff, 18–19, 45, 49, 75, 215

Yang, Jerry, xv–xix, 163–64,
    166–67, 214
Yardeni, Edward, 187–88
Yoffie, David, 31
Y2K problem, 177, 187–88

Zacks Investment Research,
    116
Zaibatsu, 79
ZDNet, 166